Reshaping

the

Graduate Education
of Scientists and
Engineers

Committee on
Science, Engineering, and Public Policy

National Academy of Sciences
National Academy of Engineering
Institute of Medicine

NATIONAL ACADEMY PRESS
Washington, D.C. 1995

NATIONAL ACADEMY PRESS • **2101 Constitution Ave., N.W.** • **Washington, D.C. 20418**

NOTICE: This volume was produced as part of a project approved by the Governing Board of the National Research Council, whose members are drawn from the councils of the National Academy of Sciences, the National Academy of Engineering, and the Institute of Medicine. It is a result of work done by the Committee on Science, Engineering, and Public Policy (COSEPUP) as augmented, which has authorized its release to the public. This report has been reviewed by a group other than the authors according to procedures approved by COSEPUP and the Report Review Committee.

The **National Academy of Sciences** (NAS) is a private, nonprofit, self-perpetuating society of distinguished scholars engaged in scientific and engineering research, dedicated to the furtherance of science and technology and to their use for the general welfare. Under the authority of the charter granted to it by Congress in 1863, the Academy has a working mandate that calls on it to advise the federal government on scientific and technical matters. Dr. Bruce M. Alberts is president of the NAS.

The **National Academy of Engineering** (NAE) was established in 1964, under the charter of the NAS, as a parallel organization of distinguished engineers. It is autonomous in its administration and in the selection of members, sharing with the NAS its responsibilities for advising the federal government. The National Academy of Engineering also sponsors engineering programs aimed at meeting national needs, encourages education and research, and recognizes the superior achievements of engineers. Dr. Robert M. White is president of the NAE.

The **Institute of Medicine** (IOM) was established in 1970 by the NAS to secure the services of eminent members of appropriate professions in the examination of policy matters pertaining to the health of the public. The Institute acts under the responsibility given to the NAS in its congressional charter to be an adviser to the federal government and, on its own initiative, to identify issues of medical care, research, and education. Dr. Kenneth I. Shine is president of the IOM.

The **Committee on Science, Engineering, and Public Policy** (COSEPUP) is a joint committee of the NAS, the NAE, and the IOM. It includes members of the councils of all three bodies.

This project was supported by the National Science Foundation, the U.S. Department of Energy, and the Kellogg Endowment Fund of the National Academy of Sciences and the Institute of Medicine.

Library of Congress Catalog Card Number: 95-69122
International Standard Book Number: 0-309-05285-8

Internet Access: This report is available on the National Academy of Sciences' Internet host. It may be accessed via World Wide Web at http://www.nas.edu, via Gopher at gopher.nas.edu, or via FTP at ftp.nas.edu.

On the Cover: The cover depicts decision trees illustrating the variety of paths scientists and engineers decide to pursue throughout their career.

Available from: National Academy Press, 2101 Constitution Avenue, N.W., Box 285, Washington, D.C. 20055 1-800-624-6242 or 202-334-3313 (in Washington metropolitan area)

Printed in the United States of America

COMMITTEE ON SCIENCE, ENGINEERING, AND PUBLIC POLICY

Study on Graduate Education

PHILLIP A. GRIFFITHS (*Chairman*), Director, Institute for Advanced Study
ROBERT McCORMICK ADAMS, Secretary Emeritus, Smithsonian Institution
BRUCE M. ALBERTS,* President, National Academy of Sciences
ARDEN L. BEMENT, Basil S. Turner Distinguished Professor of Engineering, Purdue University
ELKAN R. BLOUT, Harkness Professor, Department of Biological Chemistry and Molecular
        Pharmacology, Harvard Medical School
FELIX E. BROWDER, University Professor, Department of Mathematics, Rutgers University
DAVID R. CHALLONER, Vice President for Health Affairs, University of Florida
ELLIS B. COWLING, University Distinguished Professor At-Large, North Carolina State University
BERNARD N. FIELDS,+ Adele Lehman Professor; Chairman, Department of Microbiology and
        Molecular Genetics, Harvard Medical School
ALEXANDER H. FLAX, Senior Fellow, National Academy of Engineering
RALPH E. GOMORY, President, Alfred P. Sloan Foundation
THOMAS D. LARSON, Consultant
MARY JANE OSBORN, Head, Department of Microbiology, University of Connecticut Health Center
PHILLIP A. SHARP, Head, Department of Biology, Center for Cancer Research, Massachusetts
        Institute of Technology
KENNETH I. SHINE,* President, Institute of Medicine
RALPH SNYDERMAN, Chancellor for Health Affairs; Dean, School of Medicine, Duke University
        Medical Center
H. GUYFORD STEVER, Trustee and Science Consultant
MORRIS TANENBAUM, Vice President, National Academy of Engineering
ROBERT M. WHITE,* President, National Academy of Engineering

LAWRENCE E. McCRAY, Executive Director

Principal Project Staff

MICHAEL McGEARY, Study Director
DEBORAH D. STINE, Senior Program Officer
ALAN ANDERSON, Consultant/Writer

* Ex officio member.
+ Deceased, February 1, 1995.

PREFACE

In 1993, the Committee on Science, Engineering, and Public Policy (COSEPUP) issued a report entitled *Science, Technology, and the Federal Government: National Goals for a New Era* (the *Goals* report), which proposed a framework for federal policy to support science and technology. During the preparation of the report, it became apparent that a complete discussion of the science and technology enterprise would require an examination of the process by which scientists and engineers are educated. If scientists and engineers are to contribute effectively to national, scientific, and technological objectives, their educational experience must prepare them to do so. The present report can be considered a companion volume to the *Goals* report.

Several key questions guided the committee during its initial deliberations:

- What are typical career paths for scientists and engineers, and how have they changed in recent years?
- Given present career paths, what are the most appropriate structures and functions for graduate education?
- How can science and engineering graduate students be prepared for a variety of careers in teaching, industry, government, and other employment sectors, in addition to research?
- Are we producing the right numbers of PhDs?[1]
- What should be the nation's goals for graduate science and engineering education?

---

[1] Because of the concerns regarding PhD unemployment, the report focuses on the PhD.

In attempting to answer those questions, we found important gaps in our knowledge of employment rates and patterns. It has proved difficult, for example, to determine where PhDs are and what they are doing in nonacademic positions or to determine accurately either unemployment rates of scientists and engineers or the extent of underemployment, especially among recent graduates, because of the lack of timely data. In fact, we were sufficiently troubled by the lack of generally available information to conclude that students', professors', and mentors' lack of accurate, timely, and accessible data on employment trends, careers, and sources of student support is a serious flaw in our education system.

This deficiency makes it difficult for potential and current graduate students to make well-informed decisions as to whether and where to enter graduate school. It also hampers the faculties at our universities in preparing their students adequately for the full range of professional careers in science and engineering. Therefore, the committee faced a dilemma—whether to make recommendations despite gaps in current understanding or to counsel delay until such understanding is attained. It proceeded to make recommendations now because students, universities and colleges, professors, mentors, funding agencies, employers, and others must make decisions today that will affect the careers of science and engineering students for the rest of their lives.

The recommendations in this report reflect a common theme. Many of the job opportunities of the future will favor students with greater breadth of academic and career skills, so the universities and their partners in the graduate-education enterprise should therefore cooperate to broaden curricular options for graduate students.

We hope this report will be useful not only for university presidents, provosts, deans, and others in the decision-making structure of universities, but also for all institutions and individuals who are part of the graduate-education enterprise: federal and state government,[2] industry and business, and faculty, mentors, and students at both the graduate and undergraduate levels.

The committee acknowledges the invaluable information and opinions received from a variety of sources. We convened more than a half-dozen panels of experts from academe, government, industry, foundations, and other sectors. The panel members are listed in Appendix E. A call for comments to scientists, engineers, administrators, students, and educators across the country drew more than 100 thoughtful replies, many of them reflecting exceptional care; some correspondents even conducted informal surveys within their own institutions. Those responding to the call for comments are listed in Appendix D and their thoughtful responses are provided in Appendix F. In addition, Appendix G summarizes a survey we sent to graduate students asking what information they need to make decisions. The committee also made use of continuing work by the National Research Council's Office of Scientific and Engineering Personnel.

---

[2] There is a lack of adequate information about educational and funding activities at the state level. The states have supported graduate education for many years, and a number of state governments and agencies have initiated innovative ways to broaden graduate education through interactions with industry, government, and community groups.

The production of the report was the result of hard work by the committee as a whole and by the extra effort of the Guidance Group (consisting of Arden Bement, Mary J. Osborn, David Challoner, Alexander Flax, and me), which convened between regular committee meetings. The project was aided by the invaluable help of COSEPUP professional staff: Michael McGeary, study director, who provided research and analytical support, as illustrated in Appendixes B and C and Chapter 2, and drafted major portions of Chapters 3 and 4; Deborah Stine, senior program officer, who managed the committee's outreach efforts and contributed in a major way to Chapter 2; Alan Anderson, consultant/writer, who helped draft and revise the text throughout the project; and Lawrence McCray, executive director of COSEPUP, who oversaw the committee's activity. Wise guidance was provided by Philip M. Smith as a consultant. National Research Council staff members Dimitria Satterwhite, Jeffrey Peck, and Patrick Sevcik ably assisted the project. The committee also thanks its diligent editor, Norman Grossblatt.

PHILLIP A. GRIFFITHS
Chair
Committee on Science, Engineering, and Public Policy

CONTENTS

APPENDIXES

LIST OF FIGURES

LIST OF TABLES

EXECUTIVE SUMMARY

FRAMING THE ISSUE

Scientists and engineers with PhD and other advanced degrees play a central and growing role in American industrial and commercial life. The traditional process of graduate education to the doctoral level, organized around an intensive research experience, has served as a world model for the advanced training of scientists and engineers.

Graduate education is basic to the achievement of national goals in two ways. First, our universities are responsible for producing the teachers and researchers of the future—the independent investigators who will lay the groundwork for the paradigms and products of tomorrow and who will educate later generations of teachers and researchers. Second, graduate education contributes directly to the broader national goals of technological, economic, and cultural development. We increasingly depend on people with advanced scientific and technological knowledge in our collective efforts in developing new technologies and industries, reducing environmental pollution, combating disease and hunger, developing new sources of energy, and maintaining the competitiveness of industry. Our graduate schools of science and engineering are therefore important not only as sources of future leaders in science and engineering, but also as an indispensable underpinning of national strength and prosperity—sustaining the creativity and intellectual vigor needed to address a growing range of social and economic concerns.

As we approach the 21st century, our graduate schools face challenges both within and outside the academic setting. Many disciplines of science and engineering are undergoing rapid and pervasive change, and many aspects of modern life are increasingly dependent on emerging technologies and the scientific frameworks from which they evolve. New national-security challenges, expanded economic competition, urgent public-health needs, and a growing global awareness of environmental deterioration bring new opportunities for varied careers in science and engineering. We expect our graduate scientists and engineers to continue the expansion of fundamental knowledge and to make that knowledge useful in the world. A world of work that has become more interdisciplinary, collaborative, and global requires that we produce young people who are adaptable and flexible, as well as technically proficient.

A TIME OF CHANGE

The US system of graduate education in science and engineering is arguably the most effective system yet devised for advanced training in these fields. By carrying out graduate education in institutions where a large portion of the nation's best research is done, the universities have created a research and training system for scientists and engineers that is one of the nation's great strengths.

The present US system of graduate education evolved when the demand for research was either stable or rising. The national-security demands of the Cold War and domestic priorities, such as health, stimulated and supported a strong science and technology infrastructure, including graduate education. Our dominant economic and technological position in the world allowed us to exert clear international leadership and permitted us to influence both the progress of science and the rate of technology development and introduction.

That situation is now changing. The end of the Cold War, the rapid growth of international competition in technology-based industries, and a variety of constraints on research spending have altered our market for scientists and engineers. Furthermore, the United States has traditionally opened its doors to students from other countries. In recent years, the number of foreign science and engineering students enrolled in US graduate schools and the number receiving PhDs have risen unusually rapidly.

The demand for scientists and engineers has remained strong. However, there are indications that there is a slowdown in the growth of university positions and that we can expect a fundamental change in science and engineering employment—a reduction in the demand for traditional researchers in some fields. This employment situation has already contributed to a frustration of expectations among new PhDs. Major industrial sectors have also reassessed their needs and reshaped their research, development, and business strategies. And new research and development needs have arisen in emerging production, service, and information enterprises. The increasing rate of change suggests a need for scientists and engineers who can readily adapt to continuing changes.

Government laboratories and other facilities are also undergoing change. In some instances, research and development foci are shifting. In others, government and its contractor scientists and engineers are being challenged to build linkages with industry and universities. Some departments and agencies are reorganizing and shrinking. Moreover, government spending on research and development is expected to be constrained in the next few years. That places direct pressure on research and development performed by universities and government and indirect pressure on research and development performed by industry under government contracts.

Hence, the three areas of primary employment for PhD scientists and engineers—universities and colleges, industry, and government—are experiencing simultaneous change. The total effect is likely to be vastly more consequential for the employment of scientists and engineers than any previous period of transition has been. Some believe that the nation's teaching institutions are entering a period when the number of new PhDs should somehow be capped (we return to this point later). Although many recent graduates are frustrated by their inability to find basic-research positions, it appears that the growth in nonresearch and applied research and development positions is large enough to absorb most graduates. However, such employers complain that new PhDs are often too specialized for the range of tasks that they will confront and that they have a difficult time in adapting to the demands of nonacademic work.

A broader concern is that we have not, as a nation, paid adequate attention to the function of the graduate schools in meeting the country's varied needs for scientists and engineers. There is no clear human-resources policy for advanced scientists and engineers, so their education is largely a byproduct of policies that support research. The simplifying assumption has apparently been that the primary mission of graduate programs is to produce the next generation of academic researchers. In view of the broad range of ways in which scientists and engineers contribute to national needs, it is time to review how they are educated to do so.

The approach that is presented in this report is based on reshaping the current PhD experience and improving students' ability to make good career choices. Alternative approaches were examined during the study but were not endorsed. One would be to control graduate enrollments directly, presumably on the basis of expected employment needs. Among the problems with this approach are the questionable reliability of employment forecasts and the practical difficulty of implementing it. Another strategy would be to create a new type of degree—a "different doctorate," perhaps—that entails less intensive research experience and is intended to prepare students for nonresearch careers. Employers told us, however, that they value the requirement for original research that is a hallmark of the PhD, and we see little demand for a hybrid degree. Our approach, we believe, will make the current system self-adjusting at a time when change is certain but the nature of the change cannot be predicted.

SUMMARY OF RECOMMENDATIONS

The process of graduate education is highly effective in preparing students whose careers will focus on academic research. It must continue this excellence to maintain the strength of our national science and technology enterprise. But graduate education must also serve better the needs of those whose careers will not center on research. *More than half of new graduates with PhDs*—and much more than half in some fields, such as chemistry and engineering—*now find work in nonacademic settings*. This fraction has been growing steadily for 2 decades.

We recommend that the graduate-education enterprise—particularly at the department level—implement several basic reforms to enhance the educational experience of future scientists and engineers who will work in either academic or nonacademic settings. If programs offer a wider variety of degree and curricular options that are valued by their faculty, students will be better served. In addition, we have an obligation to inform graduate students accurately and explicitly about career options so that they will be able to make better educational choices, formulate more realistic career expectations, and achieve greater satisfaction in their careers while contributing more effectively to fulfilling national goals.

In summary, the future PhD degree would be different—an improved version of the current degree. It would retain the existing strengths—especially with regard to leading to careers in academic research—while substantially increasing the information available, the potential versatility of the students, and the career options afforded to them by their PhD education.

General Recommendation 1: Offer a Broader Range of Academic Options

To produce more versatile scientists and engineers, graduate programs should provide options that allow students to gain a wider variety of skills.

Greater versatility can be promoted on two levels. On the academic level, students should be discouraged from overspecializing. Those planning research careers should be grounded in the broad fundamentals of their fields and be familiar with several subfields. Such breadth might be much harder to gain after graduation.

On the level of career skills, there is value in experiences that supply skills desired by both academic and nonacademic employers, especially the ability to communicate complex ideas to nonspecialists and the ability to work well in teams. Off-campus internships in industry or government can lead to additional skills and exposure to authentic job situations.

To foster versatility, government and other agents of financial assistance for graduate students should adjust their support mechanisms to include new education/training grants to institutions and departments.

Most federal support for graduate students is currently provided through research assistantships. Research assistantships are included as parts of grants that are competitively awarded to individual faculty members to support their research. The grant funds are then used to provide stipends to the students in those faculty members' laboratories. Such assistantships offer educational benefit in the form of research skills to the students who work on the faculty members' projects. The needs of funded projects rather than the students' educational needs, however, have tended to be paramount in guiding the students' work.

We recommend an increased emphasis on education/training grants, an adaptation of the training grants awarded by the National Institutes of Health and other agencies. These grants would be awarded competitively to institutions and departments. Evaluation criteria would include a proposer's plan to improve the versatility of students, both through curricular innovation and through more effective faculty mentoring to acquaint students with the full range of future employment options.

While urging that the nation's overall support for PhD students be maintained as a sound investment in our future, we recognize that a heightened emphasis on education/training grants could reduce the funds available for research assistantships.

In implementing changes to promote versatility, care must be taken not to compromise other important objectives.

Modifying graduate programs to enhance versatility will require care and imagination. Change should be compatible with

- *Maintaining local initiative.* We envision change that comes from local institutional initiatives and that shows considerable local variation. Each program should build on its own strengths and interests.

- *Maintaining excellence in research.* A continuing goal of graduate education is the preparation of students who will dedicate themselves to careers in research. The reforms suggested here are not intended to alter that goal. Instead, we envision complementary steps designed to reflect all employment opportunities—in both the research and the nonresearch sectors. Nor do we espouse what some call "vocationalism"—setting each student on a particular career track and "training" him or her in a narrow specialty. We need instead an educational system that prepares students for a central feature of contemporary life: continuous change.

- *Controlling time to degree.* The time to degree and, more important, the time to first employment are steadily lengthening and are already too long. We believe that it is possible to foster versatility without increasing the time that graduate students spend on campus. Although long times to degree are often decried, universities have not generally made the disciplined effort needed to shorten them. One important step toward shortening the time to degree is to ensure that educational needs of students remain paramount. *The primary objective of graduate education is the education of students.* The value of such activities as working as highly specialized research assistants on faculty research projects and as teaching assistants should be judged according to the extent to which they contribute to a student's education. A student's progress should be the responsibility of a department rather than of a single faculty member; a small supervisory group (including the student's adviser) should determine when enough work has been accomplished for the PhD degree. Each institution is urged to set its own standards for time to degree and to enforce them.

- *Attracting women and minority-group members.* It is essential to attract a fair share of the most talented students to each discipline in science and engineering, irrespective of their sex or ethnic backgrounds. Where it appears that the number of women and minority-group members is low in particular fields, deliberate steps should be taken to deal with real and perceived barriers to full participation.

General Recommendation 2: Provide Better Information and Guidance

Graduate scientists and engineers and their advisers should receive more up-to-date and accurate information to help them make informed decisions about professional careers; broad electronic access to such information should be provided through a concerted nationwide effort.

The burden of learning about realistic career options should not be left to students themselves. We recommend the establishment of a national database of information on employment options and trends. This information, intended for use by both students and their advisers, should include, by field, data on career tracks, graduate programs (including financial aid), time to degree, and placement rates. Departments should track information on their students—not only those who go into universities and 4-year colleges, but those who go into industry, government, junior and precollege education, etc.

The rapid development of the Internet makes it possible to adhere to two important principles in regard to the database: the information can retain a more decentralized, "grass-roots" character than information assembled in central compendiums, and up-to-date information would be readily available to the ultimate consumers—doctoral students, graduates, and faculty advisers.

The National Science Foundation should coordinate federal participation in the database. However, it is preferable to design and manage the database within the academic community itself so that it has accurate, timely, and credible information.

Academic departments should provide the information referred to above to prospective and current students in a timely manner and should also provide career advice to graduate students. Students should have access to information on the full range of employment possibilities.

Advice for students should be improved by a systematic tracking of the employment path of each department's graduates and by use of the national database recommended above.

In the past, when students expected to become professors, graduate school was usually seen as a step on a simple career ladder. We are concerned that this concept is still held in some places. Departments should help students to regard their progress through graduate school as a journey with branches that require decisions. One decision point is the application stage, when students need more information on job placement, salaries, and unemployment rates in various disciplines to decide whether and where to enter graduate school.

Students should be encouraged to consider three alternative pathways at the point when they have met their qualifying requirements.

At the beginning of the research phase, departmental advisers should help students to choose among three distinct options: first, to stop with a master's degree, in light of their aspirations and projected employment demand; second, to proceed toward a PhD and a position in research; or third, for a student interested in working in nontraditional fields, to design a dissertation that meets high standards for originality but requires less time than would preparation for a career in academic research. We believe that the first option is typically undervalued and the third option often neglected.

The National Science Foundation should continue to improve the coverage, timeliness, and clarity of analysis of the data on the education and employment of scientists and engineers in order to support better national decision-making about human resources in science and technology.

In preparing this report, we discovered a lack of the timely and relevant information that students, advisers, and policy-makers should have. The National Science Foundation should seek to improve timeliness, increase detail on nonacademic employment (which now occupies most new scientists and engineers), and support extramural research on actual career patterns in science and engineering.

General Recommendation 3: Devise a National Human-Resource Policy for Advanced Scientists and Engineers

A national discussion group—including representatives of governments, universities, industries, and professional organizations—should deliberately examine the goals, policies, conditions, and unresolved issues of graduate-level human resources.

In preparing our last report, *Science, Technology, and the Federal Government* (COSEPUP, 1993), we found that no coherent national policy guides the education of advanced scientists and engineers, even though the nation depends heavily on them. At present, there is neither the conceptual clarity nor the factual basis needed to support a coherent policy discussion. We are concerned that many prevailing views are obsolete or are quickly becoming so.

As a starting point, the agenda for national discussion might include national goals and policy objectives, the relationship between the process of graduate education and employment trends, and difficult current issues (such as time to degree and sources of new students) on which opinions diverge.

MAJOR RELATED ISSUES

Two other issues were discussed at some length by the committee and committee witnesses: the relationship between supply of and demand for PhDs in science and engineering and the impact of current high enrollments of foreign citizens. We do not offer recommendations on either issue, but we discuss both in Chapter 4. We present here a brief summary of the discussions.

Is There an Oversupply of PhDs?

The committee is not convinced that the current low and stable unemployment rates among scientists and engineers mean that the system is working as well as it should. In fact, there are indications of employment difficulties, especially among recent graduates. During the course of our study, we often heard concerns that we are producing too many PhDs. Reliable information is scarce, and conditions vary greatly with field, but we report three summary observations:

- *There seem to be far more seekers of jobs as professors in academe and as basic researchers[1] than there are available positions. This situation is the basis of the frustrated expectations of new PhDs.*
- Overall unemployment rates for recent PhDs have remained very low (although the 1994 survey showed a small rise). That implies that steady expansion in applied-research and nonresearch employment has ultimately provided jobs for most of the still-growing cohort of PhD graduates.
- There are some worrisome indicators of weakness in the market, such as substantially longer delays in initial placement of new graduates, the fact that some graduates are employed in positions that do not require a PhD, and the possibility that they are taking postdoctoral assignments only in hopes of better positions when employment conditions in research are brighter.

Nevertheless, we see no basis for recommending across-the-board limits on enrollment, for three reasons. First, conditions differ greatly by field and subfield. Second, we believe that an extensive, disciplined research experience provides valuable preparation for a wide variety

---

[1] However, this situation does not mean that graduate scientists and engineers can no longer do research. In terms of primary work activity, the share of positions in applied research and development is increasing. It is just that the share of people going into management of research and teaching is declining.

of nontraditional careers for which scientific and technical expertise is relevant. Third, limiting actions would have little immediate aggregate impact even if they could be orchestrated effectively. Instead, we believe that our recommendations of greatly improved career information and guidance will enhance the ability of the system to balance supply and demand. When the employment situation is poor, better-informed students will be able to pursue options other than a PhD; when the market is expanding, students will be able to move more flexibly and rapidly in the direction of employment demand.

Foreign Students

The numbers of science and engineering students and PhDs who are foreign citizens are rising rapidly. The views we encountered about that situation are mixed. Some view it positively, arguing that universities benefit by having foreign graduate students help with research and teaching, that employers benefit by finding the most highly qualified PhDs, and that to compete in a global economy US universities and industries must be able to recruit the best talent available. Others are calling for limits on the numbers of foreign students, arguing that large numbers of foreign citizens compete with US citizens for jobs (which might explain part of the employment problems of recent years); that foreign citizens who return home might work for our economic competitors; that cultural and language difficulties make foreign students ineffective in the classroom as teaching assistants and limit their ability to succeed in the labor market; and that their presence in large numbers depresses salaries and thereby generates a discouraging market signal for potential American students.

As we argue in Chapter 4, the committee does not recommend limiting the number of foreign students, for several reasons. First, there is considerable anecdotal evidence that the most outstanding foreign PhDs tend to find employment in the United States and make major contributions to our nation. Second, the sharp increase in number of foreign-citizen graduate students seems to have been caused in part by a set of political events that are unlikely to recur as well as by changes in US immigration laws. Third, one cause of the presence of many foreign students is that their home nations have lacked adequate opportunities in both education and employment; the wealth of these nations is now growing, and there is already evidence that some foreign students are finding attractive employment opportunities at home.

To the extent that there is a limit on the number of departmental "slots" for graduate students, of more fundamental importance than the presence of foreign citizens is the fact that the number of American students entering science and engineering has grown only slightly in recent years and is a declining percentage of the total number of PhDs. We suggest that the most appropriate responses to the relatively flat enrollment of American students are to implement the measures advocated in this report (which should improve the responsiveness of the PhD labor market) and to continue efforts to strengthen the teaching of precollege science. Those measures, we believe, would make graduate education more attractive, more effective, and accessible to a larger group of qualified American applicants.

1

THE CHANGING CONTEXT OF GRADUATE EDUCATION

The American system of graduate education of scientists and engineers,[1] organized around an intensive and realistic research experience, has become the world model for simultaneously conducting basic research and educating graduate scientists and engineers. Scientists and engineers with PhD and other advanced degrees play a central and growing role in American life.

Graduate education is basic to achieving national goals in two ways. First, our universities are responsible for producing the teachers and researchers—investigators in industry or academe who will lay the groundwork for the paradigms and products of tomorrow and who will in turn educate future teachers and researchers. Second, graduate scholarship and research are key contributors to meeting broad national goals of technological, economic, and cultural development. The increase in scientific and technological knowledge and the ways in which that knowledge is applied are fundamental to the pursuit of many general national objectives, including developing new technologies and industries, combating disease and hunger, reducing environmental pollution, developing new sources of energy, and maintaining the competitiveness of American industry.

Persons educated in and part of our graduate education system provide expert service to society via their development of original ideas, which are brought to fruition in teaching, industry, business, and government. Graduate students often go beyond the thinking of their professors and create a new generation of science and engineering thought. The student learns from the professor, but the professor also learns from the student. Our system of graduate education is therefore important both as a source of future leaders in science and engineering and as a source of new ideas. We must maintain the strength of this system to sustain the

---

[1] Throughout this report, the term *graduate scientists and engineers* refers to persons who have attained a master's or doctor of philosophy degree in science or engineering. *Science* is taken to include the life sciences, physical sciences, social sciences, and mathematics. *Engineering* is taken to include all specialties of engineering.

creativity and intellectual vigor that will be needed in the United States to address a growing variety of social and economic concerns.

The efficacy of our system originated in a series of policy decisions that were prompted by the major role that science and technology had in the outcome of World War II. Among those decisions were the following:

- The public, through a number of government agencies, would assume an important role in funding basic and applied research.
- Through public funding, researchers at universities throughout the country would become major contributors to the nation's scientific research expertise.
- The universities would conduct basic research and the graduate education of scientists and engineers as joint, synergistic activities.

The dual role of the graduate science and engineering enterprise was designed to benefit the nation by educating students through the active conduct of cutting-edge research. According to a report by the National Research Council in 1964, "graduate education can be of highest quality only if it is conducted as part of the research process itself" (NRC, 1964).

By educating students in the context of research, the American system of graduate education has set the world standard for preparing scientists and engineers for research careers in academe, government, and industry. And by attracting outstanding students and faculty members from throughout the world, it has benefited from an infusion of both talent and ideas.

The products of research have contributed abundantly to the health, defense, and well-being of the country, and American

> The graduate-education enterprise in the United States is diverse and decentralized. Because of the diversity of missions and agencies participating in higher education, any important changes require cooperative efforts based on a shared understanding.
>
> There are many independent participants, including more than 600 public and private universities and colleges (which offer master's or doctoral degrees in science and engineering), scientific and engineering societies (which help to define what scientists and engineers should know and do), state governments (which provide support for universities), the federal government (which supports research and education), philanthropic organizations, accreditation bodies, the Council of Graduate Schools, the Association of American Universities, and the National Association of State Universities and Land Grant Colleges.

Box 1-1: The Graduate-Education Enterprise

has generously supported the education of its scientists and engineers with both state and federal funds and with donations from industry, large nonprofit organizations, and the universities themselves.

States have the longest tradition of supporting graduate education. Beginning with the Morrill Act of 1862, states funded on-campus agricultural research to serve the public goal of bringing technology to the nation's farmers. Today, by subsidizing tuitions, they have ensured wide access to graduate education at low cost. The state universities and land-grant colleges subsidize about half the doctoral-degree recipients in the United States and employ the professors who educate them.

Federal support for graduate education of scientists and engineers, a more recent phenomenon, expanded rapidly after World War II with the establishment of the National Science Foundation (NSF), the National Institutes of Health (NIH), and other agencies. Funding for the education of graduate scientists and engineers grew rapidly in the late 1950s after the launching of Sputnik in 1957 and passage of the National Defense Education Act in 1958. The federal government has developed a number of programs for the direct support of graduate education, including fellowships, traineeships, research-infrastructure grants, and institutional development grants.

The number of graduate science and engineering students increased roughly in parallel to the amount of federally funded scientific and engineering research from 1958 to 1988. Between 1958 and 1968, the number of PhDs awarded annually to scientists and engineers tripled to about 18,000. That swift growth lasted until the early 1970s, when national policy changes

> The doctor of philosophy degree is the highest academic degree granted by North American universities. PhD programs are designed to prepare students to become scholars, that is, to discover, integrate, and apply knowledge, as well as to communicate and disseminate it.
>
> A doctoral program is an apprenticeship that consists of lecture or laboratory courses, seminars, examinations, discussions, independent study, research, and, in many instances, teaching.
>
> The first year or two of study is normally a probationary period, during which a preliminary or qualifying examination might be required. The probationary period is followed by an examination for admission to full candidacy, when students devote essentially full time to completing dissertation research. This research, planned with the major adviser and the dissertation committee, usually takes 1-3 years, depending on the field. An oral defense of the research and dissertation before a graduate committee constitutes the final examination.
>
> Source: CGS, 1990

Box 1-2: The PhD Degree

brought about the curtailment of most federal fellowships and traineeships.[2] Thus, the annual production of science and engineering doctorates peaked at near 19,400 during 1971-1973 and fell to fewer than 18,000 during 1977-1985. The production of PhDs began to rise again in the late 1980s and reached 25,000 in 1993 (see Figure 1-1). Most of the net growth after 1985 was due to an increased number of foreign students with temporary student visas (see Figure 1-2).

Since the late 1980s, the institutions that conduct research in concert with graduate education have been buffeted by a series of political, economic, and social changes. The end

---

[2] For example, the NSF training-grant program was terminated, and research fellowships were cut back to 500 (they have since returned to 2,500). Only the NIH's training-grant program was maintained, through the intervention of Congress; but even this program was reduced as overall federal funding for direct support of graduate science and engineering education fell by 80% in the early 1970s.

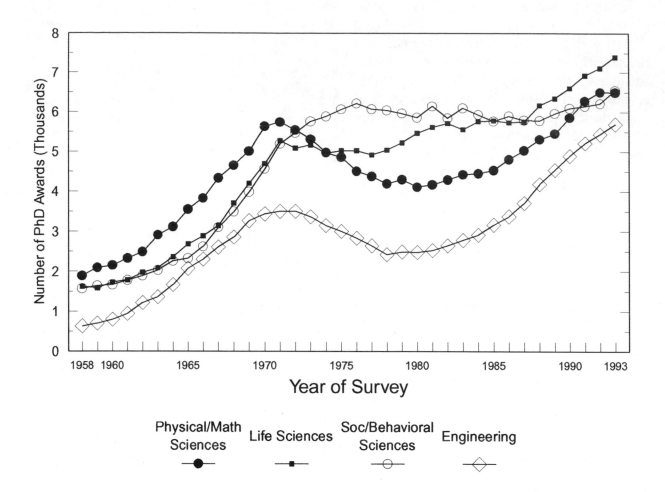

FIGURE 1-1 Number of doctorates awarded by US institutions, by broad field, 1958-1993.

SOURCE: NSF, 1994f:Table 1, for 1983-1993; unpublished "decade" tables, Office of Scientific and Engineering Personnel, National Research Council, for prior years.

NOTE: The physical/mathematical sciences include physics, chemistry, astronomy, mathematics, computer/information science, and environmental (ocean, atmospheric, earth) sciences. The life sciences include the biological, agricultural, and medical sciences. The social/behavioral sciences include the social sciences (e.g., economics, sociology, political science) and psychology. More detailed information on fields of doctorates awarded in 1983-1993 is presented in Appendix B, Table B-20.

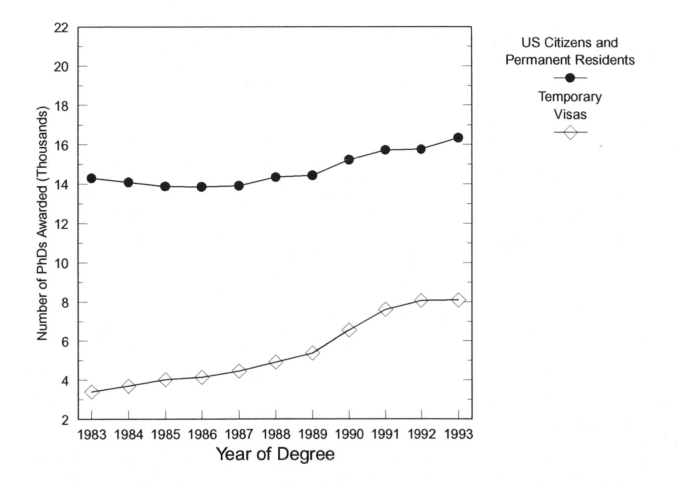

FIGURE 1-2 Trends in citizenship of recipients of doctorates from US institutions, 1983-1993.

SOURCE: Calculated from NSF, 1994f:Table 3.

NOTE: The numbers are based on those whose citizenship was known (between 92% and 98% of each year's doctorate recipients in 1983-1993).

of the Cold War has led to major cuts in defense spending, which are a source of R&D funding.[3] The cuts began in 1987, when, for the first time, the overall increase in federal funding for research stopped growing faster than inflation. Not only have fiscal constraints affected the science-oriented government agencies, but the agencies have responded to political forces by shifting toward an emphasis on "strategic" research that is oriented toward national objectives.

The last decade has seen both a rise in international economic competition and cutbacks in basic research at large industrial laboratories. Industry is said to be hiring fewer scientists and engineers and shifting emphasis toward core businesses; industrial grants to universities, an important source of research funds, are said to be reduced and increasingly directed toward incremental, low-risk programs.

State governments are tightening their budgets, with some public universities experiencing absolute decreases of 20-25% in state funding. That has reduced the ability of state universities to hire scientific and engineering faculty and to fund graduate students. Many state legislators view graduate education as a budget item that must compete with social requirements whose call on the tax dollar is at least as persuasive. Criticisms of faculty productivity are common, as is a general skepticism that the public receives an adequate return on its investment in graduate education. The Maryland General Assembly, for example, has ordered new policies that establish explicit expectations for faculty workload and responsibilities. Furthermore, state legislators have sometimes questioned the benefit of educating graduate students who leave the state on graduating.

Owing to these financial constraints, universities must use more of their own funds to support research, especially for projects considered long-term or risky. And they are less able to offer tenure-track positions to new young faculty.

As the financial support for basic research has plateaued, the graduate-education system has been criticized by the public and Congress for neglecting education and other societal needs. With the end of the Cold War and the growth of global economic competition, the nation's attention has shifted from defense to economic, environmental, and other social concerns: we are faced with the challenge of finding better ways to use natural resources, to produce energy, and to deliver health care, and we need to produce better products and services in an internationally competitive marketplace. The nation also has to deal with crime, violence, and poverty.   At the international level, we are concerned with limiting population growth, stabilizing emergent democracies, and fostering appropriate industries in developing countries, as well as with sustaining national security and global economic health. The role of research in addressing those concerns is not nearly as clear to the nation as was its role in winning the Cold War or the "space race."

In the face of these complex societal concerns, scientists and engineers have been challenged to take more active and visible roles in society—roles that require leadership,

---

[3] Universities became less dependent on Department of Defense (DoD) funding in the 1960s and 1970s. Currently, less than 14% of federal support of R&D in colleges and universities comes from DoD. A major cut in DoD R&D would affect federal funding of universities by only a few percent (Sapolsky, 1994). But this decline in defense R&D would probably be highly concentrated in particular fields (such as aeronautics and oceanography).

cooperation, and flexibility. Society expects them to contribute to new debates on public policy, to improve our competitive position in global markets, to help to create high-value jobs, and to improve the education of citizens at many levels.

To repeat: American graduate schools have done a superb job of preparing young scientists and engineers to become original researchers—to become the scientific and technical leaders of the nation. It is the purpose of this report to examine how well graduate school prepares students to integrate and disseminate their knowledge and apply it to the full range of present societal needs.

2

THE EMPLOYMENT OF GRADUATE SCIENTISTS AND ENGINEERS

2.1 CURRENT EMPLOYMENT CONDITIONS

The economy of the United States is absorbing rapidly increasing numbers of graduate scientists and engineers, but continued growth is less certain.

The number of people with science and engineering PhD degrees from US universities who are working in this country has nearly doubled since 1973, from 220,000 to 437,000 in 1991.[1] Figure 2-1 shows this growth by major field. Currently, more than 25,000 scientists and engineers earn PhDs from US institutions each year, most of whom enter the US labor

---

[1] National estimates of employment-related characteristics of scientists and engineers used here and throughout the report are from the Survey of Doctorate Recipients (SDR). The SDR is a biennial panel survey of a nationally representative sample of recipients of doctorates in science and engineering from U.S. institutions working in the United States. It is conducted by the National Research Council and has gathered employment related information since 1973 for NSF and other federal agencies. Major changes in survey timing and procedures were made in the 1991 survey that limit the comparability of estimates with those of the 1973-1989 surveys. More vigorous follow-up increased the response rate from 58% to 80%, which reduced nonresponse bias among those outside academia or who had left the country. This should have reduced overestimates of the number of U.S. PhDs remaining in the U.S. and of those employed in academia of perhaps 5% in the earlier surveys. The SDR is described more fully in Appendix C, which has a fuller discussion of changes in the 1991 and 1993 surveys and their implications for comparability of time-series data and longitudinal analysis.

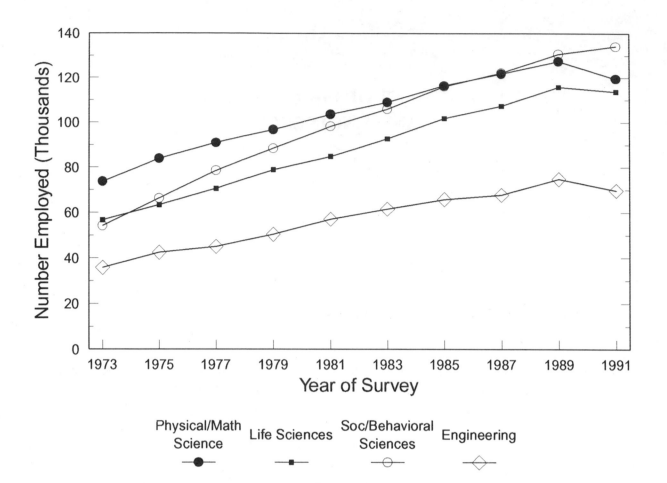

FIGURE 2-1 Growth in employment of doctoral scientists and engineers in the United States, 1973-1991.

SOURCE: NSF, 1991:Table 1, for 1973-1989; NSF, 1994d:Table 1, for 1991.

NOTES: In this figure, postdoctoral appointees are included in the labor force.

The data are national estimates of the numbers of scientists and engineers with doctorates from US institutions. The estimates are derived from the biennial sample Survey of Doctorate Recipients conducted for the National Science Foundation by the Office of Scientific and Engineering Personnel, National Research Council.

In 1991, survey procedures and timing were changed in ways that improved the estimates but introduced major comparability problems. The response rate, which had fallen steadily during the 1980s (from 66% in 1979 to 58% in 1989), increased to 80% in 1991. Nonresponse bias in the earlier surveys had led to overestimates of 5% or more in the total number of scientists and engineers in the United States. The new procedures, which involved much more intensive followup of those who did not respond initially, no doubt reduced the overestimate, but the extent is not known. The drop in number of employed scientists and engineers from 1989 to 1991 is due at least in part to the change in survey procedures. For example, if the estimates in 1989 were reduced by 5%, the number of doctorates working in the United States would have increased by 3% instead of decreased by 3% from 1989 to 1991.

market either immediately or after a period of postdoctoral study.[2] Appendix C discusses employment trends among graduate scientists and engineers in more detail.

Although increasing numbers of new PhDs have been readily absorbed into the job market over the years, there are clear indications that the most recent new PhDs in some fields are not finding employment as easily as earlier ones, and graduates who have found employment have been more likely to find less-desirable or less-secure positions than earlier graduates.

Employment Trends

Among recent PhDs, there is a steady trend away from positions in education and basic research and toward applied research and development and more diverse, even nonresearch, employment.

Graduate scientists and engineers have traditionally been educated and prepared for employment positions in which the ability to perform original research is the skill of highest value. The traditional positions include research-intensive occupations in academe,[3] industry, and government laboratories where scholarship and research—especially basic research—constitute the primary focus of employment. During recent decades, such research-intensive jobs have increased steadily, and many new PhDs have been able to choose from an expanding number of such traditional jobs. However, available information on job distribution and trends in terms of both primary work activity and the location of that work indicates a persistent long-term trend away from employment in traditional research and teaching positions and toward applied research and development and non-academic employment (see Figure 2-2).

For example, the proportion of scientists and engineers engaged in basic research and teaching as their primary activity has declined while the proportion of people involved in applied research and development and other types of work has increased. According to the SDR, in 1973, 52% of scientists and engineers with PhDs from US universities were engaged in basic research or teaching activities, but, in 1991, only 37% were in such positions (Table C-3B). On the other hand, individuals employed in applied research and development increased by about one-third, and the fraction employed in business and industry increased from about 24% in 1973 to 36% in 1991. Within that group, the share of self-employed people more than quadrupled, to nearly 9% (Table C-3B).

---

[2] An unknown number of graduate scientists and engineers graduating from foreign institutions also enter the labor market.

[3] Academe is defined in this report to include 4-year colleges, universities, and medical schools, but not 2-year colleges or precollege (K-12) educational institutions.

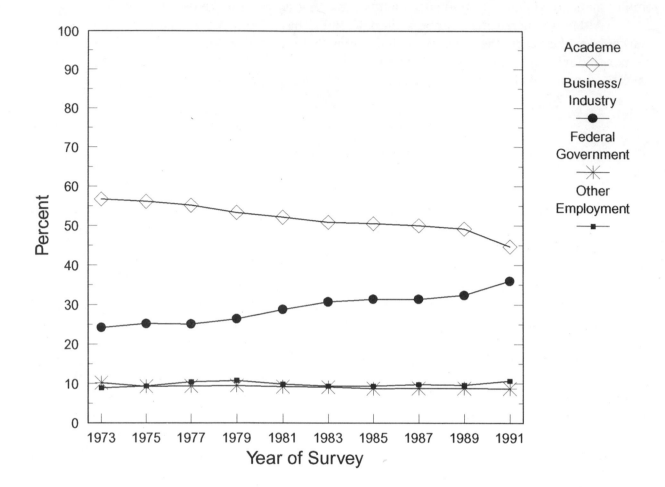

FIGURE 2-2 Scientists and engineers with US PhDs, by employment sector, 1973-1991.

SOURCE: Calculated from NSF, 1991:Table 3, for 1973-1989, and from NSF, 1994d:Table 9, for 1991.

NOTES: See notes for Figure 2-1 for important information about the comparability of 1991 estimates with the estimates for previous years.

Academe includes those employed at 4-year colleges, universities, and medical schools (including university-affiliated hospitals and medical centers).

Business/industry includes those who are self-employed.

Other employment includes other education (junior colleges, 2-year colleges, technical institutes, and elementary, middle, and secondary schools); state and local governments; hospitals and clinics; private foundations and other nonprofit organizations; other employers; and those who did not respond to the employment-sector question.

Furthermore, the fraction of total PhDs in science and engineering who are employed in academe has declined to less that half in recent years (see Figure 2-3). In addition, basic-research positions in some industry and national laboratories have also been declining. As a result, the activities and employment sectors that scientists and engineers with PhDs have been going into have been diversifying.

Those long-term trends are the basis for a major conclusion of this report, i.e., that **PhDs are increasingly finding employment outside universities and more and more are in types of positions that they had not expected to occupy.**

It should be noted that different fields and subfields of science and engineering vary widely with respect to employment patterns, job availability, and degree requirements. For example, in chemistry and engineering, many PhDs have long worked in industry; in other fields, many still work in universities.

Within nearly all fields, however, the broad trend is consistent: a smaller proportion of PhDs is going into universities and the federal government, and a larger proportion is going into business and industry (engineering was the only field in which the proportion of PhDs entering universities increased substantially. With the SDR data, it is possible to compare cohorts of scientists and engineers 5-8 years after receipt of PhD, i.e., after most of them have completed a period of postdoctoral study. More than half the 1969-1972 science and engineering PhDs were employed in universities in 1977, compared with less than 43% of the 1983-1986 PhDs in 1991 (Figure 2-4). Only 26% of them were employed in business and industry in 1973, compared with 35% in 1991.

Appendix C provides an in-depth analysis of the employment distribution of new and recent science and engineering PhDs by discipline. This is an original analysis based on data from the SDR. Information on a sectoral basis is also provided in the next section of this chapter.

Employment difficulties are most acute among new PhDs, many of whom are unable to find desirable positions in their field. Barry Hardy, who has done postdoctoral work at the National Institutes of Health and is currently a postdoc at the University of Oxford in England, has spoken out about these difficulties and offered suggestions for change. With several other members of the Young Scientists' Network Internet discussion forum, he wrote an open letter to Harold Varmus, director of the National Institutes of Health, outlining options for change.

At the committee's invitation, Dr. Hardy offered a series of suggestions for improving the graduate education experience:

● Include young scientists and engineers on policy panels, especially those affecting the funding of graduate students.
● Improve the evaluation of training grant programs.
● Fund an Internet-based information gathering and sharing system.
● Modify graduate student programs so they are more flexible and diverse.
● Improve employment conditions for postdocs so they can support their families and expect reasonable job security.
● Increase participation of young scientists at conferences.
● Reduce constraints on expression by graduate students.
● Balance immigration policies and fair treatment of foreign students.
● Develop computer simulation models to better predict science and technology employment patterns.

Box 2-1: The plight of the new PhD - Suggestions for change

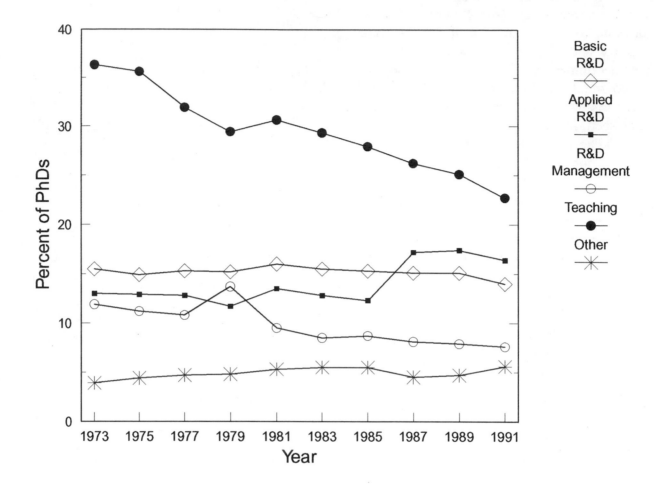

FIGURE 2-3 Primary work activity of scientists and engineers with PhDs from US universities, 1973-1991.

SOURCE: Calculated from NSF, 1991:Table 3, for 1973-1989 and from NSF, 1994d:Table 10, for 1991.

NOTES: See notes for Figure 2-1 for important information about the comparability of 1991 estimates with the estimates for previous years.

The other activities surveyed, which accounted for nearly 20% of the PhD scientists and engineers in 1973, increasing to almost one-third in 1991, included management of non-R&D activities, consulting, professional services, statistical/data analysis/reporting, and "other" and "no report."

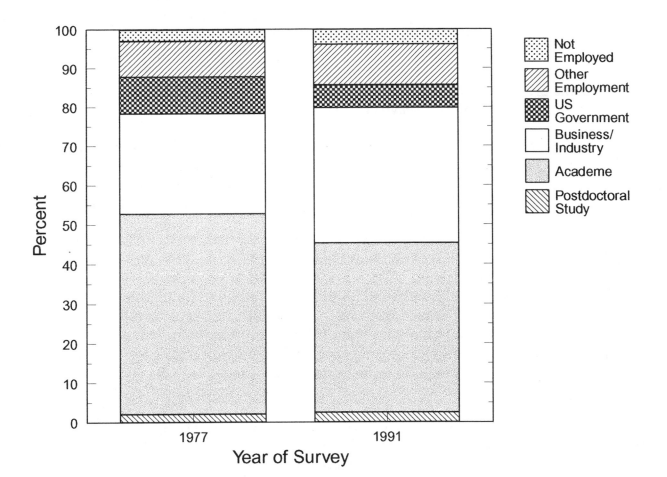

FIGURE 2-4 Change in employment sector of scientists and engineers 5-8 years after receipt of US doctorates, 1977 and 1991.

SOURCE: Special runs of data from the Survey of Doctorate Recipients on employment sector of US doctoral scientists and engineers 5-8 years after receiving the PhD (in this case, 1969-1972 PhD recipients in 1977 and 1983-1986 PhD recipients in 1991). Psychology PhDs, many of whom go into clinical psychology, are not included in the totals.

NOTES: See notes for Figure 2-1 for important information about the comparability of 1991 estimates with the estimates for previous years.

Academe includes those employed at 4-year colleges, universities, and medical schools (including university-affiliated hospitals and medical centers).

Business/industry includes those who are self-employed.

Other employment includes other education (junior colleges, 2-year colleges, technical institutes, and elementary, middle, and secondary schools); state and local governments; hospitals and clinics; private foundations and other nonprofit organizations; other employers; and those who did not respond to the employment-sector question.

Not employed includes the unemployed (seeking work) and those not seeking employment, retired, or otherwise out of the workforce or not reporting workforce status.

Unemployment and Delayed Employment

Recent graduate scientists and engineers have been experiencing increasing delays in securing permanent employment.

The employment picture for scientists and engineers, especially for recent graduates, is not clear, partly because the pertinent national surveys of new and recent PhD recipients lag by several years. The picture is complicated by wide differences among fields, some of which are shrinking as others grow. Nonetheless, we find clear evidence of employment difficulties in many disciplines.

Such difficulties are hard to detect with traditional measures, such as the SDR. According to SDR data, unemployment rates for PhD scientists and engineers have remained steady and low for the last decade, compared with those in other segments of the economy. Unemployment rates for PhD scientists and engineers were about 1% in the 1980s surveys and about 1.5% in the 1990s. Unemployment rates for the most recent 2 years of science and engineering PhD graduates were about 1.5% in the 1980s, but rose to 2% in 1993, the last year for which data are available—a disquieting increase that bears watching.[4] The latter rate compares favorably not only with the overall unemployment rate (above 6% in the early 1990s), but also with unemployment among professional occupations generally (2.6% in 1992 and 1993) and among those with at least a college degree (around 3% in the early 1990s) (see Figure 2-5).

The evidence obtained through committee panels and submitted comments (see Appendix G) and through surveys of recent PhDs by some of the scientific societies shows that an unusually high percentage of scientists and engineers are still looking for employment at the time of or soon after receiving their doctorates. Results of surveys by the professional societies of physicists, chemists, and mathematicians indicate that graduates in some fields are experiencing double-digit unemployment for increasing periods after graduation. **Recent scientific and engineering PhDs do eventually find employment, but in some fields the process is taking much longer than it did for their predecessors.**

For example, the mathematical societies conduct surveys of new PhDs each summer and update them in the spring. The percentage of new PhD mathematicians still looking for positions in the summer was about 5% during most of the 1980s but in 1990 began to rise to more than 12% for the classes of 1991-1993.[5] According to the American Mathematical Society (AMS) the percentage of new mathematicians looking for employment the summer after receiving their PhDs was 14.4% for the class of 1994, even though the number of new PhDs was 12% smaller than the class of 1993 (AMS, 1994b). Similarly, the percentage of new PhDs still unemployed in the next spring was about 3% in the late 1980s, 5% for the class of 1991, 7% for the class of 1992, and 9% for the class of 1993 (AMS, 1994a). The American Institute

---

[4] It is not known how much of this increase in unemployment rates should be attributed to a change in survey methods.

[5] A class is defined as those graduating each year from June to June.

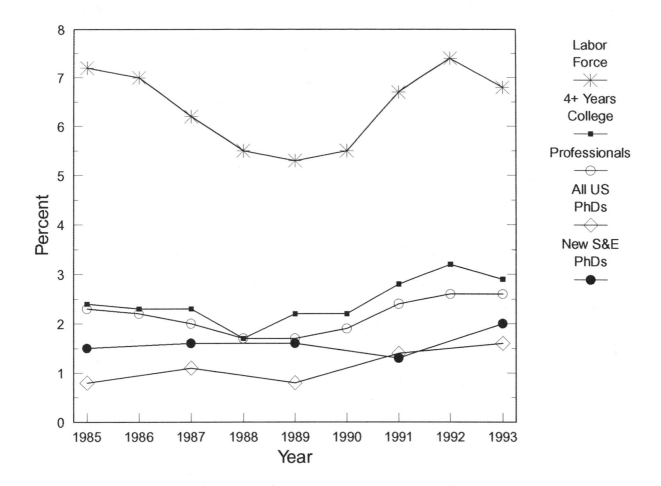

FIGURE 2-5 Unemployment rates among different occupational and educational groups in the civilian noninstitutional labor force, 1985-1993.

SOURCES: US Bureau of the Census, 1994:Table 616, for average monthly unemployment of the civilian noninstitutional labor force aged 16 or older.

US Bureau of the Census, 1994:Table 650, for average monthly unemployment of the civilian noninstitutional labor force aged 25 or older with 4 years or more of college.

US Bureau of the Census, 1994:Table 649, and unpublished Bureau of the Census tables, for average monthly unemployment among civilian noninstitutional labor force aged 16 or older in professional specialty occupations (includes S&Es).

NSF, 1991, NSF, 1994d, and unpublished SDR tables, for unemployment among S&Es with doctorates from US universities.

Unpublished SDR tables, for unemployment among S&Es 1-2 years after receiving PhD from US university.

of Physics (AIP), which also surveys new PhDs each year, found that in 1993, 14% of new doctoral physicists looking for employment had not received a job offer around the time of graduation, a figure that dropped to 6% six months after graduation. Preliminary estimates for the class of 1994 indicate that those numbers were about 12% and 4% respectively (unpublished AIP data). An American Chemical Society survey of new chemists found that more than 16% of the PhD class of 1993 were seeking employment during the summer of 1993 (Table B-1a in ACS, 1993).

Underemployment and Underutilization

When recent graduates do find employment, they are increasingly underemployed or underutilized.

Doctoral students trained in American universities are traditionally well educated for permanent or tenure-track positions in which they conduct significant research in universities, industry, or government agencies. In the recent past, the US science and technology enterprise has grown so rapidly that most advanced-degree holders could expect such a position after graduation. Testimony provided to the committee, however, indicates that today many more new science and engineering PhDs are able to obtain only part-time positions, short-term non-tenure-track positions, postdoctoral positions that are extended for nonacademic reasons, or positions that are not of the expected type and for which one does not explicitly require a PhD degree.[6]

The National Science Foundation (NSF) uses two technical categories to describe such conditions. The **underemployed** are defined as those working part-time but seeking full-time work or those working in a nonscience and nonengineering job but desiring a science or engineering job. The **underutilized** are the **unemployed** (those who do not have positions but are seeking positions) **plus the underemployed** (NSF, 1994d:69). When considering the employment trends that graduate scientists and engineers have generally had since World War II, underutilized recent PhDs might be described as scientists and engineers whose present employment positions have not matched their career expectations.

The SDR includes both underemployment and underutilization rates. In 1991, for example, 89.7% of scientific and engineering PhDs were employed and 1.4% were unemployed (together, these are considered the total scientific and engineering labor force).[7] Of those employed, 1.7% were underemployed as defined above. Therefore, of the total labor force, 3.1% were underutilized. The underemployment rate was 1.3% in 1985, 1987, and 1989 and

---

[6] Data limitations prevent quantitative analysis and verification of some of these claims.

[7] The remaining 8.9% were retired, not looking for work, or otherwise out of the workforce. It is important to note that the survey retains people in the sample for 42 years, so some people are past common retirement ages.

1.7% in 1991.[8] The underutilization rate was 2.1% in 1985, 2.4% in 1987, 2.1% in 1989, and 3.1% in 1991. Those figures, of course, differ by field.

Anecdotal information also indicates that although recent scientific and engineering PhDs are seldom working in jobs for which their graduate work is not relevant (e.g., working in a restaurant), they are increasingly able to obtain only part-time or temporary positions. Data collected by the scientific societies are also useful. For example, results of the AMS survey cited earlier indicate that beyond the 9% unemployment rate, an additional 5.5% of recent PhDs were able to obtain only part-time positions, and more than half those taking faculty jobs were in non-tenure-track positions (AMS, 1994a). About 10% of the physics PhD class of 1992 was working in temporary or part-time positions (Kirby and Czujko, 1993:23).

Another statistical indicator of underutilization is the rising percentage of new PhDs taking postdoctoral positions. A postdoctoral position is intended to provide further depth of education and job preparation, but it can also act as a safety net when the labor market is poor. The number of scientists and engineers in postdoctoral positions has grown substantially, from less than 15,000 in 1982 to more than 24,000 in 1992 (see Table B-38). From 1991 to 1992, the number increased by 5%.

Surveys do not determine the extent to which young scientists and engineers take postdoctoral positions for lack of regular employment. In chemistry, for example, the pool of postdoctoral scientists and engineers is estimated to have doubled during the last 10 years to more than 4,000. This is equivalent to the number of chemists who receive PhDs in 2 years (Rawls, 1994). Some attribute at least part of this increase to the preference of employers—especially pharmaceutical companies—for chemists with 3 or 4 years of postdoctoral experience.

2.2   EMPLOYMENT TRENDS BY SECTOR

Most of the long-term growth in employment demand for graduate scientists and engineers has occurred in business and industry.

Professional careers are becoming increasingly varied and nonacademic, although this varies somewhat by discipline (see Figure 2-6). More and more scientists and engineers are being exposed to nonacademic fields before, during, or after their academic preparation. In

---

[8] As this report was going to press, NSF released a *Data Brief* citing 4.3 percent underemployment among doctoral scientists and engineers in 1993. This rate should not be compared with the reported 1991 rate of 1.7 percent, however, because the definition of underemployment was broadened between the 2 survey years. In 1991, individuals were counted as underemployed if they were working part-time or outside of science or engineering when they desired a science or engineering position. In 1993, the requirement was expanded to include those working part-time or outside their doctoral field when they desired a position within their doctoral field.

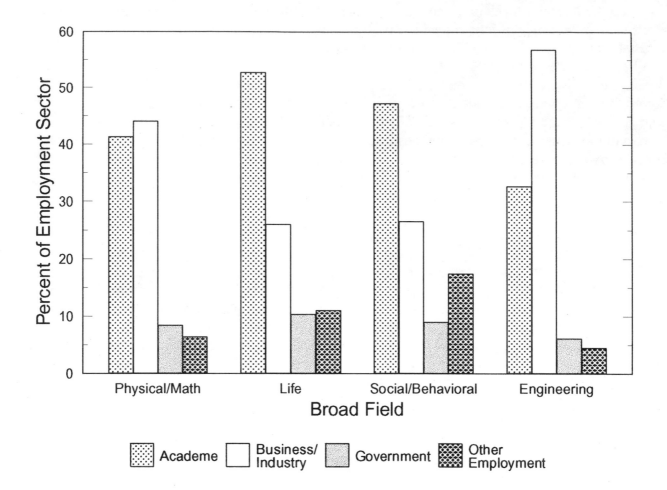

FIGURE 2-6 Employment sectors of scientists and engineers with US PhDs, by broad field, 1991.

SOURCE: Calculated from NSF, 1994d:Table 9.

NOTES: *Academe* includes those employed at 4-year colleges, universities, and medical schools (including university-affiliated hospitals and medical centers).

Business/industry includes those who are self-employed.

Other employment includes other education (junior colleges, 2-year colleges, technical institutes, and elementary, middle, and secondary schools); state and local governments; hospitals and clinics; private foundations and other nonprofit organizations; other employers; and those who did not respond to the employment-sector question.

addition, because more courses are offered as evening or "distance learning" programs, many graduate students work part- or full-time as they study.

Although most graduate scientists and engineers remain in the same general field as that of their bachelor's degree, many switch fields and thereby obtain interdisciplinary training. Furthermore, throughout their careers, graduate scientists and engineers commonly change subjects, kinds of employment, and employment sectors, moving, for example, between educational, industrial, business, and government organizations.

The following sections attempt to describe the direction of employment trends by sector. Although not included in the following section because of the lack of information on their activities, an additional 29,000 PhDs work in nonprofit institutions—including 9,000 in research and development, 9,500 in professional services, and 6,000 in administration (NSF, 1991).

Education

Of students who earn science and engineering PhDs, the proportion who enter academe has declined to less than half, and this long-term decline is likely to continue. However, there is likely to be increasing demand for teachers in precollege positions.

In the educational sector, according to the 1989 SDR, 48% of the 22,000 people working in universities said their primary activity was teaching and 36% said research and development (24% basic research, 12% applied research and development). Of the 10,000 employed in other educational institutions (precollege and community college), 59% were teachers and 15% were administrators (calculated from Table 27 in NSF, 1991). In 1992, of the 176,777 faculty and staff (regardless of degree) with instructional responsibilities in natural sciences[9] and engineering in postsecondary institutions,[10] 71% were full-time and 29% were part-time (NCES, 1994).

As shown in Table 2-1, between 1977 and 1991, the proportion of scientists and engineers with US doctorates who were employed in colleges and universities declined from 51% to 43%.[11] This trend was true for all fields except mathematics (which had a 1-year rise in 1991 after years of decline) and engineering. Only 31% of those who received PhDs in 1983-1986 were in tenure-track positions or had tenure as of 1991, whereas more than 35% of those who received PhDs in 1973-1976 were in such positions or had tenure in 1981.

---

[9] "Natural sciences" are defined by the US Department of Education to include biological sciences, physical sciences, mathematics, and computer sciences.

[10] "Postsecondary institutions" include junior colleges, 4-year colleges, and universities.

[11] Note that some of this change might be due to an overestimation of the numbers of persons employed in academe in earlier surveys. This analysis was done for persons 5-8 years after they received their PhDs to account for the time taken in postdoctoral study, which varies by field.

TABLE 2-1 **Changes in Percentages of Scientists and Engineers Employed in Academe 5-8 Years after Receiving US PhD, by Broad Field, 1977 and 1991**

	1977	1991
TOTAL	50.7	42.9%
PHYSICAL SCIENCES	46.5	37.3
Mathematical sciences	74.4	76.0
Computer sciences	45.8	41.8
Physics/Astronomy	45.9	38.3
Chemistry	32.1	21.2
Earth/Environmental sciences	50.2	45.1
LIFE SCIENCES	58.2	46.5
Agricultural sciences	55.4	47.1
Medical sciences	56.5	50.7
Biological sciences	59.1	45.7
SOCIAL SCIENCES	74.4	55.4
Psychology	45.7	26.0
ENGINEERING	28.8	32.2

NOTES: See notes for Figure 2-1 for important information about the comparability of 1991 estimates with the estimates for previous years.

Academe includes those employed at 4-year colleges, universities, and medical schools (including university-affiliated hospitals and medical centers).

SOURCE: Special runs of data from the Survey of Doctorate Recipients of employment sector of US doctoral scientists and engineers 5-8 years after receiving the PhD (in this case, 1969-1972 PhD recipients in 1977 and 1983-1986 PhD recipients in 1991). Psychology PhDs, many of whom go into clinical psychology, are not included in the totals.

Consider, however, our precollege-education system as an alternative employment market. Employment of master's-degree recipients and PhDs at the precollege level is expected to grow, and the salaries of entry-level teachers at the PhD level in many precollege school systems are not strikingly different from those of entry-level professors. According to Department of Education projections for the year 2002, the total number of science-related pre-college teachers is about 480,000 and is expected to increase by 1.3-1.6% per year, which would create thousands of new positions annually (plus those created by retirement or attrition). The average entry-level salary of a precollege teacher with a PhD is about $35,800, and that of an entry-level professor is about $36,600 (NCES, 1991;1993).

Some might question whether this is an appropriate occupation for someone with a PhD science or engineering education. However, it is generally agreed that a basic education in science and mathematics will be essential to prepare all Americans for effective participation in our increasingly scientific and technical society in the 21st century. The national science-education standards prepared by the National Research Council call for hands-on inquiry-based science to become a core subject for all Americans starting in kindergarten (NRC, 1995 forthcoming). Who will lead this effort in each of the 16,000 school districts in the United States? And who will teach our children inquiry-based science? Large numbers of scientifically trained teachers are needed if science and mathematics

Gerald Stancil received his PhD in physical chemistry from Johns Hopkins University in 1976. Today he is a high-school physics teacher in Orange, New Jersey. Is he disappointed? No, because when Dr. Stancil came to Orange High School, there was one physics class with 13 students. Today, there are three physics classes with 75 students.

He is doing what he wants to do. But he was not guided to this path in graduate school, where he learned that PhDs do not work in public schools. Nor was he schooled in the skills and abilities he uses most today—communication skills and social skills—or in an understanding of youth or a love of sharing his knowledge with others.

Dr. Stancil entered the high-school classroom 4 years ago through a New Jersey program called Alternate Route, set up specifically to attract people with graduate degrees to public-school teaching. In his comments to the committee, he noted that such alternative-teaching certification programs are becoming more common. In the past, many educators opposed hiring people at the graduate level; today, they recognize the growing need for better-prepared teachers in science and engineering.

In the New Jersey program, a 1-year course leads to provisional certification. Then the new teacher works with a mentor and after 2 years receives full certification. Other states, including Maryland, New York, and Pennsylvania, have initiated similar programs.

Dr. Stancil believes that PhDs can make a great contribution to precollege education. He told the committee that many public-school students don't even know what a PhD is; for example, they ask him for medical advice. He believes that because of such ignorance, many potential scientists and engineers are lost at around the eighth grade. As a black man, he is able to serve as a model for minority-group students, who might have little understanding of how to approach a career in science and engineering.

He does not have to make a financial sacrifice to do what he is doing. He told the committee that people with PhDs teaching high school make salaries comparable with the median salaries at most universities. Starting teachers with PhDs make about $36,000 in New Jersey, and senior PhD teachers like him earn a salary of about $55,000 for 9 months of work a year.

Box 2-2: A High-School Teacher with a PhD

are to be core subjects for all precollege students; however, current graduate-education programs do not provide sufficient knowledge, validation, or training regarding education for graduate scientists and engineers to make a transition from scientific and engineering research to teaching at these lower levels.

Some states offer innovative certification programs in precollege teaching for those with advanced degrees (see Box 2-2). As indicated by one committee witness, such programs can enliven precollege education and offer unique rewards to teachers. Furthermore, the talent of motivated graduate scientists and engineers should raise the overall level of science education for younger students who might eventually enter science and engineering.

Government

Positions for graduate scientists and engineers in government are decreasing, and this trend is likely to continue. However, there is likely to be more demand for scientists and engineers to work in particular fields, such as those related to environmental protection.

In the government sector, of the 29,000 PhDs working for the federal government in 1989, half were in research and development and one-fourth were administrators. Of the 16,000 in research and development, one-third were in basic research and more than half in applied research. In the case of the 11,000 PhDs working in state government, about one-fifth were in research and development and one-third were in management (calculated from NSF, 1991).

The federal government has long been a major source of employment for scientists and engineers. However, as shown in Table 2-2, this trend is decreasing for all fields except earth/environmental sciences. As of September 1993, 112,543 engineers and 99,239 scientists were federal employees.[12] Of the engineers, 3,681 had doctorates and 25,482 had master's degrees; of the scientists, 18,109 had doctorates and 25,744 had master's degrees.

In 1989, the federal government hired more than 13,000 new scientists and engineers—1,100 with PhDs, 2,600 with master's degrees, and more than 9,000 with other degrees.

By 1993, low turnover, program cuts, and hiring freezes had reduced the number of newly hired scientists and engineers to barely 4,000, or about 71% fewer than in 1989 (81% fewer engineers, because of staff reduction in the Department of Defense, and 50% fewer scientists). Moreover, those being hired were a little older, probably because the federal agencies had a choice of people with more experience.

---

[12] Data on federal employment of scientists and engineers were provided by Leonard Klein, Associate Director of the Office of Personnel Management, Career Entry and Employee Development Group, in a presentation to the Committee on Science, Engineering, and Public Policy at its April 6-7, 1994 meeting at the National Academy of Sciences in Washington, D.C.

TABLE 2-2   Changes in Percentages of Scientists and Engineers Who Are Civilian Employees of the Federal Government 5-8 Years after Receiving US PhD, by Broad Field, 1977 and 1991

	1977	1991
TOTAL	9.5	5.9
PHYSICAL SCIENCES	9.1	5.5
Mathematical sciences	3.5	1.9
Computer sciences	9.5	0.8
Physics/Astronomy	13	9.5
Chemistry	6	2.4
Earth/Environmental sciences	18.0	22.7
LIFE SCIENCES	9.7	6.7
Agricultural sciences	16.1	11.7
Medical sciences	7.8	5.7
Biological sciences	8.3	5.7
SOCIAL SCIENCES	5.8	5.1
Psychology	3.8	2.4
ENGINEERING	12.9	5.4

NOTES: See notes for Figure 2-1 for important information about the comparability of 1991 estimates with the estimates for previous years.

SOURCE: Special runs of data from the Survey of Doctorate Recipients of employment sector of US doctoral scientists and engineers 5-8 years after receiving the PhD (in this case, 1969-1972 PhD recipients in 1977 and 1983-1986 PhD recipients in 1991). Psychology PhDs, many of whom go into clinical psychology, are not included in the totals.

There are niches of opportunity in specific fields, such as energy and environment, but the overall numbers are steady or declining because of staff reductions and low turnover.

Business and Industry

Over the long term, demand for graduate scientists and engineers in business and industry is increasing; more employment options are available to graduate scientists and engineers who have multiple disciplines, minor degrees, personal communication skills, and entrepreneurial initiative.

In the business and industry sector, according to the 1989 SDR, of the 113,000 working in for-profit organizations, half listed research and development as their primary activity. Most—35,000—were in applied research, and another 18,000 did development work. Another large group—29,000—were administrators and managers (primarily of research and development). Less than 3% of the PhDs in industry were doing basic research. Of the 32,000 who were self-employed, half were in professional services and one-fourth were consultants (calculated from NSF, 1991).

As shown in Table 2-3, the proportion of scientists and engineers employed in business and industry for all fields has increased from 26% in 1977 to 35% in 1991.

Some PhDs are now adapting to fields once considered remote from science and engineering. Albert Bellino, an executive at Banker's Trust in New York, told the committee that investment banking is one such field in which advanced scientists and engineers are held in high esteem.

Mr. Bellino is a managing director at Banker's Trust, one of a number Wall Street firms that hire a total of perhaps 100 PhDs in science each year. His firm, for example, hires about 10-15 PhDs each year. In total, the company now employs approximately 150 PhDs among its 5,000 employees. Most newly hired employees have traditionally been economists, but the number of PhDs in physical sciences and mathematics is rising. The company believes that such training is excellent preparation that is easily transferred to financial markets.

There have been other changes in the qualities desired at Banker's Trust. In the past, said Mr. Bellino, the bank looked for these traits: "hardworking, reliable, local, team player, consistent performer." Now, it prefers "smart, intense, driven, problem solver, entrepreneur, quixotic, a little abrasive." It used to seek out people who were involved in jogging, swimming, tennis, and travel; now, it looks for bridge, chess, crossword puzzles, trading of baseball cards or stamps, linguistics, and music.

Mr. Bellino explained that the latter traits are desirable because investment banking has become an "ideas business." It wants people who have the best ideas, who know how to implement ideas, and who can manage risk on behalf of their clients and themselves. It also seeks those with an interest in markets (for example, someone who ran a family fund or had such a hobby as trading baseball cards) and those whose communication skills enable them to be effective in a less-hierarchical organization.

Box 2-3: Investment Banking

In some fields—such as chemistry, engineering, and computer science—graduate scientists and engineers have long found employment in nonacademic markets. But survey data, buttressed by testimony of committee witnesses and correspondents, show that this trend now applies to

TABLE 2-3   Changes in Percentages of Scientists and Engineers Employed in Business/Industry 5-8 Years after Receiving US PhD, by Broad Field, 1977 and 1991

	1977	1991
TOTAL	25.6	34.5
PHYSICAL SCIENCES	30.4	44.2
Mathematical sciences	12.2	18.6
Computer sciences	42.0	50.3
Physics/Astronomy	25.1	38.2
Chemistry	45.5	60.9
Earth/Environmental sciences	18.6	22.7
LIFE SCIENCES	12.9	26.4
Agricultural sciences	17.9	30.8
Medical sciences	15.9	26.4
Biological sciences	11.4	25.4
SOCIAL SCIENCES	5.6	13.1
Psychology	15.4	36.5
ENGINEERING	50.5	56.7

NOTES: See notes for Figure 2-1 for important information about the comparability of 1991 estimates with the estimates for previous years.

SOURCE: Special runs of data from the Survey of Doctorate Recipients of employment sector of US doctoral scientists and engineers 5-8 years after receiving the PhD (in this case, 1969-1972 PhD recipients in 1977 and 1983-1986 PhD recipients in 1991). Psychology PhDs, many of whom go into clinical psychology, are not included in the totals.

other fields as well (see Table 2-1). For example, in biological sciences, the percentage employed in business and industry increased from 11% in 1977 to 25% in 1991.

The evidence received by the committee indicates that the trend will continue and that most job creation for scientists and engineers in coming years will occur in business and industry. However, for a variety of reasons, some large industries are modifying or closing their central research laboratories: some have become smaller, and some have shifted into enterprises that emphasize development, marketing, and R&D activities that are designed primarily for short-term economic gain. Hence, although industries will continue to perform research and to offer employment, they might not support traditional research to the degree that they have in the past.

In small and medium-size companies, new and emerging technologies develop rapidly. Such companies provide one of the few increases in R&D funding. Because staff sizes in such companies are limited, successful science and engineering employees are those who can cross disciplinary boundaries and have talents in product development, manufacturing, or technical services.

Jobs in industries that depend on emerging technologies show steady increases (which, however, can fluctuate with the business cycle). Within those industries are fields that are expanding, such as manufacturing simulation, information science, computational simulation, software engineering, data processing, visualization, forensic science, and electronic networking.

2.3   EMPLOYER PERSPECTIVES

As part of its outreach effort, the committee sent out a call for comments to over 1,000 persons: graduate students, postdoctoral researchers, professors, university administrators, industry scientists and executives, and representatives of scientific societies. The 100 responses received (50% of which came from industry) are summarized in Appendix F. This section provides an overview of graduate education from an employer perspective.

Why do organizations employ individuals with a scientific background? Here is a view from the president of a biotechnology company:

> We employ people with a scientific background in almost all aspects of our operations: general management, marketing and sales, business development, regulatory and quality affairs, clinical development, manufacturing and, obviously, research and research management. We find that a scientific education prepares people well for a number of careers, because it teaches them to be analytical, adaptable, and pragmatic problem-solvers. Furthermore, the spirit of scientific enterprise encourages them to be entrepreneurial which is an increasingly valuable personal quality across the breadth of today's commercial environment.

What do employers think of the current science and engineering graduate education program? Generally, industry and academic administrators responded favorably to the current concept of graduate education, although they expressed some concern as to the relationship between that education and the positions eventually attained. The following statement typifies the general sentiment: "We may see some specific difficulties in the relationship between academe and the profession it is intended to serve, but the structure itself is sound."

Some concerns were also expressed about the level of additional education that is needed to enable recent graduates to become fully participating employees. Consider the response from one major industrial employer who hires several hundred people with graduate science and engineering degrees in laboratories each year from many universities and in many disciplines:

> Even "the best of the crop" take anywhere from 6 months to 2 years to become good, productive industrial researchers. Most recent graduates, particularly those who have not summer-interned, do not have the foggiest idea of what industrial research is all about. Some even think that using or developing technology to do something useful is not research and if it is a product that makes a profit, is even slightly dishonorable.

Those from the academic arena had concerns as well—focused primarily on the teaching and mentoring skills of students trained in the science and engineering graduate system. The following comment is from a graduate dean and provost:

> I have long been concerned about the teaching expectations of graduate students—all graduate students, not just in the sciences and engineering. How we can expect that an individual will intuit teaching skills is an amazement. While teaching is somewhat an art, there are many skills and techniques that need to be learned before an individual should be turned loose to teach a course. We do our graduate students no service, and certainly provide no service to the teachers, if we expect them to function in that capacity....They also need to be prepared to be academic advisers. It is not enough to walk into a class and conduct that experience. If graduate students are to be teachers, they need to know how to interact outside the classroom with undergraduate students, providing them the support that they should have during their undergraduate experience.

A common subject was the changing environment—in both the industrial and the academic world. The following is from the dean of a major graduate school:

> Graduates are not necessarily being well trained to participate in much of our higher educational system as faculty: facilities for front-line research in sciences are not likely to get less costly. Not many colleges and universities will be able to afford the kinds of equipment required for faculty to make significant contributions to science in many areas. If this is true, most academic PhD positions will be in institutions which do not have essential facilities for what is viewed by these fields as cutting-edge research. Either the faculty in such institutions will have to carve out areas of research which don't rely on expensive equipment, or they will have to change their expectations of being significant players on the national and international science scene. It may be that there should be some effort devoted to training PhDs for research appropriate to those other institutions, either for enhancing their instructional roles or for providing them with realistic lines of research.

These are from an industry perspective:

> In my judgment, educating and training students to do research as well as conducting basic research are still the primary objectives of graduate programs. However, [the programs] must be responsive to changing national policies and industrial needs.... I would agree that the American graduate system has been/is a great success. However, to ignore the indicators that show change is needed would be a mistake. Clearly, the challenge ahead is to retain the best of the system while making the changes that will strengthen the nation's outstanding research universities and make them more responsive to the nation's needs.

*   *   *   *   *   *   *

> The days when a person could do a PhD thesis in surface thermodynamics (as I did) and reasonably expect to work in the field for a career are over—and I think will never return. One must be ready with the skills to change one's area of focus several times over a career. Most PhD education is training people in the exact opposite direction, and I think this needs to be changed promptly.

This comment from a university graduate dean shows both perspectives:

> Unfortunately, the training the graduates receive in universities is not directed to any specific career path. Most of the time, after some necessary training in their background, graduate students are pushed into narrow specialization. The consequence of such training is that many of them lack the breadth for work in industry. From what I have seen from the job offers received by our engineering students, they are successful with relatively less effort if their research topic and/or their assistantship experience is closely related to the prospective job description.
>
> The universities are not doing any better in training PhDs for academe either. Except for the recent initiatives taken by some universities in giving them pointers on effective teaching, generally their training is in a narrow area of research and they are faced with on-the-job training.

There was also a general concern that although the scientific and technological education received was sufficient, the skills training that is part of that educational experience was not. The following comment is from a major consulting firm:

> It is our general finding that US graduate schools successfully continue their tradition of producing well-educated scientists and engineers that are capable of making important contributions in their chosen fields. We also believe that the effectiveness of these graduates could be enhanced through practical ("hands-on") experiences/traineeships, functioning as a member of a (multidisciplinary) team, strengthened interpersonal skills, ability to communicate clearly the purpose (including the "strategic" value and relevance) of the activity in question, and substantial knowledge of the business environment/culture (including project-management fundamentals, time/effort/budget deliverables, sensitivity to human-resource concerns, safety, intellectual property, etc.).

These are from international corporations:

> Why are industries such as ours not more accepting of PhDs with little or no experience? Because many fresh PhDs see their research area as their sole focus, at least for the immediate future. They generally tend to be very narrow. And, more important, they generally have no meaningful understanding of the *business* of business. Some might say that such understanding is the responsibility of

business to provide. I say no. A highly trained scientist or engineer cannot be very effective if she/he has no knowledge at all of how a company is organized and why, lacks understanding about the principal staff and operating functions, is ignorant of the rudiments of accounting and finance, is unaware of product-liability issues that directly affect product development, etc., etc. Industry cannot be expected to deliver such training and education in a short period of time. True, with years of experience working in industry such knowledge is slowly acquired—but it is an extremely inefficient transfer mechanism. Meanwhile, in the early years when the new technologist is working without awareness of these forces and boundary conditions, that person cannot be as effective as she/he otherwise might be. Careers are throttled.

*   *   *   *   *   *   *

Most of the new PhDs that we hire seem to be relatively well prepared for careers in our organization. I would urge, however, that rather than move towards increasing specialization, which occurs very early in their training, the students should be given a broad array of courses in related areas early in their training. I have the impression that, also from day one in their program, students are now put into laboratories and given a research project so that they can develop the knowledge and skills in their specific area of activity to allow them to compete for grants in the future. However, it has been my observation that this type of training limits their ability to participate in multi-disciplinary teams that are often necessary in the industrial setting.

*   *   *   *   *   *   *

We look for top-notch technical skills and some evidence of ability to "reduce to practice" the technologies the candidate has been involved in. If we look at new graduates, we look for curiosity about and an appreciation for practical applications of science. As we move away from independent, stand-alone research and toward more team projects, we screen and hire candidates based on their ability to work in teams, to lead collaborations and teams in an effective way. Skills like project management, leadership, planning and organizing, interpersonal skills, adaptability, negotiation, written and oral communication and solid computer knowledge/utilization are critical for an industrial R&D scientist/engineer. If you walk on water technically but can't or won't explain or promote your ideas and your science, you won't get hired. If you do get hired, your career will stall.

Expectations are slightly different for those with master's degrees and PhDs. Here is an overview from a major company:

> In the case of PhDs we are looking for high intelligence and creativity, the ability to originate and conduct independent research, a research background involving at least a solid thesis research experience, and the potential breadth of talent to move from one research field to another. The flexibility required by the latter point is important to us because we cannot hire new talent every time we wish to enter new research fields.

> We are also looking for excellent communication and interpersonal skills, so that with proper training they can develop into potential management candidates both in the research organization and in management positions in our operations. We have had a good track record in our research organization in supplying high-caliber talent to our operations.

> In the case of master's-degree candidates, we are looking for the same kind of talents, except we do not expect experience in conducting research.

In summary, the anecdotal information collected via the committee's call for comments indicates that although employers are generally pleased with the result of US graduate education, they have some specific concerns as to its breadth, versatility, and skill development. In particular, employers do not feel that the current level of education is sufficient in providing skills and abilities to the people that they are interested in employing, particularly in

A number of universities are attempting to improve the preparation of graduate students who plan to become professors. One example is a pilot program at North Carolina State University, "Preparing the Professoriate." N.C. State found in focus-group discussions that doctoral students wanted "opportunities to prepare more fully for the academic life of a professor...to learn to teach in the same way that they learn to do research in a significant and extensive advising atmosphere."

The program uses "mentoring pairs," each of which teams a doctoral candidate with a current or emeritus professor. Throughout an academic year, the mentors work with their graduate students ("teaching associates") to develop individualized plans for substantive teaching experiences; these range from course preparation and planning to final course evaluation.

Students document their experience by developing a professional portfolio, which can include student evaluations, letters of recommendation that specifically address teaching, and evidence of course planning and preparation with videotapes. The portfolio may be used when a student applies for a position in academe.

Box 2-4: Preparing Professors

- Communication skills (including teaching and mentoring abilities for academic positions).
- Appreciation for applied problems (particularly in an industrial setting).
- Teamwork (especially in interdisciplinary settings).

They are also concerned that the graduate-education system—although acceptable for the past employment world—is less and less acceptable in today's more global world.

2.4   THE CHANGING CONTEXT OF EMPLOYMENT

During the preparation of this report, the committee heard sufficient testimony to be convinced of the considerable pain and dislocation among new PhDs. One forum for such discussions is the Young Scientists' Network (YSN), through which junior scientists and engineers discuss employment and other issues on an Internet bulletin board. For example, the YSN recently posted an open letter that said, in part: "Jobs in research are more than scarce today: advertised research positions routinely attract hundreds of excellent applicants." The tone of the letter carried the urgency and anxiety that the committee heard during panel discussions with members of the YSN and with other young scientists and engineers.

The changes in the employment market described earlier suggest that the most effective graduate-education programs are the ones that prepare students not only for independent careers in academic research, but also for nontraditional employment in a variety of nonacademic settings (see Box 2-5). Universities and their professors need to revise the science and engineering graduate curriculum so that students are educated and prepared for the opportunities available. For example, although employers prefer to hire

These are some nontraditional positions and employment sectors identified for physicists with graduate degrees (APS, 1994). A list could be developed for other fields.

Medicine: medical-physics practitioner, radiological technician, CAT scan and MRI technician.
City, state, and federal government: science adviser, science attache, state-level educator or administrator, transportation staff, environment staff, statistics personnel, computational staff, World Bank staff, international trade personnel, International Atomic Energy Commission (UN) staff.
Computing: software developer, business-data handler, securities broker, banking personnel.
Small business: consultant, computational staff, forecaster, data analyzer, instrumentation expert, indexer, abstracting staff.
Law: patent attorney, expert witness.
Education: precollege teacher, community and technical college staff, museum staff, librarian, educational-materials developer, district-level school administrator.
Science journalism: newspaper journalists, scientific journalist.

Box 2-5: Nontraditional Positions and Employment Sectors

people who have a strong background in basic

principles and reasoning, graduate research activities often focus on specialized training and techniques.

In addition, more opportunities are available to graduates who are flexible enough to shift careers. The field that is "hot" when a student enters graduate school might cool by the time of graduation. The first permanent job will seldom be the last, as workers in all fields are expected to change positions and even careers with greater frequency. Job-seekers who do not limit their educational preparation—or their job search—to traditional research positions might be better able to take advantage of a vocational environment that is changing rapidly.

As indicated in Appendix F, committee testimony and written comments from a variety of employers supported that point of view—that employers favor potential employees who

- Can collaborate across disciplines, in various settings, and learn in fields beyond their specialty.
- Can adapt quickly under changing conditions.
- Work well in teams and demonstrate leadership ability.
- Can work with people whose languages and cultures are different from their own.

In some cases, multiple advanced degrees or multidisciplinary backgrounds will be useful. For example, a student who combines a degree in life sciences with a law degree might be well qualified for the specialty of patent law within biotechnology. Likewise, a minor in geology might help an ecologist to obtain employment. Other growing multidisciplinary fields are biostatistics, numerical analysis, operations research, and digital signal processing. In some fields, single projects require multiple skills. For example, engineers with specialties in interdisciplinary fields like transportation are more likely to find employment than their mechanical- or civil-engineering counterparts.

Others have emphasized the extent to which strong scientific training—with its emphasis on analytical problem-solving, experimental strategy, and creativity—prepares a person for productive roles in government, business, and industry beyond roles that require the specific scientific or technical expertise acquired in the education process.

It is impossible to predict whether the rapid growth of traditional positions will resume during the 1990s, as was widely predicted in the late 1980s (Atkinson, 1990; Bowen and Sosa, 1989; NSF, 1989). History has shown that employment trends for graduate scientists and engineers are particularly difficult to forecast (Fechter, 1990; Leslie and Oaxaca, 1990; Vetter, 1993). Public spending on R&D and employment of scientists and engineers can change suddenly in response to unexpected events, such as the launching of Sputnik in 1957 and the collapse of the Soviet Union and the economic recession of the early 1990s. The continuing debate over employment of scientists and engineers clearly requires a continuing re-evaluation of the graduate education and training of scientists and engineers.

3

THE EDUCATION OF GRADUATE SCIENTISTS AND ENGINEERS

3.1 OVERVIEW

The recent increase in annual production of scientists and engineers with graduate degrees extends a trend of steady growth.

In 1993, more than 25,000 scientists and engineers received PhDs from US universities, up from about 18,400 in 1983 (NSF, 1994f). In the same year, some 80,000 scientists and engineers received master's degrees from US universities (including those who intended to continue toward the PhD degree), a number that has increased steadily from about 65,000 a year in the early 1980s (NSF, 1994b).

Most of the recent increase in the number of science and engineering PhDs awarded annually can be accounted for by an influx of foreign students (discussed later in this chapter). Including those students, average growth in the total science and engineering graduate-student population has averaged about 2.5% per year since 1982. The total number of graduate students in science and engineering in the United States rose from 339,600 in 1982 to 431,600 in 1992, an increase of 27% (Table 5 in NSF, 1994a). Figure 3-1 shows this growth by major field.

In 1992, most graduate science and engineering students (87%) were enrolled in universities that grant doctorates, a percentage that has varied only slightly since the Survey of Doctorate Recipients began in 1975 (NSF, 1994a). Most (67%) were full-time students.

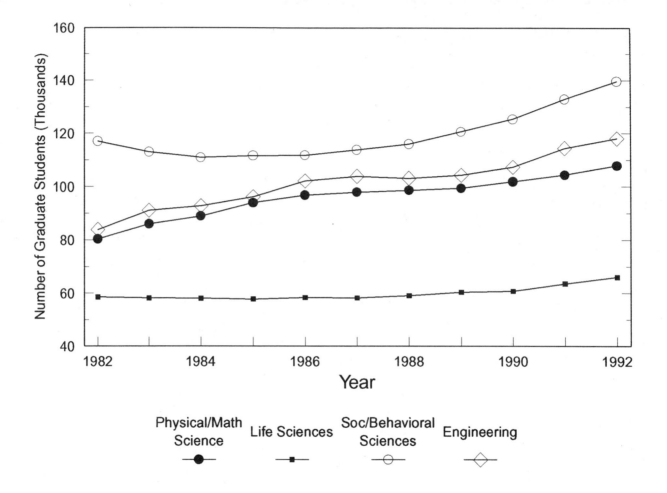

FIGURE 3-1 Science and engineering graduate student enrollment, by broad field, 1982-1992.

SOURCE: Calculated from NSF, 1994a:Table 1.

NOTES: The broad fields are defined as in the notes to Figure 1-1.

3.2 THE MASTER'S EXPERIENCE

In some fields, a master's degree is the professional norm.

A master's degree generally entails 2 years of coursework. Some master's-degree programs require a research thesis, others do not. In the latter case, the master's degree is not so much a terminal degree as a recognition of the coursework and qualifying examinations completed after about 2 years in a doctoral program.

In recent decades, the 2-year master's degree has served in some fields as the terminal degree. For example, the American Society for Engineering Education in 1987 reaffirmed the appropriateness of the master's degree for engineering students not expecting to enter careers in research or university teaching (ASEE, 1987). About 4.6 times as many master's degrees in engineering are awarded each year as engineering PhDs (for comparison, the ratio in the physical sciences is close to unity) (NSF, 1994b). The master's degree is also a customary end point in public health, computer science, and bioengineering and for those who want to teach in high schools and community colleges.

Data on the number of master's degrees by field, sex, race, and citizenship are included in Tables B-16 through B-19 in Appendix B and on the employment of new master's-degree recipients in Appendix C.

3.3 THE DOCTORAL EXPERIENCE

Acquisition of research skills is central to the doctoral experience.

The typical PhD program constitutes a two-part experience of great depth and intensity that lasts 4 or more years. The first part consists of about 2 years of course work. The second part focuses on a doctoral dissertation based on original research that might take 2 or 3 years or more to complete. The dissertation, as a demonstration of ability to carry out independent research, is the central exercise of the PhD program. When completed, it is expected to describe in detail the student's research and results, the relevance of that research to previous work, and the importance of the results in extending understanding of the topic (CGS, 1990).

It is customary in most fields of science and engineering for a doctoral candidate to be invited to work as a research assistant (RA) on the project of a faculty member; an aspect of this research project often becomes the subject of the student's dissertation. A traditional expectation of many students (and their professors) is that they will extend this work by becoming university faculty members. If they do, promotion and tenure depend to a great extent on continuing research publication.

A properly structured requirement for demonstrated ability to perform independent research continues to be the most effective means to prepare bright and motivated people for research careers. Original research demands high standards, perseverance, and a first-hand understanding of evidence, controls, and problem-solving, all of which have value in a wide array of professional careers.

In the course of their dissertation research, doctoral students perform much of the work of faculty research projects and some of the university's teaching. Therefore, institutions and individual professors have incentives to accept and help to educate as many graduate (and postdoctoral) researchers as they can support on research grants, teaching assistantships, and other sources of funding. By the time they receive PhDs, 63% of science and engineering graduate students have been RAs and half have been teaching assistants. This system is advantageous for institutions, to which it brings motivated students, outside funding, and the prestige of original research programs. And it is advantageous for the graduate students, for whom it supports an original research experience as part of their education.

Although the research component of the doctoral experience is dominant, other components are also important. They include a comprehensive knowledge of the current state of knowledge and techniques in a field and an informed approach to career preparation. Because of the recent trend toward large group projects in some disciplines—in which a research topic is divided among a number of students, postdoctoral fellows, and faculty—a PhD candidate can become so focused on a particular technique that there might be little opportunity for independent exploration of related fields or career options. When a graduate student becomes essential to a larger research project, completion of the degree can be unduly delayed. Furthermore, students working on tightly focused research might conclude that this is the only valued achievement for scientists and engineers.

Carnegie-Mellon University in Pittsburgh is one institution that is experimenting with a number of reforms. Paul Christiano, provost of the university, offered the committee a summary of trends affecting graduate education in science and engineering:

- More cross-fertilization between disciplines to exploit new opportunities.
- Somewhat greater emphasis on master's-degree programs.
- Greater interest in advanced nondegree programs.
- More teaching practice for faculty and graduate students, complemented by a new teaching center.

Dr. Christiano said that new commercial and societal needs invite innovative approaches to graduate education. He cited a need for more interdisciplinary programs and for an appreciation of the value of graduate education by potential students and employers.

He also identified some obstacles to change, including reduced interest of US students in science and engineering, institutional inertia, and the short-term view of industry sponsors. For example, in the case of industry, he has found that graduates of Carnegie-Mellon's research center for engineering design have not always been well accepted by some employers, because its graduates are not linked to a traditional field. He felt that such obstacles could be reduced by better communication and more interaction between universities and industry, which would demonstrate the benefits of interdisciplinary centers.

Box 3-1: Experimentation and obstacles to reform

In many fields, nonresearch jobs are accorded lower status by faculty; students who end up in such jobs, especially outside academe, often regard themselves as having failed (that is less true in engineering and chemistry, in which nonacademic employment is often the norm). If the number of academic-style research positions continues to level off or contract, as seems likely, a growing number of PhDs might find themselves in nonacademic careers to which they have been encouraged to give little respect.

3.4   TIME TO DEGREE

The average time to complete a doctoral degree has increased for graduate students in all science and engineering fields.

Over the last 30 years, the average time it takes graduate students to complete their doctoral programs, called the "time to degree" (TTD), has increased steadily. One measure, the median time that each year's new PhDs have been registered in graduate school, has increased in some fields by more than 30%. (The time to master's degree does not seem to have increased, although no one collects national statistics on it.)

The lengthening of the period of graduate work is accompanied by a second trend. It has become more common for new PhDs in many fields to enter a period of postdoctoral study (discussed at the end of this chapter), to work in temporary research positions, and to take 1-year faculty jobs before finding a tenure-track or other potentially permanent career-track position.

We are concerned about the increasing time spent by young scientists and engineers in launching their careers. Spending time in doctoral or postdoctoral activities might not be the most effective way to use the talents of young scientists and engineers for most employment positions. Furthermore, because of the potential financial and opportunity costs, it might discourage highly talented people from going into or staying in science and engineering.

The median number of years between receipt of the bachelor's degree and the doctorate in science and engineering has increased from 7.0 years during the 1960s to 8.7 years for those who received doctorates in 1991 (Table 5 in NSF, 1993b). Graduate students in the physical sciences have shorter-than-average overall completion times—about 7 years—and social scientists have longer-than-average completion times—about 11 years (see Figure 3-2). The remaining science and engineering fields average between 8 and 9 years.

The median time registered in doctorate programs is shorter than total TTD (the interval from receipt of a bachelor's degree to receipt of a PhD) because many graduate students take some time between college and graduate school to work, and some take time off during graduate school. Because time out between college and graduate school can be valuable for gaining work experience and more mature decision-making about careers, an increase in years from bachelor's

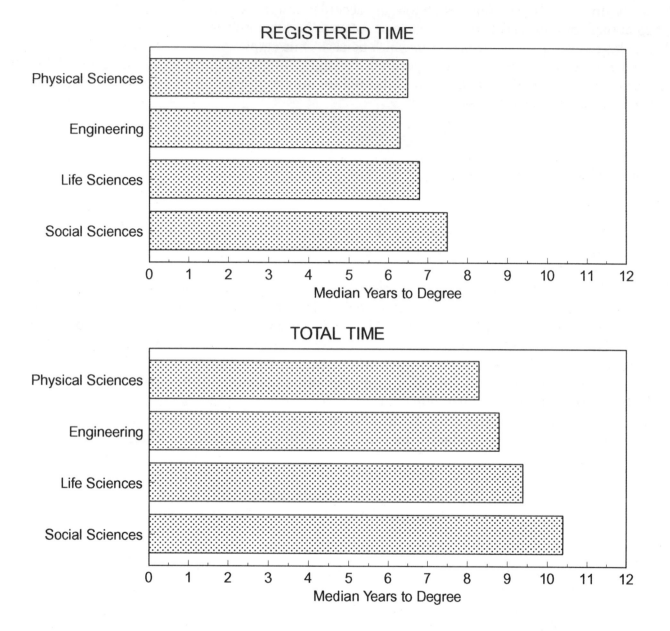

FIGURE 3-2 Median years to degree for doctorate recipients, by broad field, 1993.

SOURCE: Appendix Table B-29.

NOTES: *Total time* is the number of years between receipt of the bachelor's degree and receipt of the PhD.

Registered time is the amount of time actually enrolled in graduate school (thus, it might be less than the time elapsed from entry into graduate school and completion of the PhD).

degree to doctorate is not a problem. But registered time to degree (RTTD)[1] has also increased steadily over the last 30 years. The median RTTD for engineering PhDs increased from 5.0 years in 1962 to 6.2 years in 1992. In 1992, it was 6.7 years for PhDs in the life sciences, 6.5 years in the physical sciences, and 7.5 for the social sciences (Table 6 in NRC, 1993).

Our understanding of factors that affect TTD is incomplete. One finding, reported for psychology, is that TTDs are longer when there are many students per faculty member or many students overall (Striker, 1994). The National Research Council's Office of Scientific and Engineering Personnel in 1990 tested a five-variable model over 11 fields of science and could find no cause or set of causes to explain the trend (Striker, 1994; Tuckman et al., 1990).

Some researchers explain the increase in TTDs by pointing to the increasing complexity and quantity of knowledge required for expertise in a given field. Another possible explanation is the tendency of some faculty to extend the time that students spend on research projects beyond what is necessary to meet appropriate requirements for a dissertation. The Council of Graduate Schools (CGS) reports that lack of financial support during the dissertation phase substantially extends TTD, as do difficulties in topic selection, unrealistic expectations for the amount of work that can be completed in a dissertation, and inadequate guidance by advisers. Still other reasons are poor undergraduate preparation, student reluctance to leave the congenial life of academe, and postponement of graduation in the face of uncertain employment prospects (CGS, 1990).

There has been little research on how students spend the extra time that they take to earn a degree—whether in classwork, studying for general examinations, doing thesis research, working as teaching assistants or research assistants, etc. In a tight labor market, students might hope that the extra time might provide them with a better thesis and thus a better chance at a research position, but information on this is not readily available.

3.5   MECHANISMS OF ASSISTANCE FOR GRADUATE EDUCATION

Research grants, whose primary purpose is to support research, exert a powerful influence on the format of graduate education.

Table 3-1 provides an overview of the sources of graduate school support for doctorate recipients by broad field in 1993. Master's-degree students are mainly self-supporting (and often hold full-time jobs while studying), but most PhD students offset the cost of graduate education with grants and other forms of support from state and federal governments, industries, universities, nonprofit groups, and others. The amount and kind of support vary widely by field (see Appendix B, Table B-7).

---

[1] *Registered time* is the amount of time actually enrolled in graduate school (thus, it might be less than the time elapsed from entry into graduate school and completion of the PhD).

TABLE 3-1 Source of Graduate-School Support for Doctorate Recipients, by Broad Field, 1993

CATEGORY	Total Number	Total Percent of Total	Physical Sciences Number	Physical Sciences Percent of Total	Engineering Number	Engineering Percent of Total	Life Sciences Number	Life Sciences Percent of Total	Social Sciences Number	Social Sciences Percent of Total
Federal Fellow/Trainee	2,352	6.3	215	3.5	132	2.5	1,360	19.4	445	7.3
GI Bill	412	1.1	35	0.6	36	0.7	53	0.8	105	1.7
Other Federal Support+	1,647	4.4	314	5.1	234	4.4	320	4.6	325	5.3
State Government	393	1.1	47	0.8	37	0.7	94	1.3	79	1.3
Foreign Government	1,631	4.4	236	3.8	402	7.5	339	4.8	247	4.0
National Fellow (nonfederal)	1,953	5.2	223	3.6	189	3.5	351	5.0	441	7.2
University Teaching Assistant	19,407	52.0	4,510	73.5	2,392	44.7	2,789	39.8	3,650	59.8
University Research Assistant+	19,564	52.4	4,714	76.8	4,211	78.7	4,604	65.7	2,934	48.1
University Fellow	6,328	16.9	967	15.7	643	12.0	1,088	15.5	1,347	22.1
Other University	4,145	11.1	312	5.1	282	5.3	642	9.2	975	16.0
Business/Employer	2,538	6.8	351	5.7	453	8.5	308	4.4	337	5.5
Own Earnings	21,537	57.7	2,073	33.8	1,912	35.7	3,088	44.1	4,331	71.0
Spouse's Earnings	10,789	28.9	1,180	19.2	878	16.4	1,847	26.4	2,082	34.1
Family Support	9,659	25.9	1,316	21.4	1,526	28.5	1,605	22.9	2,045	33.5
Guaranteed Student Loan (Stafford)	8,522	22.8	827	13.5	469	8.8	1,428	20.4	2,474	40.6
Perkins Loan (NDSL)	2,193	5.9	152	2.5	93	1.7	275	3.9	780	12.8
Other Loans	1,349	3.6	116	1.9	92	1.7	181	2.6	411	6.7
Other Sources	1,621	4.3	159	2.6	179	3.3	365	5.2	307	5.0
Unduplicated Total*	37,344		6,140		5,349		7,004		6,101	

NOTE: In this table a recipient counts once in each source category from which he or she received support. Since students indicate multiple sources of support, the vertical percentages sum to more than 100%.

+ Because federal support obtained through the university cannot always be determined, no distinction is made between federal and university research assistants in this table. Both types of support are grouped under "University Research Assistant." Federal loans are counted in the categories for loans.

* The 2,410 PhDs who did not report sources of support are omitted from this total. Percentages are based only on known responses.

SOURCE: NRC, 1995

In 1992, according to a survey of graduate departments, 41% of the 126,000 full-time graduate science and engineering students received their primary support from their institutions, 31% provided most of their own funds (including funds from federally guaranteed loans), and 20% depended primarily on federal sources, primarily in the form of research assistantships, graduate fellowships, and training-grant positions (Table 12 in NSF, 1994a). However, federal support for students in the biological and physical sciences was higher (34% and 36%, respectively). One-fourth of those with institutional support received it in the form of research assistantships, half received teaching assistantships, and the remaining one-fourth were supported by a mix of fellowships, traineeships, and other forms of support.

The preceding discussion underestimates the importance of federal support, especially to RAs, because they were measured at one time (1992). Typically, graduate students depend on different sources of support in different phases of graduate work—perhaps as teaching assistants (TAs) in the first 2 years and then as RAs while doing dissertation research. By the time students receive the doctorate, nearly two-thirds have been RAs and half TAs (see Figure 3-3). The students reporting this information are not always sure of the ultimate source of their RA funds, and the reported data do not distinguish between federal and institutional RAs (Table A-5 in NRC, 1993). But we believe that most RAs are supported by federal research grants and contracts.

Since the early 1970s, virtually all growth in federal support of scientists and engineers in academe has been in the form of grants, contracts, and cooperative agreements for R&D projects (Figure 3-4). Federal fellowship and traineeship programs were cut back substantially in the early 1970s. The research-assistantship mechanism began to grow in importance as faculty used their research grants to support graduate students. Federal support of graduate fellowships and traineeships fell steadily as a percentage of overall federal funding (Figure 3-5). **As a result, the federal government has supported graduate education for the last 2 decades primarily through its support of faculty research projects, rather than direct support of graduate students.**

There are no clear guidelines for distributing the various types of federal support. The research assistantship has become dominant, but not as a result of an education policy. The number of PhDs produced now reflects more closely the availability of research funds than the employment demand for PhDs. There are several drawbacks to this dependence on research grants. One is that the pressure to produce new research results extends to graduate students, who easily gain the impression that hard, goal-oriented work on a specific project is the most important aspect of graduate education. As already noted, PhD students can become so involved in the work of the faculty investigators under whose grants they conduct their dissertation research that little time is left for independent exploration or other educational activities. Even the best-intentioned professors might lack the time to impart a broad appreciation of their discipline or to encourage their RAs to investigate the discipline thoroughly or plan their careers. Efforts should continue to be made to make this experience as profitable and broadening as possible so that graduate scientists and engineers are prepared for all kinds of careers.

In addition, the peer-review process, effective as it is at judging the research ability of academic researchers, does not try to evaluate the educational value of the research projects that can constitute the central activities of graduate students (although contribution to education is

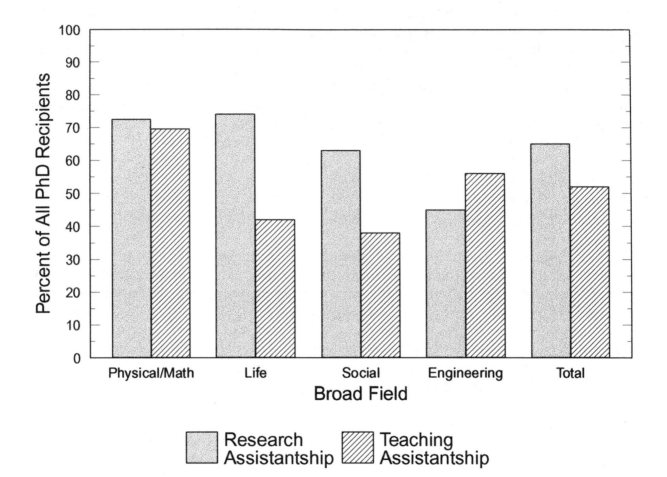

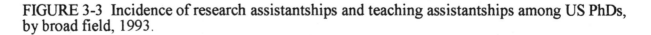

FIGURE 3-3 Incidence of research assistantships and teaching assistantships among US PhDs, by broad field, 1993.

SOURCE: NRC, 1995:Table A-5.

NOTES: 1993 doctoral recipients also reported many other sources of support (see Table 3-1).

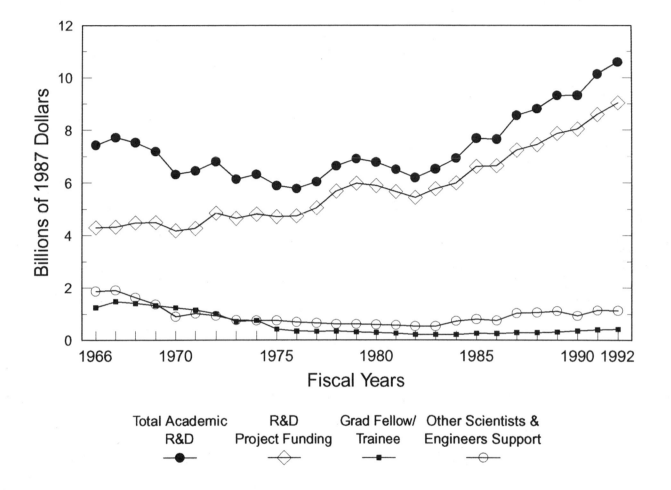

FIGURE 3-4 Types of support for academic R&D, 1966-1992 (billions of 1987 dollars).

SOURCE: NSF, 1994c:Table 5.

NOTES: Research assistantships are included as part of R&D projects. Other includes R&D plant, scientists and engineers facilities, general scientists and engineers support, and other scientists and engineers activities.

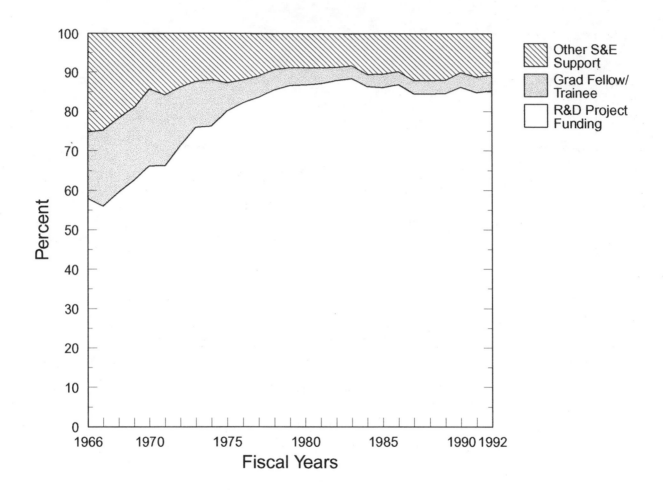

FIGURE 3-5 Mix of federal support for academic scientists and engineers, 1966-1992

SOURCE: NSF, 1994c:Table 5

NOTES: Research assistantships are included as part of R&D projects. Other includes R&D plant, scientists and engineers facilities, general scientists and engineers support, and other scientists and engineers activities.

technically one of four criteria used to judge National Science Foundation grants). And a project or research environment of high educational merit will not necessarily impress a peer-review committee charged with judging the scientific merit of a proposed research topic and the ability of a principal investigator to carry it out.

3.6   CAREER INFORMATION AND GUIDANCE

Graduate students do not routinely receive accurate, timely, and complete information on the array of available careers in science and engineering.

Several government agencies and private organizations collect and publish information relevant to the careers of graduate students, including the National Science Foundation, the Bureau of Labor Statistics, and the National Research Council. Those data are of interest to three more or less distinct communities:

● The professionals who generate the data, including universities, professors, students, and professional societies.

● The National Science Foundation, which arranges and presents data to be used by others.

● A small number of people who study and use human-resources data.

In general, the data that are available are not presented in formats designed for use by students or faculty advisers in choosing and planning careers in science and engineering. Moreover, in most cases, there is a lag of several years between the gathering of data and their publication. As a result, graduate students lack adequate information to

New employment trends are already obliging some universities to pay more attention to PhD placement. Theodore Poehler, vice provost for research at Johns Hopkins University, told the committee that his university used to pay little attention to placement of graduate scientists and engineers. However, now that they are paying more attention, they are finding that one incentive for doing so is that increasing numbers of students are considering unconventional careers. For example, of the six new PhDs in one graduate program at Hopkins last year (three US women, three foreign men), two went to small companies, two went to postdoctoral positions, one had numerous offers from around the world, and one became a NASA program manager.

Because of that experience, Johns Hopkins is trying to provide graduate students with more educational options to prepare them for a wider range of career opportunities. For example, the university offers more faculty and graduate students more opportunities for interdisciplinary research and education and for "life-long learning."

In addition, when funding is available, the university encourages graduate students to travel to national meetings where they can present their research results and to workshops where they can meet representatives of small companies and other potential employers.

Box 3-2: Enhancing Graduate Student Career Opportunities

- Design their own education and career-development strategies.
- Gain a realistic understanding of employment prospects.
- Recognize likely future demand for scientists and engineers, by field.
- Understand the dynamics, structure, and evolution of the scientific-research system.

More-effective guidance is clearly required. A prevailing belief in higher education is that faculty members "naturally" know how to be dissertation advisers through their own experience as students and teachers. That might be true when it comes to advising students who will enter academic careers, but many (if not most) faculty members have little experience with or awareness of nonacademic job opportunities and so cannot be effective advisers for other students.

3.7   THE GRADUATE EDUCATION OF WOMEN AND MINORITY-GROUP STUDENTS

The presence of women and minority-group students, although increasing, is still small relative to the population as a whole in nearly all science and engineering fields. In the long run, it is in the interest of all to recruit a fair share of the most-able members of society into science and engineering. Meanwhile, efforts should continue to ensure that all people with talent have an equal <u>opportunity</u> to enter science and engineering careers.

Women and minorities are underrepresented as graduate students and particularly as

Feniosky Pena, a doctoral candidate in engineering at MIT who is performing an internship with industry, told the committee that he experienced a troublesome culture gap when he began his studies.

As a native of the Dominican Republic, he had been taught to respect authority. At MIT, he was reluctant to question his adviser, who in turn thought that Mr. Pena lacked a grasp of his subject. Furthermore, the adviser used a technique of persistent interrogation, which Mr. Pena found humiliating. He heard this difficulty described by others at minority-group conferences, where students told him that they felt "stupid" when dealing with their advisers, classmates, or teachers.

He suggested that if faculty were familiar with other cultures, such misunderstandings could be avoided. He said that minority-group students need more "nurturing" if they are to reach a good understanding of the education environment in the United States.

Mr. Pena added that the racial diversity that minority-group members bring to campuses is not valued by everyone. He suggested training for both the minority and the majority so that each gains a better understanding of the other's culture.

Box 3-3: Minority Issues: the Culture Gap

faculty, researchers, academic officers, administrators, and policy-makers. The proportion of new entrants into the workforce who are minority-group members and women has risen and will continue to rise, and the quality and extent of their education should have high national priority.

Statistically, the position of **women students** in advanced science and engineering is improving, in part because of special efforts. From 1982 to 1992, the total number of women in graduate schools rose by about 3% a year, compared with a rise of 1% a year for men. In 1982, women received 23.7% of science and engineering doctorates; in 1992, they received 28.5% (see Appendix B, Table B-22). In 1993, women constituted 33% of all full-time faculty (and 37% of combined full-time and part-time faculty) but only 6% of the full-time faculty in engineering, 20% in the natural sciences, and 27% in the social sciences (Table 6 in NCES, 1994).

Women have been most successful at entering the social and life sciences. In 1992, 54% of graduate students in the social sciences and 44% of those in the life sciences were women (see Appendix B, Table B-3). Fewer women enroll in the physical sciences or engineering. In 1992, 15% of engineering graduate students and 27% of those in the natural sciences were women, but their percentage gains over the preceding decade have been greatest in those fields.

Linda Wilson, president of Radcliffe College, was asked by the committee to comment on issues pertaining to women in graduate science and engineering education. Dr. Wilson chairs the National Research Council's Office of Scientific and Engineering Personnel.

Dr. Wilson said that the unsatisfactory position of women in graduate education indicates the need to change the system for both men and women, both minority and majority. In her view, the key elements requiring improvement are access, including expectations and encouragement; mentoring and career guidance; recognition and respect; and accurate information about career paths.

She recommends changing the university into a more supportive culture, moving toward a "continuous learning system," and maximizing our "human capital investment" by including more women and minority-group members throughout the science and engineering enterprise.

Dr. Wilson said that key assumptions about graduate school are seldom tested, such as the notion that scientists do their best work when young and that independent work is more important than collaborative work. She suggested that more careful scrutiny of such assumptions might lead to constructive policy changes.

Box 3-4: Improving access for women and minority-group students

Entry into science and engineering graduate schools is lowest among **minority-group students**. The percentage of science and engineering doctorates awarded to members of underrepresented minorities increased from only 4.1% in 1982 to only 5.5% in 1992 (see Appendix B, Table B-24). In 1992, fewer than 29,000 (9%) of science and engineering graduate students were US citizens who belonged to underrepresented minorities (black, Hispanic, and American Indian) (see Appendix B, Table B-4). That is related to their low representation on college faculties: 8% of full-time faculty in 1993—6% in engineering, 7% in the natural sciences, and more than 9% in the social science (Table 6 in NCES, 1994). By comparison, in 1991, 22% of Americans were black, Hispanic, or American Indian. Committee witnesses indicated that a "critical mass" of students is particularly important for minority-group members, who as students often suffer from a "one and only" syndrome.

As the demographics of the workplace shift rapidly, it is clearly in the national interest to encourage and facilitate the entry of women and minority-group members, with white men, into science and engineering fields.

3.8   FOREIGN GRADUATE STUDENTS

The number of foreign science and engineering students enrolled in US graduate schools and the number receiving PhDs have both risen more rapidly than the comparable numbers of US citizens.

The number of science and engineering doctorates earned annually by people who are not US citizens and have temporary visas increased sharply from 3,400 in 1983 to almost 8,100 in 1993. This group received 18.5% of the doctorates in 1982 and 32% in 1992 (see Appendix B, Table B-25) and accounted for most of the net increase in the number of doctorates awarded since 1986 (see Figure 1-2).

> Overall enrollment of scientists and engineers grew by just over 2% a year from 1982 to 1992, but foreign enrollment grew by more than 5% a year. Foreign participation varies widely by field: non-US citizens make up 46% of all full-time graduate students in engineering, 39% of those in the physical and mathematical sciences, 27% of those in the life sciences, and 17% of those in the social sciences.
>
> In 1992, foreign students earned more than half the new PhDs in engineering (up from 39% 10 years earlier), more than one-third of the PhDs in physical and mathematical sciences, and one-fourth of those in the life sciences.

Box 3-5: Distribution of Foreign Graduate Students

One reason for the marked increase has been a series of political events that have encouraged in immigration. The Immigration Reform Act of 1990 gave visa preference to applicants with science and engineering skills (NSB, 1993). The arrival of many of those students results from one-time political events, but American universities continue to attract students for whom comparable education is not available at home. The issues raised by the increase in the number of foreign students in American graduate schools and earning US doctorates are discussed in Chapter 4 (Section 4.2). As discussed in Chapter 4, the decision of an increasing number of those students to seek permanent jobs in the United States increases the talent available to our country, although it adds to the employment-related pressures on advanced scientists and engineers.

3.9   POSTDOCTORAL EDUCATION

The postdoctoral population has increased faster than the graduate-student population. Some of the increase might be due to employment difficulties.

According to the latest National Science Foundation (NSF) survey of science and engineering graduate departments (unpublished), there were 24,024 science and engineering postdoctoral appointees[2] in doctorate-granting institutions in the fall of 1992, compared with 14,672 in 1982—a 63.7% increase, compared with a 26.7% increase in the number of graduate students. Part of the growth can be assumed to reflect the legitimate need for postdoctoral study and exploration to prepare for the increased complexity of modern science; in biology, chemistry, and physics, for example, postdoctoral study has become the norm. But committee testimony and other anecdotal evidence indicates that many postdoctoral appointees are extending their studies because permanent positions in academic or industrial research are not available.

An important additional factor is the increasing percentage of postdoctoral appointees who are foreign students—53% in 1992, compared with 42% in 1985 (NSF, unpublished). More foreign citizens than American citizens have had postdoctoral appointments in US universities since 1991 (Tables C-29 and C-30 in NSF, 1993a).

However, surveys do not determine the extent to which young scientists and engineers take postdoctoral positions because they cannot find regular employment. One measure of the impact of employment-market problems on the growth of the postdoctoral pool would be an increase in the length of postdoctoral time before a permanent position is found or an increase in the percentage of scientists and engineers who take second or third postdoctoral positions. Another indication would be an increasing percentage of scientists and engineers taking postdoctoral appointments at the institutions where they received their doctorates; this would indicate that professors are retaining their former students as RAs when they cannot find regular jobs.

The Survey of Doctorate Recipients can be analyzed to address the question. The comparative analysis of cohorts of scientists and engineers 5-8 years after receipt of their PhDs, done for this report, indicated that the percentage still in postdoctoral positions grew from 2% in 1977 to 3% in 1989; the increase was greater and smaller in specific fields (see Appendix C, Table C-2).[3] In 1979, more than 600 (4.9%) of the biologists who received PhDs in 1971-1974 held postdoctoral appointments; in 1989, nearly 1,300 (9.2%) of those with PhDs from 1981-1984 were in postdoctoral positions. The percentage of each cohort in the faculty tenure system fell from 40% in 1979 to 25% in 1989.

The above changes might partially explain the finding that the percentage of young biologists (aged 36 and younger) who applied to the National Institutes of Health for individual-investigator research grants fell by 54% from 1985 to 1993 (NRC, 1994a); clearly, fewer of them were in a position of independent investigator, from which they are permitted to apply for research grants.

---

[2] Both numbers include foreign citizens, but the postdoctoral total includes doctorates in science or engineering from foreign universities. Part of the larger increase in the number of postdoctoral fellows over the last decade, therefore, might be ascribed to a greater propensity of foreign scientists and engineers to immigrate at the postdoctoral than the predoctoral stage, rather than to an increase in the pool of postdoctoral fellows who cannot find a job.

[3] The 1989 data from the Survey of Doctorate Recipients are used because, owing to a change in the timing of the survey, the 1991 data on postdoctoral appointments are not comparable.

Regardless of the proportion of postdoctoral appointees who are in a vocational "holding pattern," their numbers are rising, and each year they vie with the new class of graduating PhDs for available positions. The postdoctoral appointees have an advantage in being able to offer more research experience and publications in competing for available research positions. That competition, in turn, increases the trends among new PhDs toward postdoctoral study and nontraditional jobs.

4

DISCUSSION OF MAJOR RELATED ISSUES

Three of the issues raised in Chapters 2 and 3 (whether the United States is producing too many science and engineering doctorates, the effect of enrollment of foreigners, and the long time from starting graduate study to first job) are closely related to the design of graduate-education programs for scientists and engineers. Those contemporary issues have been discussed extensively by the committee and by the witnesses and correspondents who have contributed to the content of this report. Each of these related topics deserves extended study and debate in its own right. We present the issues and their possible implications for graduate-education programs in this chapter.

4.1 THE "RIGHT" NUMBER OF SCIENCE AND ENGINEERING PHDS

Having read accounts of scarcity in academic research positions, some readers might expect this report to conclude that we are producing too many PhDs and should take immediate steps to cut back PhD programs in science and engineering. We are aware of the reports of unemployment and underemployment among new doctorate recipients, and survey data indicate that recent PhDs are finding it harder to make the transition from graduate school and postdoctoral study to career positions (see Chapter 2). The current situation probably results in part from the increase in annual PhD production to 25,000 in 1993 from the 18,000-19,000 per year in 1976-1986. In response, some graduate programs have begun to accept fewer new students. But forecasting demand for science and engineering PhDs is difficult, and, because it takes a long time for changes in graduate enrollment to manifest themselves in PhDs, past efforts either to increase production in response to perceived shortages (in the 1960s and 1980s) or to reduce production (in the 1970s) ended up not having beneficial effects, in that graduate students and programs had already made substantial adjustments. Because of the lag times between policy action and changes in the system and for reasons enumerated below, we do not think it possible to determine appropriate production targets. A better way to keep supply and demand in balance appears in the next chapter.

The Current Unemployment Situation

The committee is not convinced that the current low and stable unemployment rates among science and engineering PhDs, even new ones, that are documented in Chapter 2 prove that the system is working as well as it should. It is true that science and engineering PhDs have prospered in an increasingly diverse labor market. But as we illustrated in Chapter 2, there are indications of employment difficulties, especially for recent graduates. For example, the percentage of scientists and engineers looking for jobs in the first months after PhD receipt has risen dramatically in some fields, and there is evidence that an increasing percentage of those counted as "employed PhDs" have taken temporary positions in either postdoctoral fellowships or short-term jobs. The unemployment rate as of 1993 (the last year for which there were national data) was still low at 1.6% but was increased from the roughly 1.0% of the 1980s and 1.4% in 1991 (Figure 2-3). Unemployment among new science and engineering PhDs reached 2% in 1993, compared with the roughly 1.5% of the 1980s.

Nor do the available employment data take into account the nature of jobs held by recent PhD recipients. Statistically, a PhD physicist working in a job outside science and engineering is counted equally with a physicist on the staff of AT&T Bell Laboratories or a tenure-track assistant professor at a research university. Moreover, some PhDs who are finding good jobs in nontraditional fields might be doing so regardless of their PhD training, not because of it. The predominant view of the employers that we heard from during the course of our study was that PhD work, including original research, made students more effective employees. However, these graduates might be attractive to some employers simply because they are members of a highly qualified, hard-working, and carefully selected group of people. The time spent in or the content of a PhD program might not be well matched to some science and engineering graduates' jobs.

The committee cannot measure employment difficulties precisely, but the evidence received from witnesses and other contributors is persuasive that problems exist in at least some sectors. Some recent PhDs have indicated that they regretted having spent time and money on doctoral work that turned out not to be useful in their permanent jobs. Some even reported "hiding" their doctorates so as not to appear overqualified, unbusinesslike, or too theoretical in their approach to work.

We believe that the slow but steady shift[1] in demand for doctoral scientists and engineers over the last 2 decades away from academe and toward a greater variety of employment has

---

[1] This shift seems dramatic to many observers, but employment data portray slow change over the last 20 years.

accelerated somewhat in the early 1990s at the same time that the number of new graduates (many of them foreign students) has increased rapidly. For a variety of reasons, the number of academic positions and traditional industrial research positions is steady or shrinking, in accord with anecdotal reports that an unusually high number of new PhDs had to change career plans on graduating or after several years in postdoctoral positions.

To some extent, the science and engineering employment situation is cyclical, and it might already be adjusting. The recent recession ended slowly, but economic growth has resumed, and the demand for skilled people is increasing even in some industries that have undergone substantial reduction and restructuring. In addition, the high rate of increase in the number of PhDs awarded to foreign citizens in the United States, which averaged more than 12% per year in the late 1980s, began to fall after 1990 and was 0.3% in 1993 (calculated from Table 3 in NSF, 1994f). The number of doctorates awarded to foreign citizens with temporary visas fell slightly in physics/astronomy, chemistry, environmental sciences, and computer sciences from 1992 to 1993 (NRC, 1995: Appendix Table A-2).

However, we have already cited some indications of basic structural changes that lower demand, including cuts in defense spending, industrial restructuring, and reductions in growth of federal R&D spending. There is no evidence that these trends of the last several years will end soon. Thus, even if PhD production does fall in the near term, science and engineering graduate students might do well to prepare themselves for an increasingly diverse set of career paths.

Limitations of Supply-Demand Models for Forecasting Science and Engineering Personnel Needs

Supply-demand models are not now adequate for predicting whether there will be an undersupply or oversupply of trained scientists and engineers (Fechter, 1990; Leslie and Oaxaca, 1990; NSB, 1993; Vetter, 1993). That conclusion was also expressed by the panel on estimation procedures of the Committee on National Needs for Biomedical and Behavioral Research Personnel, which found that previous supply-demand models for basic biomedical, behavioral, and clinical research scientists had not proved accurate (NRC, 1994b).

At least two types of limitations of such models severely reduce their reliability, especially over the 5- to 10-year periods needed to carry out graduate-education plans. Internally, they are not based on an adequate understanding of the behavior of the students, faculty, and other people whose collective decisions affect the supply of new scientists and engineers; externally, they cannot always predict the impact of major changes in key variables outside the graduate system itself that affect demand for scientists and engineers.

For example, predictions of a huge oversupply of scientists and engineers in the early 1970s did not come true, because as a result of the predictions the students changed plans, administrators reduced programs, and graduates found new ways to use their training—all behavioral changes that were not included in the models. More recent studies have forecast shortages of college and university faculty, beginning in the middle 1990s. These shortages have not occurred. The forecasters could not anticipate the behavioral effects of recession and tight government budgets: fewer faculty have elected to retire, and universities and colleges have begun to fill faculty openings temporarily or leave them unfilled.

As an example of unanticipated external events affecting science and engineering employment, the buildup of physical scientists and engineers in the late 1980s stimulated by increased defense spending earlier in the decade was followed by the end of the Cold War, which reduced demand for scientists and engineers; similarly, no one could predict the immigration of experienced scientists and engineers from the former Soviet Union and eastern Europe. The intensified pressures of international economic competition have also had unexpected effects, which have led some large high-technology companies to reduce their research staffs and redirect those who remain toward more-applied research with near-term payoffs.

Conclusion

With current techniques, it is not possible to forecast the future demand for or supply of scientists and engineers. We can tell with some confidence whether there are immediate mismatches between supply and demand; but in the absence of reliable long-range models, we do not know whether a situation is temporary and self-correcting or whether stronger action is required. In other words, there is little basis for trying to control the production of new science and engineering PhDs by limiting enrollments nationally through some central control mechanism.

There are ways to improve the likelihood of a balance between supply and demand that do not involve central planning and all the information requirements on which such planning depends. We believe that a combination of greater breadth and flexibility in graduate curriculums, better information and guidance, and financial support mechanisms whose primary purpose is education will provide scientists and engineers who can move more flexibly toward employment demand. Our recommendations are presented in greater detail in Chapter 5.

Meanwhile, efforts should continue to improve the collection and analysis of employment-related information by the National Science Foundation (NSF), other agencies, and the scientific societies and associations. Understanding the dynamics of and trends in career paths of scientists and engineers with advanced degrees in the various employment sectors is especially important. The results should be disseminated to prospective graduate students, to graduate students, to postdoctoral fellows, and to the faculty who advise them. Better supply-demand modeling of PhD labor markets is also important. We offer specific recommendations in Chapter 5.

4.2   THE ISSUE OF FOREIGN STUDENTS

As noted in Chapter 3, foreign-citizen students accounted for most of the increase in the numbers of science and engineering graduate students and numbers of PhDs since about 1986. In 1992, for example, foreign citizens were nearly one-third of graduate students in science and engineering, up from less than one-fourth in 1982. By 1993, 57% of the PhDs in engineering and more than one-third in physics, computer science, and mathematics were awarded to foreign-born scientists and engineers (Table 3 in NSF, 1994f). All together, the increase in foreign graduate students with temporary visas accounted for 65.5% of the net increase in annual science and engineering PhD awards 1986 to 1993, and an increase in the number of foreign-citizen PhDs with permanent visas contributed almost another 11% to the increase. Foreign citizens achieved a majority of science and engineering postdoctoral appointments in the United States in 1991.

Support of Foreign Graduate Students

Immigration laws have been changed to place some restrictions on foreign citizens with temporary student visas who are enrolled in US graduate science and engineering programs. They are required to be full-time students, and they and their dependents are prohibited from taking jobs. They are prohibited from taking most fellowships and traineeships or applying for federally guaranteed loans and other forms of direct federal assistance. They can be employed as research assistants on federally funded research projects. Many foreigners receive support for the first year of their graduate study from their home countries, but the universities usually support them after that, generally with research assistantships and teaching assistantships (much of the support comes from federal research grants) (CRS, 1992).

As a result, universities provide a greater degree of financial support to foreign students than to US citizens. In 1992, for example, universities provided support to 87% of the graduate students in the physical sciences with temporary visas, 84% of those with permanent visas, and 72% of those who were US citizens. In engineering, university support went to 76%, 73%, and 61%, respectively. The pattern was similar in the life and social sciences.

Where Do Foreign-Citizen PhDs Go?

It has been generally possible under the immigration laws for new PhDs of foreign citizenship to find entry-level positions in the US labor force (NSF, 1990b). Historically, about half the foreign citizens with American doctorates in science and engineering have left the United States after getting their PhDs or later postdoctoral appointments (CRS, 1992).[2]

What Are the Effects?

Opinions about the effects of an increasing number and percentage of foreigners in American graduate science and engineering programs have been mixed (see CRS, 1992, for review and citations). Some people say that the United States benefits from high graduate enrollments of foreign students because they help with research and teaching, counter the declining interest of American students in science and engineering, and fill the employment needs of industrial laboratories. They argue that in a global economy, US universities and industries should be able to recruit the best talent available.[3] Some value the contribution of foreign students to a multicultural educational environment. Others point out that US companies later hire foreign students to help open new markets in their country of origin.

Other people have begun to argue that the numbers of foreign students should be limited, on several grounds. They charge that increasing numbers of foreigners with US PhDs who remain in this country (many of whom become US citizens) are competing with American graduates for jobs; that might explain some part of the employment problems that recent PhDs have complained of in the last several years. Meanwhile, some return home and work for our economic competitors. Critics of increased graduate enrollment of foreigners also have charged that cultural and language differences make many of them ineffective in the classroom and limit their ability to succeed in the labor market, that their graduate training has been unfairly subsidized by American taxpayers, that they depress salaries and thus interfere with an important market signal that would attract more American students, and that their presence discourages defense-related research in industry and on campus (CRS, 1992). A bill was introduced in 1992

---

[2] In addition, an unknown number of foreign citizens come to work in the United States after receiving their PhDs from foreign institutions. They are a subset of the immigrant scientists and engineers of all degree levels reported by the US Department of State to NSF. In 1992, that number jumped to nearly 23,000, compared with 11,000-12,000 a year during the 1980s (NSB, 1993:82). More than half were from East Asia, and two-thirds to three-fourths have been engineers. The increase probably resulted from the Immigration Act of 1990, which was passed in response to predictions by NSF and others in the late 1980s that a shortage of scientists and engineers was impending.

[3] It is interesting to note, for example, that approximately 20% of the individuals elected to National Academy of Sciences membership each year since World War II have been foreign-born US citizens.

in the second session of the 102nd Congress requiring universities to give preference to US students in filling federally sponsored research positions.[4]

Conclusion

The sharp jump in number of foreign-citizen graduate students in recent years, as described in Chapter 3, has probably been caused in part by a set of political events that are unlikely to recur, as well as changes in US immigration laws. And many foreign students are in the United States because their home nations lack adequate educational infrastructures. As the wealth of developing nations grows, so will these infrastructures, providing more attractive employment opportunities at home. Already, the aggregate of undergraduate science and engineering enrollments in six economically important Asian nations exceeds undergraduate science and engineering enrollment in the United States (NSF, 1993c).

The number of American students entering science and engineering graduate schools is not rising. There is no evidence that this situation would be changed by limiting foreigners. In fact, artificial limits could have the detrimental effect of disrupting the supply of scientists and engineers in key fields.

To the extent that there is a limit on the number of departmental "slots" for graduate students, we are inclined to believe that the real issue is the lack of US students, rather than the increasing presence of foreign students in our graduate science and engineering programs, but it is difficult to assess the claim that the easy access to foreign students has prevented an adequate response of the system to declining US student interest. If graduate programs are filled with foreigners, the programs do not have to make adjustments in enrollments or in content to make them more relevant to US students. Nor do businesses have to increase salaries to increase their supply of American students.

The committee suggests that the most appropriate response to flat or declining graduate enrollments of American students is to implement the measures advocated in this report, which should improve the functioning of the PhD labor market, and to continue efforts to strengthen the teaching of precollege and undergraduate science. Those measures, we believe, would make graduate education in science and engineering more attractive, more effective, and accessible to a larger group of qualified American applicants.

---

[4] The American Math and Science Student Support Bill, HR 4595, was introduced on March 26, 1992. It did not pass, but neither did a bill (S 44) to allow any foreign citizens earning degrees in the natural sciences, engineering, or computer science from US institutions to obtain permanent resident visas.

4.3   TIME TO EMPLOYMENT

For a variety of reasons that are not well understood, it has been taking longer for PhDs in science and engineering to begin their careers with "potentially permanent" jobs—i.e., post-PhD jobs that are not postdoctoral fellowships and are not temporary. According to an NSF analysis of the Survey of Doctorate Recipients, the median age of PhD recipients entering their first permanent positions increased in all fields from 1971 to 1991—by more than a year for PhDs in engineering (from age 30 to 31), by 2 years in the physical and mathematical sciences (from 30 to 32), by 3 years in the life sciences (from 30 to 33), and by nearly 4 years in the social and behavioral sciences (from 30 to 34).

The committee is concerned about the longer time to first permanent job. The prospect of many years of graduate study might discourage qualified candidates from attempting a PhD. Also, extending the years of schooling burdens PhDs who enter nonacademic employment with a disadvantage compared with their contemporaries, who are years ahead in workplace experience and seniority. Finally, long times to degree (TTDs) and more postdoctoral study increase the time required for the supply of PhDs to respond to shifts in market demand; this has both social and individual costs.

There are many possible reasons for the lengthening of time to first regular position, some of them positive (e.g., time spent working between college and graduate school, which adds experience and maturity), some negative (e.g., discouragement of graduation by faculty who need research assistants or teaching assistants and an oversupply of PhDs relative to demand for academic positions), and some unavoidable (more time devoted to child-care responsibilities and a greater amount of material to learn in graduate school and in postdoctoral appointments). Increasing TTDs of all types (registered, elapsed, and total time) have been defined and documented in Chapter 3, and entering graduate students on the average are probably older to begin with. The median age of new PhDs has increased in all fields since 1971—by 1 year in physics and astronomy, by 1.5 years in engineering and chemistry, by 2 years in biology, by 2.5 years in mathematics, and by more than 3 years in the social sciences (Table 4 in NSF, 1993b). A growing proportion of graduate students come from groups that take longer to finish—women, underrepresented minorities, and foreign citizens (Stricker, 1994:570).

The committee discussed the issue of longer time to first permanent position, the possible causes, and the significance. We are concerned about the costs of increased time to first permanent position and the role of increased TTD in it, but we hesitate to recommend a particular time limit for completion of the PhD or a particular length of postdoctoral study, partly in recognition of the great diversity of graduate students, disciplinary requirements, and educational institutions missions. Instead, we believe that clearly understood quantitative guidelines for PhD completion times should be set by individual institutions after discussions among students, faculty, and professional societies.[5]

---

[5] Institutional policies should include criteria for exceptions to standards. For example, students who work or have children should be allowed to negotiate reasonable schedules without prejudice to their standing.

The committee notes that many institutions already have guidelines intended to limit time to degree. At the Georgia Institute of Technology, for example, chemical engineers are expected to complete a PhD in 4 years, and flexibility is granted as appropriate. Other institutions allow students to receive teaching assistantships for only 4 years; still others limit the time that a student can work on a single research project.

Whatever the institutional guidelines are, they must be implemented, monitored, and enforced to ensure that graduate students are never used to provide inexpensive labor on research projects or in teaching. As the report of the Association of American Universities/Association of Graduate Schools puts it, "policy changes alone are insufficient; the commitment to implement them is crucial" (AAU, 1990). Each institution should adopt standards appropriate to its mission and student body and should charge graduate schools and their deans with oversight. That could be done at the departmental or program level. Departmental rules should be developed with the active participation of the faculty who carry out graduate education, and they must be clearly communicated to students, faculty advisers, and dissertation committees.

4.4   INFORMATION AND ANALYSIS NEEDS

It is characteristic of the issues described in this chapter, particularly time to employment or first permanent job, that more information on and better understanding of them is needed, despite the problems and sensitivities involved in addressing the issues of employment, foreign students, and institutional policies concerning time to degree. Accordingly, appropriate recommendations aimed at NSF, which has the lead responsibility for gathering and analyzing information about the science and engineering enterprise, are included in the next chapter.

5

CONCLUSIONS AND RECOMMENDATIONS

America's system of graduate education in science and engineering has set the international standard, especially in preparing students to work successfully at the cutting edge of research, and it must continue to do so. Graduate schools have also, increasingly in recent years, contributed to filling the nation's growing need for advanced expertise in diverse nonresearch positions.

Nevertheless, the committee believes that there is room for substantial improvement in graduate education and that some immediate changes are needed in programs, information, and attitudes. These changes are recommended, in part, in response to contemporary stresses. In many important fields, employment in basic-research positions has not kept pace with expanding graduate enrollments, and this has led to unmet expectations among many graduates who have aspired to such positions. The available evidence on unemployment rates indicates that demand by less-traditional employers is growing fast enough to absorb most graduates. However, we note broad criticism from many such employers concerning graduates' immediate suitability for entry jobs—criticism that is often based on a belief that students are too specialized, in view of the variety of tasks that they will confront, and that it is hard for them to adapt to the demands of nonacademic work. With only one-third of new PhDs expected to enter the academic tenure system, the needs of these alternate employees should be given more attention.

There is also a broader concern: Although it is clear that human resources are the primary key to the nation's strength in science and technology, we have not, as a nation, paid adequate attention to the graduate schools as a system for meeting the full range of needs for advanced talent in science and engineering. That is perhaps seen most clearly in the fact that the United States has effectively lacked human-resources policy for advanced scientists and engineers. In effect, human resources have been taken for granted as a byproduct of our policies for the support of research. The simplifying assumption—both inside and outside the university community—has been that the dominant function of graduate programs is to produce the next generation of academic researchers. It is time for a fuller recognition, by academics and policy officials alike, of the changing way that graduate education in science and engineering contributes to the wide array of national needs. For many of these needs, it is a career in professional service, applied research, development, or consulting that graduates will find open to them.

The committee concludes that improvement of three kinds is needed. First, graduate programs should add emphasis on **versatility**; we need to make our students more adaptable to changing conditions. This is mainly a matter of local initiative by the universities themselves, but there is a supporting role for government, too. Second, much better **information** should be routinely provided to students and their advisers so that students can make more realistic career decisions than is now practical. Third, there needs to be a deliberate **national reconsideration** of graduate education so that the open policy questions, the current information gaps, and the contemporary stresses are systematically addressed by a suitable blend of university, industry, professional society, and government. Those improvements can be made without disruption of the traditional commitment to excellence in basic research that has been, and must continue to be, a hallmark of the US system of graduate education.

Although the universities are primarily responsible for implementing those changes, national and state government, industry, business, and others can help by providing opportunities to gain experience and exposure to a variety of occupations via internships, alternative certification programs, etc. We do not minimize the difficulty of effecting reform in a system as complex and diffuse as that of US universities. But we already have many relevant examples of the application of local imagination and initiative. We believe that most university leaders will find it in their own interest to reshape graduate education to meet students' career needs better and to ensure universities' vital role in the nation's steady progress toward a knowledge-based society.

5.1   NATIONAL OPTIONS

The committee arrived at its preferred national strategy—emphasizing versatility and information—after considering alternative approaches.

For example, it might seem tempting to remove any apparent imbalance between supply and demand by adjusting student enrollment. The reasons not to move toward anything like national enrollment quotas have been presented above (see Section 4.1). We found these arguments as persuasive when applied to discipline or fields as would be implied in suggestions to cut physics enrollments by X% or to increase the numbers of master's degrees in microbiology by Y%. Identifying the "right" number of graduates is chancy, to say nothing of administering nationwide compliance.

Another version of this suggestion is that we should set out to adjust the mix of master's degrees and PhD degrees that are awarded. Some question, for example, whether PhD-holders are not overeducated for the positions they fill—especially for nonresearch jobs—and whether a master's degree would suffice. But can one actually conclude that the PhD experience is unnecessary for such positions? From the information gathered by the committee (see Section 2.7 and Appendix F), the opposite seems to be true. Employers themselves appear to be seeking the intellectual standards, resourcefulness, and initiative that come with the successful completion of original research in a PhD program. The complexity and sophistication of more and more positions appear to require the qualities gained in the advanced coursework and original-problem formation of graduate programs.

Another possibility is the creation of a new form of degree—a "different doctorate," perhaps, or a degree that is intermediate between a master's and a doctorate. In theory, a new degree could be better tuned to the class of nontraditional jobs that PhDs are increasingly filling-—for example, it might require less-intensive or different types of research and dissertation experience and as a consequence take less time to complete.

In practice, however, we are convinced that this approach would not work well. The proposal is reminiscent of the doctor of science (DSc) degree that some institutions have offered with the hope that it would catch on as the preferred degree for doctoral students who seek nontraditional careers. A key point is that employers report that they value the research experience required for the PhD degree. Without ready demand for a newly introduced degree, students risk investing substantial effort only to find that they receive a diploma regarded as inferior—one that critics might think of as "PhD-lite." It is more realistic, we conclude, to adapt the PhD degree than to try to invent and introduce a hybrid degree.

In opting for a strategy of making graduates much more versatile and informed, we believe we have a solution that allows the system to self-adjust continuously in a way that does not depend on the accuracy of an assessment of the number of graduates needed in the national aggregate or in particular fields. Thus, for example, if better-informed students conclude that the PhD is inappropriate or unnecessary for the jobs they want, enrollments will decline accordingly.

5.2   TOWARD GREATER VERSATILITY

Once enrolled, a graduate student might find many reasons to select a relatively narrow subject for intensive study. A student might be fascinated by a particular field of knowledge and see specialization as the surest route to a research position. If the selected field aligns with the research interests of a professor, the student might have an exciting and educationally enriching chance to work as an assistant on a path-breaking research team; this can enrich the student's educational experience immeasurably and can provide fresh ideas and energy to the research team as well.

The disadvantages of overspecialization in graduate school, although not immediately apparent, are real for both the student and the nation, whether or not the student becomes a researcher. Excessive concentration in a particular subfield can limit a person's later research contributions and affect later career choices. It is difficult to gauge whether a specialty chosen early in graduate school will be desirable in the job market or still be in the exciting forefront of research when the graduate years conclude. And midcareer changes might be desirable later, whether or not the person starts off in a research position; too narrow an educational experience makes later changes difficult, especially in the direction of nontraditional types of employment.

5.2.1. To produce scientists and engineers who are versatile, graduate programs should provide options that allow students to gain a wider variety of academic and other career skills.

Graduate programs should offer options that equip students for a wide array of eventual career opportunities. These options are beginning to appear on some campuses but need to be expanded to promote students' ability to adapt. Adaptability can be enhanced in two ways.

First, graduate students can benefit from a wider variety of **academic preparation.** For students who choose to enter a research career within the discipline studied in graduate school, it is important to have a grounding in the broad fundamentals of the field and some personal familiarity with several subfields—a breadth that might be much harder to gain after graduation. For such positions, if students become overspecialized in graduate school, they can later suffer from an inability to recognize and enter newly emerging kinds of research. For nonresearch positions, too, one's value to employers is likely to be enhanced by breadth in a related field, gained through coursework or, better, a minor. For example, a chemist might minor in computer science or a biologist in mathematics. Second, there is value in experiences that supply **career skills** beyond those gained in the laboratory and classroom. More students should, for example, have off-campus experiences to acquire the skills desired by an increasing number of employers, especially the ability to communicate complex ideas to nonspecialists and the ability to work in teams of interdependent workers.

The internship in off-campus settings is one option that needs to be expanded. Project-oriented teams in corporations provide potential opportunities for collaborative interactions and exposure to challenging practical problems. Joint industry-university projects should be explored as part of some students' preparation, with the possibility that students complete their dissertation

A number of universities have set up innovative programs designed to promote interactions between academe and industry. One example is the Leaders for Manufacturing Program at the Massachusetts Institute of Technology, organized around the School of Engineering and the Sloan School of Management.

The program seeks to create collaborative processes for problem identification, discovery, and knowledge transfer. It attempts to promote leadership skills (communication, motivation, decision-making, and change management), practice, and reflection. A survey of industry partners involved in the program estimated that in the first 5 years they had saved more than $28 million and incorporated 40% of the thesis work into practice.

Box 5-1: University-Industry Interactions

work off campus. Such projects also acquaint faculty members with the needs and organizational cultures of nonacademic employers.

Graduate programs should also expand on-campus opportunities to allow their students to attain a broader range of career skills. Outstanding people in a large variety of careers can be brought to campuses for presentations and made available to students. And communication skills might be sharpened through organized presentations to people outside the discipline and through older students' mentorship of younger students, for example.

5.2.2. To foster versatility, government and other agents of financial assistance for graduate students should adjust their support mechanisms to include new "education/training grants" that resemble the training grants now available in some federal agencies.

The United States has a sound tradition of investing generously in the graduate education of scientists and engineers. Federal agencies, private foundations, industries, and other granting agencies can support the efforts of both students and their graduate programs to enhance the versatility of new graduates.

Most federal support for students is provided through research assistantships. Research assistantships have proved important for bringing graduate students into federally funded research projects, and they will continue to remain a major form of federal assistance.

> "Compared with fellowships and traineeships, research assistantships are a very imprecise instrument for producing human resources for science and engineering. First, because students are in effect bound to their faculty mentors for financial support, they have less flexibility to pursue innovative learning experiences, such as participating in collaborative research with private corporations. In addition, research funding could play a larger strategic role in developing human resources for science and technology, particularly in attracting and cultivating more students from groups in the U.S. population that have traditionally been underrepresented in science and engineering. This has taken on added importance now that the majority of new entrants to the workforce are women and [members of] minorities."
>
> Source: Good and Lane, 1994.

Research assistantships can bring great educational benefits to students, but they are not specifically designed to enhance the versatility of graduate students. Assistantships are usually administered by the faculty researchers who receive the research grants, so the needs of the funded projects themselves are likely to be paramount in guiding students' work assignments.

We recommend increasing the relative emphasis on education/training grants, a concept adapted from the training grants[1] that are now awarded in selected agencies. Training grants are awarded competitively to institutions and departments, which use them to enrich students' educational experience in diverse ways. They have been used effectively to meet a variety of national objectives, and they can be tuned to the goal that we emphasize: the development and sustenance of locally conceived program innovations that enhance versatility in the graduate population. We recognize that, in a period of constrained funds, increased emphasis on education grants could reduce the number of research assistantships that are available.

The essential features of education/training grants would be:

- The grants are awarded, on the basis of competitive proposals, to *departments and programs*, rather than to individual faculty members.
- *Evaluation criteria* feature the proposer's plan to improve the versatility of students, both through program and curriculum innovations and by upgrading faculty advice to acquaint students with the full range of future employment options.

In recent years, the engineering directorate of the National Science Foundation (NSF) has developed innovative programs that support the goals outlined in this report. One example is the Industry Partnerships in Research and Education program, which includes 18 engineering research centers, 25 science-technology centers, and 53 cooperative research centers. The purpose of these activities is to increase industry-university interactions.

NSF recently announced a new program to allow students receiving NSF postdoctoral fellowships in chemistry to work in a US industrial laboratory. The purposes of the program are to facilitate the transfer of knowledge and technology between industry and academe and to give new PhDs experience in private industry. Applicants are required to negotiate agreements on intellectual property with the sponsoring company and to write a research plan that can be pursued after the fellowship is completed.

Box 5-2: New NSF Graduate-Education Initiatives

The experience with training grants at the National Institutes of Health over the last few decades shows that this type of mechanism can be successful in establishing productive interdisciplinary programs and in encouraging students to enter emerging fields of research. We encourage the growth of this program in a way that further enhances students' command of subjects and skills needed by nontraditional employers.

---

[1] *Training grant* is the traditional term to describe many grants to universities and departments. However, we propose the term *education/training grant* as more appropriate for the mechanism set forth in this report. The difference in meaning between education ("learning how to think and learn") and training ("learning how to do") underlies our preference for adding the word *education*. Training grants are used to meet several ends. Education/training grants, in contrast, would be aimed at one goal: greater student versatility.

The National Science Foundation (NSF) is reviving the training-grant program that it supported until the 1970s. In its initial stage, only a few hundred of the 20,000 students supported by NSF grants are receiving traineeships. By means of its training grants, NSF hopes to serve a variety of distinct purposes, including promotion of emerging fields, interdisciplinary programs, industry involvement, and the participation of women and minority-group members. We encourage deliberate expansion of this effort for the special purpose of fostering broader graduate experiences, which could well include industry involvement and emerging research that is particularly valued in expanding job markets. Some of the new education/training grants should be administered as demonstration grants for particularly innovative programs; if successful, demonstration grants should be expanded at NSF and replicated in other agencies.

What would be a "winning" education/ training-grant proposal, according to the committee? A winning proposal might include (1) an interdepartmental or program activity that would improve the versatility of graduate students, such as an interdisciplinary degree program that allowed a mathematics PhD student to obtain an MS in engineering; (2) a program element, such as an internship program, that improved the adaptability of graduate students by increasing their exposure to different ways of working in different employment sectors; (3) a program element that exposed students to the wide variety of employment opportunities open to them via career-opportunity and skill seminars, job fairs, and graduate career counseling; and (4) a program to reduce time to degree by 1 year.

One example of a winning proposal would be a grant that would be provided to both a university and an industry for a collaborative research program. One could imagine a collaborative program between the University of Washington and Boeing Corporation to develop a program in which the University of Washington would provide solid grounding in elementary and particle physics and Boeing would provide background in aerospace applications of physics. Another possibility is a grant to a university and a state K-12 authority to provide teacher leadership training in science curricula.

Box 5-3: Education/Training-Grant Proposal

Other federal agencies could use education/training grants effectively. The Atomic Energy Commission and the National Aeronautics and Space Administration once used what they called training grants to help to augment the national pool of nuclear and aerospace engineers; today, the Environmental Protection Agency and the Department of Energy, for example, could use this type of grant to induce more young researchers to address issues in environmental protection and remediation. Similarly, one goal of the recently launched technology-transfer programs—the Advanced Technology Program and the Technology Reinvestment Program—is to foster science-based technologies in industry. Those programs now operate by means of cost-shared research grants, but a worthy national objective could be the development of human resources as a component of technology transfer, and a portion of program funds could be devoted to education/training grants.

Education/training grants need not be restricted to federal agencies. For example, corporate sponsors could design grants to expose students to industrial research, development, and problem-solving. Foundations and state governments could fund graduate education/training grants with the aim of producing secondary-school teachers and science-curriculum specialists.

In summary, these suggestions are intended to encourage a **better balance** among the alternative types of grants: continuing *fellowships* for the top research-oriented students, expanding *education/training grants* to catalyze the development of innovative programs, continuing a substantial number of *research assistantships*, and continuing institution-supported *teaching assistantships*.

5.2.3. In implementing changes to promote versatility, care must be taken not to compromise other important objectives.

Introducing measures to enhance versatility will require care and imagination. They should be instituted in a way that allows universities to attain other ends—enumerated below—at the same time.

Maintaining Local Initiative. The changes that we recommend will likely come from local institutional initiatives and should show considerable local variation. We would not expect or want all universities to offer the same or similar options to their students. Programs should build on their own strengths and interests. Some universities and departments might want to focus on particular career paths (e.g., secondary-school teaching or subject fields of interest to local business and industry). Others might emphasize the development of particular career skills or cross-disciplinary combinations. Different university programs across the United States play different roles now, and that should continue.

At Drexel University, PhD programs are relatively new. The first efforts, beginning in the 1960s, were interdisciplinary biomedical programs. Today, Drexel produces 70-80 PhDs per year, mostly in science and engineering.

An unusual aspect of the program is that students spend 18 months of the 5-year program doing cooperative work with industry. Dennis Brown, provost at Drexel, told the committee that half the full-time faculty are involved in collaborative industry-faculty research.

In Dr. Brown's opinion, today's scientists and engineers need more knowledge about business, pedagogy, multidisciplinary approaches, and policy environments. He summarized the Drexel approach as a "value-added PhD," which includes

- More intimate knowledge of business and commerce and ability to develop and market ideas.
- Less emphasis on research during graduate school and more emphasis on education.
- Interdisciplinary PhDs in such areas as environmental science and engineering and biomedicine.
- Combining traditional PhDs with policy studies through traineeship programs.

Other current efforts at Drexel include master's-degree cooperative placements, new programs in engineering management and software development, increased employer support for advanced training, and a practice-oriented master's degree in engineering.

Box 5-4: A "Value-Added PhD"

Maintaining Excellence in Research. We are not recommending that all students be prepared for nonresearch careers. Opportunities appear to be growing in nonresearch jobs now;

but we will continue to need many of the best students to dedicate themselves to research in academic and nonacademic settings, and they will need the depth and quality of graduate experience that basic researchers have long enjoyed.

Furthermore, we are not espousing what some call vocationalism. The idea is not to slot every student into a particular career path and then "train" him or her accordingly. Among other problems, that would bind students to jobs that can change or decline in number while they are in graduate school. What is needed is not additional specialization. We need a graduate system that is well tuned to the central feature of contemporary life: continuous change. Change is happening both within the research world and outside, and work in both spheres requires constant readiness to adapt. Our objective, therefore, is a breadth of experience so that graduates can keep career options open and have the capacity to switch career tracks both at the beginning of and throughout their professional lives.

Controlling Time to Degree. The recommended changes should not be construed as additional requirements that would in themselves extend a student's time in a graduate program. The steadily lengthening time to degree—and, more important, the time to first employment—is already too long, for whatever reasons. Many ways of fostering versatility, including several noted above, can easily be introduced within the time that graduate students now spend after registration. An industrial assignment, for example, might replace—and not supplement—an on-campus research assignment.

We are aware of some strain between broadening the graduate experience and controlling its duration. Both solutions are needed, even if considerable administrative energies are required. Although long average time to degree is often decried, faculty and administrators have not generally made the disciplined effort that is needed to tighten graduate programs.

Whatever the nature of a specific graduate program, it is crucial to establish the principle that each student is the responsibility of a department, not of a single faculty member. Thus, a small faculty group (including the adviser) should meet often with each student working for a PhD degree; this faculty group, not the student's faculty adviser acting alone, should determine when enough work has been accomplished for the PhD degree.

Some observers have suggested fixed limits—5 years, perhaps, which is about 2 years shorter than the current averages—for a doctoral-education career. In the abstract, it is not obvious why such a period, which would allow 2 years of coursework and 3 years for a dissertation, should not suffice for most full-time PhD candidates. However, we are not prepared to espouse strict limits, in part because today's more-diverse student population requires flexibility to accommodate family and other personal factors.

However, we do believe that the "Two Plus Three Plus X" model for doctoral education ought to be evaluated and debated within the academic community. The idea is that preparation for a career in research has three discrete phases. The first, which should require no more than 2 years (assuming adequate preparation and suitable adjustment for part-time students), is for developing a broad command of the field. The second, for which the norm might be 3 years, is for making an original contribution to research as reflected in the dissertation. The third, for refining research skills and specialized knowledge that might be required for a first research position, should be left to postdoctoral assignments. Our concern is that the second and third phases are often merged in current practice.

We urge institutions to set their own standards on time to degree. This could be done at the departmental or program level, and it could accommodate the features of individual disciplines and the character of the student body. The standards should be clearly communicated to students and advisers, and responsibility for enforcement should be accepted by university administrators.

Attracting Women and Minority-Group Members. It is essential that a fair share of the best students be attracted to each discipline in science and engineering. If it appears that the numbers of women and minority-group members are low in particular fields, an effort must be made to determine whether there are barriers to entry, including issues perceived as barriers by members of the group in question. If so, steps to encourage increased participation should be devised and implemented.

Paula Hammond, a postdoctoral engineering student at Harvard University and recent PhD graduate of MIT, sees the need to improve the mentorship provided to all graduate students, but especially to women minority-group members. As a black woman, she has also seen how helpful are such opportunities as fellowships, student travel to professional conferences, and undergraduate training programs for minority-group members. Such activities are effective in encouraging careful planning, providing improved access to professors, and "showing minority-group students the ropes."

Box 5-5: Minority Issues: Suggestions for Improvement

5.3 TOWARD BETTER CAREER INFORMATION AND GUIDANCE

The committee is concerned about the lack of organized and timely career information and guidance that is available to students and their advisers—especially about the absence of reliable information on the less-conventional career paths of scientists and engineers.

Faculty attitudes have sometimes favored academic research careers, and some students have come to feel that other career paths were less worthy.

During their graduate years, students by themselves have access to little more than anecdotal information about career options. Many proceed through these years presuming that research jobs will be available in sufficient numbers to allow them some

"Our message is a simple one: Everyone who teaches and counsels future scientists and engineers must give careful consideration to the many profound changes in career paths in these fields and in the economy and workforce generally."

Source: Good and Lane, 1994

freedom of choice. They might see no urgency to investigate alternative careers when actual job entry is several years away and few sources of information about such careers are available. Their faculty advisers, having spent most of their time interacting with other academic researchers, might have little personal knowledge about alternatives and thus no basis to advise students about them. Former students who have taken nonresearch jobs are often less visible to their graduate departments than former students in traditional positions and are too seldom available as career models for current students. Departments generally do not adequately track information on nonacademic nonresearch employment so that it will be available to potential and current students.

The lack of reliable and timely information impedes the adjustments of the supply of graduate scientists and engineers—both upward and downward—to the demands of the job market.

The committee stresses that departments should not assume that the burden of learning about realistic career options rests with students. They have an affirmative obligation both to know what the full range of options is and to impart that knowledge to students.

Graduate students in science and engineering have insufficient current information on careers and employment. Some academic institutions and societies are now offering seminars and other programs on this topic. To judge by attendance, student interest is high.

For example, Stanford University recently held a symposium on education and careers in biomedicine. The symposium was described as "an interactive forum to address the issues that have been generated by the current shortage of academic positions and to identify alternative and traditional career opportunities as well as educational needs for both predoctoral and postdoctoral fellows." Presenters included persons in government, academe, industry, and law.

Similarly, Princeton University recently held a seminar on careers in chemistry. Industry representatives, entrepreneurs, and representatives of professional societies provided an overview of nontraditional careers. The organizers offered information on resume-writing, job-interview skills, and job-search techniques.

Box 5-6: Career Seminars for Graduate Students

5.3.1. Graduate scientists and engineers and their advisers should receive more up-to-date, accurate, and accessible information to make informed decisions about professional careers. Broad electronic access to such information should be provided.

We recommend that a national database on employment options and trends be established. The database information, intended for both students and their advisers, should include, by field, data on career tracks, graduate programs (including financial aid), time to degree, and placement rates.

Given the diversity of the information for which there is a need, it is clear that the responsibility for providing data must be shared by all partners in the graduate-education enterprise, including the universities, federal and state agencies, and professional societies.

The rapid development of information networks—collectively called the Internet—makes it possible to organize employment and career information so that two important principles are maintained: the information made available in the information system retains decentralized "grass roots" and therefore more currency than information previously assembled into central compendia; and timely information is available where it is most needed—in the hands of the ultimate consumers, doctoral students, graduates, and their mentors and advisers. In the past (for example, as recently as the downturn in aerospace employment in the 1970s), it would not have been possible to construct an employment-information system that recognized those principles. The new technologies can and should be deployed to improve nationwide access to accurate, germane, and timely education and employment information.

The National Science Foundation should coordinate the federal participation needed to organize the database. However, it is preferable that the database be designed and managed within the research community itself so that it has accurate and timely information that is credible to students and other users, some of it collected from university departments and professional societies. A national organization that covers the many fields of science and engineering could be a catalyst in establishing the database.

5.3.2. Academic departments should provide employment information and career advice to prospective and current students in a timely manner and should help students see career choices as a series of branching decisions. Students should be encouraged to consider discrete alternative pathways when they have met their qualifying requirements.

Graduate students typically devote years of intense effort to their education, and they deserve thoughtful, individual advice about career options. Many faculty members find that advising and mentoring are among the most important and most rewarding of their responsibilities. But more can be done to make sure the advice that is given is both pertinent and complete.

Advice for students should not be limited to the personal knowledge of the faculty member who serves as a student's adviser. Departments should both understand and convey the employment prospects of their graduates. One way to start is to track—perhaps with the assistance of alumni affairs offices—their own past graduates systematically.

Use of information in the national database recommended above could help. We hope, in addition, that some of the

To help graduate students to make career choices, some universities provide information on the employment of their graduates. For example, business school at the University of Chicago provides an overview of the placement, salary, and demographics of its graduates by industry, function, geographic region, undergraduate major, years of work experience, and recent employers. This information is distributed to potential and current students and to potential employers.

A few universities provide useful information about science and engineering graduates. Michigan State University indicates the employment sector, geographic distribution, salary trends, and unemployment rate of its science and engineering graduates.

Although some universities collect employment information, they rarely provide it to those attempting to decide whether to enter graduate-degree programs. Doing so could allow students to make better decisions about courses, programs, and, ultimately, careers.

Box 5-7: Employment Information for Students

demonstration effort funded under a program of education/training grants would allow departments to invent and try other novel means of improving the advice that students receive.

In the past, when most students were destined to become professors, graduate school was more accurately construed as a step on a simple career ladder. We are concerned that that perception is still held in some places. Departments should help students to conceive of their time in graduate school as a series of deliberate decision branches.

Academic departments can focus attention on the importance of career choice at two particular points. The first is the application stage. It would be helpful if more departments, in describing their programs to potential students, routinely provided more data relevant to career choice, such as location of job placements, salaries, and unemployment rates for the department and the discipline as a whole. Departments should report on the careers of all their graduates and provide the relevant information to prospective and current students. Such information could help to prevent unrealistic expectations among students.

> Leonard Carter is an older graduate student at Boston University pursuing a PhD in astrophysics. He has extensive work experience in government and for-profit and nonprofit corporations. He believes that the most-effective preparation for a career is a combination of academic studies and working apprenticeships. To this end, he suggested increasing partnerships among industry, academe, and government.
>
> In line with his own experience, he advocates flexible career preparation. Students should be encouraged to do apprentice work in a variety of areas to understand the full range of employment options and the work culture of industry.
>
> He suggests that universities assist in this effort by tracking PhDs, obtaining feedback from them 3-5 years after graduation, and providing this feedback to current students.

Box 5-8: Viewpoint of an Older Student

The second point is the beginning of the research phase, which usually begins with the passage of the qualifying examination for doctoral students. That is when departmental advisers can help students to evaluate each of three distinct options:

- Some might conclude that a master's degree is sufficient, given their aspirations and the current employment demand for PhDs.
- Some might elect to proceed toward a PhD and try for a position in research.
- Students interested in nontraditional careers could design dissertations that meet high standards for originality but require less time than would be customary for a career in academic research.

The last of those options is often neglected. Implementing the first, which is typically undervalued, might require some reshaping of the master's program to ensure that those who switch from the doctoral program receive—and are perceived to receive—something more than a consolation award. Among other advantages, this counseling approach will require that the leading faculty members come to respect the alternative careers that are available to their students.

Professional societies are often in the best position to gather nationwide employment information on scientists and engineers by field. Some—the Graduate Student Packet of the American Physical Society and American Institute of Physics is a good example—have made impressive starts in this direction. University departments should help to communicate their results to students and advisers.

5.3.3. The National Science Foundation and National Research Council should continue to improve the coverage, timeliness, and analysis of data on the education and employment of scientists and engineers to support better national decision-making about human resources in science and technology.

NSF has the responsibility for collecting, analyzing, and disseminating information on the science and engineering enterprise. In addition to the series of biennial reports on science and engineering indicators, NSF publishes a number of more specialized reports on the production and use of scientists and engineers at all degree levels. Through such activities, it holds the lead role in providing policy-related information to national decision-makers in government, industry, academe, and scientific societies. Some of the data collection related to graduate education, including the Survey of Doctorate Recipients, is done by the National Research Council.

> Scientific and engineering societies provide helpful career guidance about current trends. This information is often obtained by surveys of the membership and published by the societies.
>
> For example, the American Chemical Society annually offers data on career opportunities, an overview of the current workforce, information on jobs, job-hunting tips, an analysis of help-wanted ads, a salary survey, and sources of information on career planning.
>
> Another example is an excellent document produced by the American Physical Society (APS) and the American Institute of Physics (AIP) for graduate students in physics; entitled Graduate Student Packet (APS, 1995), it provides information on employment statistics, corporations employing the largest numbers of physicists, how to write a resume and cover letter, interview tips, a list of nontraditional positions held by physicists, and a list of resource books, bulletins, and directories. Also included are interesting biographical sketches of people in nontraditional occupations. Besides general biographical information, the persons profiled indicate what careers are like, give career path information, and give general career advice. The document is provided free by APS and AIP to anyone on request.
>
> Society information tends to be more current and specific than information published by the federal government. For graduate students who maintain membership, it offers overviews of the employment market throughout their student careers. Universities can help by disseminating this information to students who are not members.

Box 5-9: Disciplinary Societies and Career Information

In preparing this report, we have been limited in various ways by the lack of timely and relevant information that policy-makers—and students and their advisers—should have. NSF should address the following:

Timeliness. Databases and reports should be made available soon after the data are collected.

Nonacademic employment. NSF should increase the degree of detail of data on nonacademic employment, which now accounts for most new scientists and engineers. More information is also needed on the career tracks followed by scientists and engineers, both inside and outside universities.

Extramural research. In addition to strengthening its own data collection and analysis, NSF should expand its support of extramural research on career patterns in advanced science and engineering.

5.4   TOWARD IMPLEMENTATION OF A NATIONAL POLICY

In preparing our last report, *Science, Technology, and the Federal Government: National Goals for a New Era* (COSEPUP, 1993), it became clear that no coherent national policy guides the education of advanced scientists and engineers, even though the nation depends heavily on them. That recognition was an important stimulus for the present report.

A casual observer might say that federal policy should simply be to fund the best research and that sound graduate education is an automatic byproduct. There is some validity to that view, but we believe that it is time to reconsider the stewardship of our human resources separately. The nation's graduate programs must prepare scientists and engineers for contributions not only to the nation's basic research, but also to a wide array of other national objectives. Simply to let the development of human resources be guided by the workings of the relevant labor markets is an inadequate policy, given the long lead times required to make career decisions.

At present, there is neither the conceptual clarity nor the factual basis for us to lay out a coherent policy. We are concerned that many prevailing views are obsolete or obsolescent.

5.4.1. A searching national discussion that includes representatives of government, universities, employers, and professional organizations should examine the goals, policies, conditions, and unresolved issues pertaining to graduate-level human resources.

Graduate education is the responsibility of private and state-supported universities; of the federal and state governments, which support many students; of the corporate sector, which increasingly employs those who complete it; and of public and private foundations, which support its conduct and study its workings. All those parties need to be involved in a continuing reconsideration of graduate education and its national purposes.

Three kinds of issues are suggested as worthy of a searching national discussion:

- National goals and policy options.
- System characterization.
- Contemporary issues.

National Goals and Policy Options. How can we judge the overall adequacy of the national system of graduate education in science and engineering? Our 1993 *Goals* report suggested three goals to keep in mind in assessing the nation's performance in research. Goal 1 is for the United States to be among the world leaders in all major fields of research. Goal 2 is for the United States to maintain clear leadership in selected fields. Goal 3 is for the United States to cede technological leadership in no technology because of technical backwardness alone.

Whether that framework suggests a corresponding set of goals for graduate education or whether some other goals are appropriate should be considered. With better agreement on goals, participants could productively refine the roles and responsibilities of each sector—university, state and federal government, professions, corporations—in meeting them.

Policies and goals for graduate education, to be truly national, must be the shared objectives of all—the research and teaching institutions, state leaders, the federal agencies responsible for support of research and education, and Congress. Developing a shared **national view** of such goals (and not just a federal view) could lead to a series of policies and actions taken by all the partners in the system.

The science and engineering graduate-education enterprise, which serves multiple national objectives, should be measured against several yardsticks. It should ensure a steady supply of precollege and college teachers, of university faculty, and of researchers in academic, government, and industrial laboratories. It should meet the expanding need for advanced scientists and engineers in careers outside research. And it should offer a diverse vision of education and employment that inspires future generations of American students to strive for careers in science and technology.

System Characterization. What are the key trends in graduate education with respect to employment patterns, career paths, financial support from public and private sources, program evolution, and so on? What are the determinants of those trends?

The national discussion could examine whether underemployment is widespread, how nontraditional employers view new PhDs, the growth of postdoctoral positions, and how people choose careers. It could also monitor progress on innovations, such as the measures recommended in this report, and it might thus serve as a clearinghouse for information on university programs intended to foster versatility, including those stemming from demonstrations funded by education/training grants, and facilitate the development of a national database for better career decision-making.

Contemporary Issues. Finally, the national discussion could examine current issues on which opinions diverge across the sectors, including the difficult issues—time to first job and sources of new students—discussed in Chapter 4.

5.5 CONCLUSION

In conclusion, the committee believes that science and engineering graduate programs will be improved if

- Science and engineering programs are made more flexible and provide more options for students so that they are more versatile.
- Graduate-student support is shifted to education/training grants.
- Time to degree is controlled.
- More women and minority-group members are attracted to them.
- Better and more-timely career information and guidance are provided while diversity and excellence in research are maintained.

How can reforms like this work in a system as decentralized as graduate education? The committee feels that there is one especially good way: for the major participants—universities, government, industry, and foundations—to come together to discuss these issues. Although some major universities have been slow to consider reforms, there has in fact been tremendous innovation, and our specific recommendations for institutional change are being implemented somewhere. This should be better known. The committee feels strongly that having a national dialogue could strengthen an educational process that must change at least as fast as the world around it.

A

Biographical Information on Committee Members

Phillip A. Griffiths (Chair) is the director of the Institute for Advanced Study in Princeton, New Jersey. He has been professor of mathematics at Princeton University and Harvard, and provost and James B. Duke Professor of mathematics at Duke University. He earned his BS at Wake Forest University and his PhD at Princeton University in 1962. He is a member of the National Academy of Sciences. His current research centers on the geometry of differential equations.

Robert McCormick Adams is secretary emeritus of the Smithsonian Institution in Washington, D.C. and adjunct professor of anthropology at the University of California, San Diego. He is a member of the National Academy of Sciences (NAS) and has been a councilor of the NAS twice. From 1955 to 1984 he was a member of the University of Chicago faculty. He earned a PhB in 1947, an AM in 1952, and a PhD in 1956, all at the University of Chicago.

Bruce M. Alberts is president of the National Academy of Sciences (NAS) and is a biochemist who has been recognized for his work in both biochemistry and molecular biology. He graduated from Harvard College with a BS and earned a PhD in 1965 at Harvard. Dr. Alberts has long been committed to the improvement of science education and serves on the advisory board of the NAS's National Committee on Science Education Standards and Assessment.

Arden L. Bement is Basil S. Turner Distinguished Professor of Engineering and director of the Midwest Superconductivity Consortium at Purdue University. He was vice president for science and technology at TRW, Inc. He earned a professional degree of Metallurgical Engineer (EMet) at the Colorado School of Mines, a MS at the University of Idaho, and a PhD from the University of Michigan. He is a member of the National Academy of Engineering and a recipient of the Distinguished Civilian Service Medal of the Department of Defense.

Elkan R. Blout is director emeritus of the Division of Biological Sciences at Harvard School of Public Health and Edward S. Harkness Professor of Biological Chemistry, Emeritus, at Harvard Medical School. He earned an AB at Princeton University in 1939 and a PhD in chemistry at Harvard in 1942. He is a member of the National Academy of Sciences and the Institute of Medicine.

Felix E. Browder is university professor of mathematics at Rutgers University and former vice president for research. He is also Max Mason Distinguished Service Professor, Emeritus, of the University of Chicago. He graduated from Massachusetts Institute of Technology with a BS in 1946 and obtained his PhD in mathematics at Princeton University in 1948. His research centers on partial differential equations and nonlinear functional analysis. He is a member of the National Academy of Sciences and was elected to the council of NAS in 1992.

David R. Challoner is vice president for health affairs at the University of Florida and chairman of the board of directors of the Shands Hospital. He earned an MD at Harvard Medical School in 1961 and was dean and professor of medicine at the St. Louis University School of Medicine before taking his post in Florida. His clinical specialty is internal medicine with a subspecialty interest in endocrinology. He is a member of the Institute of Medicine.

Ellis B. Cowling is University Distinguished Professor At-Large and director of the Southern Oxidants Study at North Carolina State University. He earned a BS and an MS at the State University of New York College of Forestry at Syracuse University (wood technology), a PhD at the University of Wisconsin (plant pathology and biochemistry), and Filosofie Licensiat and Filosofie Doktor degrees in physiological botany at the University of Uppsala in Sweden. He is a member of the National Academy of Sciences.

Bernard N. Fields was the Adele Lehman Professor and chairman of the Department of Microbiology and Molecular Genetics at Harvard Medical School. He earned his AB at Brandeis University and a MD in 1962 at New York University School of Medicine. He was a postdoctoral fellow in cell biology at the Albert Einstein College of Medicine and was a member of the Institute of Medicine. He died in 1995.

Alexander H. Flax is a senior fellow at the National Academy of Engineering (NAE). He received his BS in aeronautical engineering from the Guggenheim School of Aeronautics of New York University in 1940 and a PhD in physics from the University of Buffalo. He was president of the Institute for Defense Analyses for 14 years before to coming to NAE. He is a member and former home Secretary of the National Academy of Engineering.

Ralph E. Gomory is president of the Alfred P. Sloan Foundation. He received his BA from Williams College in 1950, studied at Cambridge University, and received his PhD in mathematics from Princeton University in 1954. He was director of research for the IBM Corporation from 1970-1986, and senior vice president for science and technology from 1986-1989. He is a member of both the National Academy of Sciences and National Academy of Engineering. He has been awarded a number of honorary degrees and prizes, including the National Medal of Science.

Thomas D. Larson is a consultant and former administrator of the Federal Highway Administration. He earned his BS, MS, and PhD in civil engineering at Pennsylvania State University. He is a member of the National Academy of Engineering and the National Academy of Public Administration. He served for 8 years as secretary of transportation for Pennsylvania and as a chaired professor at Pennsylvania State University.

Mary Jane Osborn is head of the Microbiology Department at the University of Connecticut Health Center. She received a BA (physiology) from the University of California, Berkeley and a PhD (biochemistry) from the University of Washington. Dr. Osborn is a member of the National Academy of Sciences. Her research focuses on biogenesis of bacterial membranes.

Phillip A. Sharp is Salvador E. Luria Professor in the Center for Cancer Research and head of the Department of Biology at the Massachusetts Institute of Technology. He received a BA (chemistry and mathematics) from Union College, Kentucky, and a PhD (chemistry) from the University of Illinois, Urbana/Champaign. He is a member of both the National Academy of Sciences and the Institute of Medicine and corecipient of the 1993 Nobel Prize in physiology and medicine.

Kenneth Shine is president of the Institute of Medicine and professor of medicine, emeritus at the University of California at Los Angeles School of Medicine. He is the School of Medicine's immediate past dean and provost for medical sciences. Both a cardiologist and a physiologist, he received his AB from Harvard College and his MD from Harvard Medical School.

Ralph Snyderman is chancellor for health affairs and dean of the School of Medicine at Duke University. Formerly, he was senior vice president for medical research and development at Genentech, Inc. and Frederic M. Hanes Professor of Medicine and Immunology at Duke. In 1991, he was awarded the Ciba Geigy award for lifetime achievement in inflammation research and in 1993, he was awarded the Bonazinga Award for Excellence in leukocyte-biology research. He received his BS degree from Washington College and his MD degree from the SUNY Downstate Medical Center. He is a member of the Institute of Medicine.

H. Guyford Stever is trustee at a variety of scientific agencies and a consultant on science issues. He was science and technology adviser to President Ford (1976-1977). From 1972 to 1976, he was director of the National Science Foundation. He was president of Carnegie-Mellon University from 1965 to 1972, chief scientist of the Air Force from 1955 to 1965, and professor of aeronautical engineering at Massachusetts Institute of Technology from 1946 to 1965. He received degrees from Colgate and California Institute of Technology. He is a member of the National Academy of Sciences and the National Academy of Engineering (NAE), serving as the NAE foreign secretary from 1984 to 1988. In 1991, he was awarded the National Medal of Science.

Morris Tanenbaum retired as vice chairman of the board and chief financial officer of AT&T in 1991. He earned a BA in chemistry at Johns Hopkins University and a PhD in physical chemistry at Princeton University. He pioneered the use of silicon as a commercial semiconductor material through the invention of the diffused base silicon transistor and was a leader of the group that discovered the first practical materials for superconductor magnets. He is a member and currently vice president of the National Academy of Engineering.

Robert M. White is president of the National Academy of Engineering. He holds a BA in geology from Harvard University and MS and ScD degrees in meteorology from the Massachusetts Institute of Technology. He served under five US presidents from 1963 to 1977, first as chief of the US Weather Bureau and finally as the first administrator of the National Oceanic and Atmospheric Administration. In those capacities, he brought about a revolution in the US weather warning system with satellite and computer technology, helping to initiate new approaches to the balanced management of the country's coastal zones.

B

STATISTICS ON GRADUATE EDUCATION OF SCIENTISTS AND ENGINEERS

Michael McGeary
Study Director, Committee on Science,
Engineering, and Public Policy

Contents

OVERVIEW

About 1,500 institutions of higher learning in the United States have programs leading to degrees in science and engineering. Of those, nearly 300 offer doctoral-degree programs in science and engineering. They also offer master's degrees, and more than 400 nondoctoral academic institutions offer master's-degree programs in science and engineering. In 1992, about 430,000 graduate students were in science and engineering programs; 87% of them were at the 300 doctorate-granting institutions.

In 1992, about 80,000 master's degrees and 25,000 doctoral degrees were earned in science and engineering fields. About one-fourth of the doctorates were awarded in each broad field of science and engineering: physical/mathematical sciences, life sciences, social sciences, and engineering. The median time from the bachelor's degree to the PhD was 9.2 years. More than half of the master's degrees and 90% of the PhDs are awarded by the 150 universities that receive 90% of federal academic R&D funding.

About 5% of all science and engineering doctorate recipients in 1993 (14% of life-sciences PhDs) were supported by federal fellowships and traineeships. Another 61% (including 78% of physical scientists and 69% of engineers) received external support, primarily research assistantships and teaching assistantships. Many of the research assistantships were funded by federal grants. About one-quarter of the science and engineering doctoral recipients (including one-half the social scientists) were self-supporting (including federally guaranteed loans).

More than one-third more doctorates in science and engineering were awarded in 1993 than in 1983. Seven-tenths of the net increase in doctorate awards went to foreign citizens with temporary visas, and most of the remaining increase was to US women. In 1993, nearly 30% of the doctorates were earned by women, up from about 25% in 1983. In 1992, 5.7% of PhDs were earned by members of underrepresented minorities in 1992, up from 4.1% in 1983; most of the increase was earned by Hispanics. Foreign citizens with temporary visas greatly increased their share of US doctorates, earning 18.5% in 1983 and 32% in 1993; almost all the net increase was accounted for by citizens of Asian countries. Nearly half of the engineering PhDs went to foreign citizens with temporary visas.

THE GRADUATE STUDENTS

In 1992, the National Science Foundation (NSF) estimated that about 431,600 students were enrolled in graduate science and engineering degree programs (NSF, 1994a:Table 1). Most (87%) were enrolled in doctorate-granting institutions, a proportion that has varied only slightly since the NSF survey began in 1975. Most (67%) were full-time students (this proportion was 72% in doctorate-granting institutions).

It is not possible to tell which of these graduate students were enrolled in master's degree programs and which in doctoral programs, although many PhD recipients have master's degrees (72% in 1993) (NRC, 1995:Appendix Table A-3).

Table B-1, a comparison of the distribution of science and engineering graduate students among fields by type of institution and enrollment status shows that life-sciences graduate students were somewhat more likely than science and engineering graduate students overall to be at doctorate institutions and to be enrolled full-time. Social sciences and behavioral-science graduate students had the opposite pattern: they were somewhat more likely to be part-time and at master's institutions. Engineering graduate students were slightly more likely to be at doctorate institutions but more likely to be enrolled part-time.

TABLE B-1 **Distribution of Science and Engineering Graduate Students, by Field, 1992**

Field	All Institutions, All Students	Doctorate-Granting Institutions All Students	Full-Time Students
TOTAL	431,613 (100%)	374,781 (100%)	270,984 (100%)
Physical/ mathematical sciences	106,548 (25.0%)	93,429 (25.2%)	69,053 (25.8%)
Astronomy	869	869	840
Physics	14,264	13,734	12,432
Chemistry	19,904	18,799	16,611
Physical sciences n.e.c.	459	209	128
Mathematical sciences	20,375	17,890	13,889
Environmental sciences	15,609	13,964	10,567
Computer sciences	36,396	29,042	15,554
Life sciences	66,046 (15.3%)	61,114 (16.3%)	51,676 (19.1%)
Agricultural sciences	11,609	10,891	8,907
Biological sciences	54,437	50,223	42,769
Social/behavioral sciences	139,644 (32.4%)	110,868 (29.6%)	77,464 (28.6%)
Social sciences	85,824	73,170	50,272
Psychology	53,820	37,698	27,192
Engineering	118,047 (27.3%)	108,292 (28.9%)	71,823 (26.5%)

SOURCE: Calculated from Table 1 in NSF, 1994a.

Non-US Citizens

Nearly 110,000 (25.3%) science and engineering graduate students were not US citizens in 1992. About 93,000 of them were enrolled full-time. Their distribution among fields differed from that of US-citizen science and engineering graduate students. Table B-2 shows the distribution of full-time science and engineering graduate students by citizenship and broad field in 1992. Those who were not US citizens were more likely to be studying engineering or the physical sciences and less likely to be in life-science or social/behavioral-sciences programs.

As a result, those who were not US citizens constituted relatively high proportions in some fields—46% of all full-time graduate students in engineering and 39% of those in the physical/mathematic sciences—but low proportions in other fields—27% of all full-time graduate students in the life sciences and 17% of those in the social/behavioral sciences or psychology.

TABLE B-2 **Distribution of US and Non-US Citizens, by Broad Field, 1992**

Field	Full-Time Science and Engineering Graduate Student, All Institutions	
	US Citizen	Non-US Citizen
TOTAL	198,198 (100.0%)	92,795 (100.0%)
Physical/ mathematical sciences	45,177 (22.8%)	28,983 (31.2%)
Life sciences	39,146 (19.7%)	14,652 (15.8%)
Social/behavioral sciences	73,661 (37.2%)	14,908 (16.1%)
Engineering	40,214 (20.3%)	34,252 (36.9%)

SOURCE: Calculated from Tables 13 and 14 in NSF, 1994a.

Female Graduate Students

In 1992, more than 150,000 (35%) science and engineering graduate students were women (up from 25% in 1977). As Table B-3 shows, they were more likely to be enrolled in the life sciences or the social/behavioral sciences and less likely to be in the physical sciences or engineering. In fact, half of all female science and engineering graduate students were in social sciences and psychology programs.

As a result, the majority (54%) of graduate students in the social/behavioral sciences were women, as were 44% of those in the life sciences. Only 15% of engineering graduate students and 27% of those in the natural (physical, environmental, mathematical, and computer) sciences were female.

TABLE B-3 **Female Science and Engineering Graduate Students, by Broad Field, 1992**

Field	Number	Percentage Distribution Across Fields	Percentage of All Graduate Students
TOTAL	150,411	100.0	34.8
Physical/ mathematical sciences	28,719	19.1	26.6
Life sciences	29,223	19.4	44.2
Social/behavioral sciences	75,311	50.1	53.9
Engineering	17,158	11.4	14.5

SOURCE: Calculated from Table 8 in NSF, 1994a.

Members of Underrepresented Minorities

Fewer than 29,000 (9%) of science and engineering graduate students who were US citizens were members of underrepresented minorities—black, Hispanic, or American Indian. Compared with all US-citizen graduate students, they were much more likely to be studying social/behavioral sciences (53 versus 37%) and substantially less likely to be in the life sciences (13% versus 20%). Members of underrepresented minorities constituted 13% of US citizens in the social/behavioral sciences and about 7% of those in the other broad fields (see Table B-4).

TABLE B-4 **Members of Underrepresented Minorities, by Broad Field, 1992**

Field	Number	Percentage Distribution Across Fields	Percentage of All US-Citizen Graduate Students
TOTAL	28,866	100.0%	9.0
Physical/math sciences	4,917	17.0%	6.7
Life sciences	3,615	12.5%	7.2
Social/behavioral sciences	15,335	53.1%	12.6
Engineering	4,999	17.3%	6.5

SOURCE: Calculated from Table 2 in NSF, 1994a.

Growth Trends in Full-Time Graduate Enrollment Since 1982

In 1992, there were nearly 291,000 full-time science and engineering graduate students, 30.6% more than in 1982. The growth by field is presented in the first column of Table B-5. Much of the net growth came from foreign citizens; as overall enrollment was increasing by almost 2% a year, foreign enrollment was growing by more than 5% a year (NSB, 1993:50). The second and third columns of Table B-5 compare the increases in full-time science and engineering graduate students who were foreign citizens with those who were US citizens in 1982-1992, by field.

Enrollment increases were also driven by the increased participation of women—3% a year, compared with 1% among men, during the 1980s. There were absolute decreases in the number of male graduate students in the life, environmental, and social sciences and psychology (NSB, 1993:53).

TABLE B-5 **Increases in Full-Time Graduate Enrollment, by Field and Citizenship, 1982-1992 (percentages)**

| Field | Citizenship | | |
	All	Non-US	US
TOTAL	+30.6	+68.1	+18.4
Physical/			
mathematical sciences	+33.7	+90.6	+12.2
Physical sciences	+27.8	+83.9	+7.1
Mathematical sciences	+35.5	+47.8	+28.6
Environmental sciences	-2.5	+63.3	-13.6
Computer sciences	+92.1	+170.3	+50.4
Life sciences	+14.8	+97.6	-0.8
Agricultural sciences	-6.2	+17.3	-14.1
Biological sciences	+20.4	+136.3	+2.3
Social/behavioral sciences	+26.2	+32.4	+25.1
Social sciences	+22.1	+30.1	+19.8
Psychology	+33.2	+53.9	+32.3
Engineering	+48.2	+60.6	+39.6

SOURCES: Calculated from Tables 13 and 14 in NSF, 1994a for 1992; Table B-5 in NSF, 1993a for 1982.

Growth in First-Year and Beyond-First-Year Enrollments, 1982-1992

The NSF survey of graduate students and postdoctorates in science and engineering fields began to collect information on the number of first-year full-time enrollments in 1982. The data indicate that first-year enrollments increased at a lower rate than total full-time enrollments until about 1989, after which they increased more rapidly for several years. During 1982-1992, first-year enrollments increased by 17% and beyond-first-year enrollments by 37% (Table B-6). It is difficult to interpret those data. Are the recent large increases in first-year enrollments the result of reports in the middle to late 1980s of impending shortfalls in the number of PhDs or the tendency of more college graduates to go to graduate school when economic conditions are poor? Also, how much of the higher rate of growth among beyond-first-year graduate students until recently was simply the manifestation of the steadily increasing degree requirements among science and engineering PhDs, and how much was due to graduate students' deliberately delaying completion of their degrees as short-term responses to poor job-market prospects?

TABLE B-6   **Trends in First-Year and Beyond-First-Year Full-Time Enrollments in Doctorate-Granting Institutions, 1982-1992**

Year	First Year	Beyond First Year
1982	70,351	152,419
1983	72,152 (2.6%)	157,786 (3.5%)
1984	70,604 (-1.8%)	160,986 (2.0%)
1985	71,395 (1.1%)	163,100 (1.3%)
1986	73,167 (2.5%)	169,941 (4.2%)
1987	71,255 (-2.6%)	176,265 (3.7%)
1988	70,930 (-0.5%)	180,036 (2.1%)
1989	74,478 (5.0%)	182,677 (1.5%)
1990	76,405 (2.6%)	189,355 (3.7%)
1991	81,140 (6.2%)	196,211 (3.6%)
1992	82,481 (1.7%)	208,512 (6.3%)

SOURCES: Calculated from Tables B-34 and B-35 in NSF, 1992a for 1982; Tables B-24 and B-25 in NSF, 1993a for 1983-1994; unpublished NSF Tables for 1985-1992.

Sources and Mechanisms of Financial Support

In 1992, science and engineering graduate students were supported in a number of ways by a variety of sources. For each full-time student, the NSF survey asks for the "major" (i.e., largest) source of support (e.g., federal, institutional, and self) and the type (e.g., fellowship, and/or research assistantship). Table B-7 shows that the sources of support vary considerably from field to field. Although on the average 20% of full-time science and engineering graduate students received their major support from a federal source, this was the largest source of support for 32% of graduate students in biology and nearly 36% of graduate students in the physical sciences. Only 7% of graduate students in the social or behavioral sciences and 10% of those in the mathematical sciences were supported primarily by federal funds. Nearly two-thirds of mathematical scientists and half of those in the physical sciences received their major support from their institutions (mostly in the form of research and teaching assistantships), but institutional funds were also an important source of graduate support in the other disciplines—between 32 and 45%. "Own funds" (including, however, federally guaranteed loans) were the major source of support for large fractions of graduate students in some fields—46% of those in computer science and 40% of those in the social and behavioral sciences—but for relatively few in physics, astronomy, and chemistry (6%) or the biological sciences (13%). Only a few percent received foreign support (although those completing the survey might not always have known whether those funding their own way—thus classified as self-supporting—were receiving foreign support). Finally, about 7% overall were receiving support from industry and domestic sources other than federal and institutional. About 11% of students in engineering and agricultural science were receiving such support.

TABLE B-7 **Sources of Major Support for Full-Time Science and Engineering Graduate Students in All Institutions, by Field, 1992**

Field	Total No.	Federal	Institu- tional	Other US	Foreign	Self
TOTAL	290,993	20.0%	41.3%	6.9%	2.1%	29.7%
Physical/ mathematical sciences	74,160	25.0%	47.0%	5.8%	1.6%	20.6%
Physical sciences	30,730	35.7%	50.0%	7.0%	1.1%	6.4%
Mathematical sciences	14,663	10.2%	65.1%	2.4%	2.0%	20.3%
Environmental sciences	11,150	30.9%	39.2%	7.1%	2.2%	20.6%
Computer sciences	17,617	15.0%	31.7%	5.9%	1.8%	45.6%
Life sciences	53,798	31.8%	43.4%	7.9%	2.3%	14.5%
Agricultural sciences	9,280	21.1%	38.7%	11.5%	6.2%	22.5%
Biological sciences	44,518	34.0%	44.4%	7.2%	1.5%	12.9%
Social/behavioral sciences	88,569	7.0%	42.0%	3.5%	1.7%	45.7%
Social sciences	54,183	6.3%	45.0%	3.7%	2.7%	42.3%
Psychology	34,386	8.1%	37.4%	3.2%	0.2%	51.1%
Engineering	74,466	22.1%	33.3%	11.4%	2.7%	30.5%

SOURCE: Calculated from Table 11 in NSF, 1994a.

The pattern of sources of support has not changed much over the last 10 years, as seen in Table B-8; federal, institutional, and other US sources of support were up by several percentage points each, offsetting relative declines in foreign and own sources of support.

TABLE B-8 Sources of Major Support for Full-Time Science and Engineering Graduate Students, 1982 and 1992

Year	Total No.	Federal	Institu-tional	Other US	Foreign	Self
1982	208,954	19.3%	41.5%	6.6%	4.0%	28.6%
1992	290,993	20.0%	41.3%	6.9%	2.1%	29.7%

SOURCES: Calculated from Table C-18 in NSFa, 1992 for 1982; and Table 11 in NSF, 1994a for 1992.

The sources of *federal* support for full-time science and engineering graduate students also varied by field (see Table B-9), although the pattern has not changed since 1982 (compare NSF, 1992: Table C-18).

National Institutes of Health (NIH) NIH is the primary source of support for nearly 70% of federally supported graduate students in the biological sciences and also accounts for one-third (34%) of federally funded graduate students in psychology. Overall, NIH is the major source of support for more than one-fourth of the federally supported science and engineering graduate students. Other Health and Human Services (DHHS) agencies pick up a few percent more.

United States Department of Agriculture (USDA) The majority (55%) of federally supported agricultural-science students are funded by USDA. USDA is the primary supporter of few other graduate students (a little more than 5% of federally funded students).

Department of Defense (DoD) Nearly half (45%) of those with major federal support in the computer sciences and more than one-fourth of those in the mathematical sciences are funded by DoD. Overall, DoD is the major source of support for 15% of federally funded graduate students.

National Science Foundation (NSF) Almost one-third of the graduate students in physical sciences who receive their major support from federal sources are funded by NSF. Overall, NSF supports more than a one-fifth of the federally funded graduate students.

Other Other federal agencies are the major source of support for 29% of federally supported graduate students, especially in the social (44%) and environmental (44%) sciences. The only fields that do not receive much support from other federal agencies are the biological (8%) and the computer (14%) sciences.

TABLE B-9 Federal Sources of Support for Full-Time Science and Engineering Graduate Students in All Institutions, by Field and Agency, 1992

Field	Total No.	DoD	NIH	Other HHS	NSF	USDA	Federal Sources
TOTAL	58,309	15.0%	25.6%	2.2%	22.7%	5.4%	29.1%
Physical/ mathematical sciences	18,539	17.5%	12.1%	0.8%	34.2%	1.0%	34.4%
Physical sciences	10,956	10.8%	18.6%	1.2%	32.9%	0.6%	35.9%
Mathematical sciences	1,499	25.8%	4.1%	0.5%	30.5%	1.7%	37.6%
Environmental sciences	3,449	13.7%	1.2%	0.2%	38.4%	2.6%	43.9%
Computer sciences	2,635	45.3%	3.7%	0.2%	36.3%	0.2%	14.3%
Life sciences	17,102	1.5%	61.9%	2.8%	8.3%	12.8%	12.7%
Agricultural sciences	1,961	0.9%	1.5%	0.1%	4.3%	55.0%	38.2%
Biological sciences	15,141	1.5%	69.8%	3.1%	8.8%	7.3%	9.4%
Social/behavioral sciences	6,193	5.9%	19.9%	9.1%	14.7%	6.7%	43.8%
Social sciences	3,408	6.7%	8.6%	3.6%	18.3%	11.6%	51.1%
Psychology	2,785	4.8%	33.7%	15.7%	10.2%	0.7%	34.9%
Engineering	16,475	29.7%	5.2%	0.6%	27.7%	2.2%	34.6%

SOURCE: Calculated from Table 11 in NSF, 1994a.

As for the *mechanisms* of support (including nonfederal), the latest detailed data by field are for 1991 (Table B-10).

Fellowships Fellowships are awarded to individual graduate students on the basis of merit. Table B-10 shows that about 10% of the 259,000 full-time science and engineering graduate students were supported by fellowships in 1991, and fellowship support was spread fairly evenly across the disciplines (about one-fourth of the fellowships were federally funded).

Traineeships Traineeship programs are competitively awarded to universities, which select the graduate students to support. About 4% of science and engineering graduate students were trainees, most of them in the biological sciences. (About 60% of the trainees were federally supported; 30% were institutionally funded.)

Research Assistantships About 30% of full-time science and engineering graduate students were supported as research associates on research grants awarded to faculty supervisors. The proportion varied by field. Graduate students in the some of the physical sciences and the life sciences were more likely to be research associates; those in the mathematical sciences and social and behavioral sciences were less likely. (About half the research assistants were supported by federal funds and one-third by institutional funds.)

Teaching Assistantships More than one-fifth (23%) of graduate students were supported primarily as teaching assistants. Graduate students in mathematics and in the physical sciences were especially likely to be teaching assistants; those in engineering and agricultural sciences were less likely than average to have teaching assistantships.

Other Support "Other support" includes loans, personal funds, and tuition payments by industry and government agencies. It accounts for more than a third (33%) of graduate students. It was especially important in some fields; about half those in computer science, psychology, and social sciences were supported other than by fellowships, traineeships, and research or teaching assistantships. Graduate students in biology or the physical sciences were less likely to rely on other types of support.

TABLE B-10 **Mechanisms of Major Support for Full-Time Science and Engineering Graduate Students in Doctorate-Granting Institutions, 1991**

Field	Total No.	Fellow-ships	Trainee-ships	Research Assistant-ships	Teaching Assistant-ships	Other Types of Support
TOTAL	259,484	9.6%	3.9%	30.4%	23.3%	32.8%
Physical/ mathematical sciences	67,352	8.6%	1.8%	31.0%	36.3%	22.3%
Physical sciences	29,364	9.1%	2.6%	41.0%	38.9%	8.4%
Mathematical sciences	13,525	9.9%	1.6%	9.4%	55.2%	23.9%
Environmental sciences	9,880	9.1%	0.9%	42.5%	22.9%	24.5%
Computer sciences	14,583	5.8%	0.8%	23.3%	22.6%	47.5%
Life sciences	50,075	10.3%	10.3%	42.6%	18.1%	18.6%
Agricultural sciences	8,793	4.9%	0.9%	55.4%	9.0%	29.9%
Biological sciences	41,282	11.5%	12.3%	39.9%	20.1%	16.2%
Social/behavioral sciences	73,132	11.3%	3.8%	14.0%	21.9%	49.0%
Social sciences	47,080	14.0%	3.4%	13.5%	22.7%	46.3%
Psychology	26,052	6.4%	4.4%	14.8%	20.5%	53.8%
Engineering	68,925	8.1%	1.6%	38.4%	15.9%	36.0%

SOURCE: Calculated from Tables C-19 and C-20 in NSF, 1993a.

Science and Engineering Graduate Students in Master's-Granting Institutions

In 1992, nearly 57,000 science and engineering graduate students were in institutions whose highest degree is the master's. Most of them (65%) were enrolled part-time. Table B-11 gives their distribution and enrollment status by field and compares them with graduate students at doctorate-granting institutions. The table indicates that graduate students in master's degree institutions were much more likely to be in the social sciences and psychology and much less likely to be in the life sciences. In fact, 26% of all graduate students in the social sciences and psychology were in master's-degree institutions, compared with 11% of the remaining science and engineering graduate students.

TABLE B-11 Science and Engineering Graduate Students in Master's Degree Institutions and Doctorate Institutions, by Enrollment Status and Field, 1992

Field	Master's-Granting Institution		Doctorate-Granting Institution	
	All Students	Full-Time	All Students	Full-Time
TOTAL	56,832	20,009	374,781	270,984
Physical/ mathematical sciences	13,369 (24%)	4,139 (21%)	94,507 (25%)	70,021 (26%)
Physical sciences	1,885	719	33,611	30,011
Mathematical sciences	2,485	774	17,890	13,889
Environmental sciences	1,645	583	13,964	10,567
Computer sciences	7,354	2,063	29,042	15,554
Life sciences	4,932 (9%)	2,122 (11%)	61,114 (16%)	51,676 (19%)
Agricultural sciences	718	373	10,891	8,907
Biological sci	4,214	1,749	50,223	42,769
Social/behavioral sciences	28,776 (51%)	11,105 (56%)	110,868 (30%)	77,464 (29%)
Social sciences	12,654	3,911	73,170	50,272
Psychology	16,122	7,194	37,698	27,192
Engineering	9,755 (17%)	2,643 (13%)	108,292 (29%)	71,823 (27%)

SOURCE: Calculated from Tables 20 and 21 in NSF, 1994a.

THE INSTITUTIONS

In 1991, there were 3,611 institutions of higher education in the United States; they enrolled 14 million students and granted 1.9 million degrees, of which about one-fourth (470,000) were in science and engineering fields (NSB, 1993:38). The Carnegie Foundation for the Advancement of Teaching has classified those institutions into categories according to the size of their bachelor's-degree and graduate programs, amount of research funding, and—for liberal-arts colleges—selectivity of admissions. Table B-12 shows how many institutions were in each category in 1991.

TABLE B-12 **Number of Academic Institutions with Science and Engineering Programs, by Highest Degree Level, 1991**

Carnegie Foundation Category	Science and Engineering Program		
	Bachelor's	Master's	Doctorate
TOTAL	1,448	738	299
Research I	67	68	71
Research II	34	34	34
Doctorate-Granting I	46	48	48
Doctorate-Granting II	56	57	53
Comprehensive I	419	318	36
Comprehensive II	167	50	1
Liberal Arts I	138	30	4
Liberal Arts II	389	42	0
Two-Year	20	0	0
Specialized	94	69	38
Other	15	20	13
Not classified	3	2	1

SOURCE: Calculated from Appendix Table 2-6 in NSB, 1993.

Although comprehensive and liberal-arts institutions were the majority of institutions granting science and engineering bachelor's and master's degrees, the research and doctorate institutions accounted for large fractions of the degrees granted: 54% of all science and engineering bachelor's degrees and 53% of the master's degrees. Degree production is especially concentrated at the doctoral level (see Table B-13): nearly two-thirds of the science and engineering PhDs awarded in 1991 came from the 71 Research I universities, four-fifths from the 105 Research I and II universities; and nine-tenths from the 153 Research I and II and Doctorate I universities. The same set of 153 universities also receives 90% of all academic R&D funding (NSB, 1993:40; Appendix Table 2-5).

TABLE B-13 **Concentration of Science and Engineering Degree Awards by Type of Institution, 1991**

Carnegie Foundation Category	Total No. and Cumulative Percentage of Science and Engineering Degrees Awarded		
	Bachelors	Masters	Doctorate
TOTAL	337,675	78,368	23,979
Research I	29.3	37.6	65.2
Research II	39.1	49.2	79.5
Doctorate-Granting I	47.2	59.0	89.4
Doctorate-Granting II	53.7	68.0	94.7
Comprehensive I	83.5	91.4	96.2
Comprehensive II	87.0	93.2	96.2
Liberal Arts I	93.6	94.3	96.4
Liberal Arts II	97.7	95.3	96.4
Two-Year	97.9	95.3	96.4
Specialized	99.3	98.1	98.4
Other	99.9	99.9	99.9
Not classified	100.0	100.0	100.0

SOURCE: Calculated from Appendix Table 2-6 in NSB, 1993.

The 105 Research I and II universities produce nearly 80% of the science and engineering doctorates awarded each year (see Table B-14). This concentration of PhD production differs some by broad field, although the 71 Research I institutions accounted for at least the majority of PhDs granted in each.

TABLE B-14 Concentration of 80 Percent of Science and Engineering PhD Production in the 105 Research Universities, by Field, 1991

Carnegie Foundation Category	Natural Sciences	Math & Computer Sciences	Social & Behavioral Sciences	Engineering
TOTAL	10,152	1,837	6,778	5,212
Research I (n=71)	67.3%	70.3%	55.4%	71.9%
Research II (n=34)	81.9%	84.5%	71.0%	84.2%

SOURCE: Calculated from Appendix Table 2-5 in NSB, 1993.

There was substantial growth in the number of institutions with graduate degree programs since 1961 (see Table B-15). The number of institutions granting doctorates doubled between 1961 and 1991; the number of master's-degree institutions more than doubled.

TABLE B-15 Number of Institutions by Highest Degree Level Since 1961, by Decade

Year	Highest Degree Granted	
	Master's	Doctorate
1961	189	153
1971	287	229
1981	361	293
1991	442	299

SOURCE: Calculated from Appendix Table 5-1 in NSB, 1985 for 1961-1981; and Appendix Table 2-6 in NSB, 1993 for 1991.

SCIENCE AND ENGINEERING MASTER'S DEGREES

Master's Degrees in Science and Engineering

The number of master's degrees awarded in science and engineering has grown every year since 1966 except in the 1979-1981 period (Table 1 in NSF, 1994b). In 1991, over 78,000 science and engineering master's degrees were awarded, up from 41,000 in 1966. Science and engineering master's degrees were 29% of all master's degrees awarded in 1966, a percentage that declined to less than 21 in 1976, increased to 25% in 1987, and fell again to 23% in 1991.

According to Table B-16, about one-third of science and engineering master's degrees are awarded in the social and behavioral sciences, three-tenths in engineering, one-fourth in the natural sciences, and one-tenth in the life sciences (NSF, 1994b). (Compared with 1966, the social/behavioral sciences increased their share by almost 9 percentage points, gaining 5 points from the life. sciences, 3 from engineering, and 1 from the natural sciences.)

TABLE B-16 Science and Engineering Master's Degrees Awarded, by Field, 1966-1991

Field	1966	1971	1976	1981	1986	1991
TOTAL	41,059 (100.0%)	56,454	65,007	64,366	71,831	78,368 (100.0%)
Physical/ mathematical sciences	9,975 (24.3%)	13,131	11,927	12,029	17,124	18,232 (23.3%)
Physical sciences	4,275	5,115	3,880	3,366	3,649	3,777
Mathematical/ computer sciences	5,010	6,789	6,466	6,787	11,241	12,956
Environmental sciences	690	1,227	1,581	1,876	2,234	1,499
Life sciences	5,865 (14.3%)	7,604	9,223	9,107	8,027	7,406 (9.5%)
Agricultural sciences	1,641	1,848	2,602	3,092	2,983	2,600
Biological sciences	4,224	5,756	6,621	6,015	5,044	4,806
Social/behavioral sciences	11,514 (28.0%)	19,352	27,812	26,779	25,584	28,717 (36.6%)
Social sciences	9,091	14,914	19,953	18,740	17,221	18,915
Psychology	2,423	4,438	7,859	8,039	8,363	9,802
Engineering	13,705 (33.4%)	16,367	16,045	16,451	21,096	24,013 (30.6%)

SOURCE: Calculated from Table 1 in NSF, 1994b.

Women

Women earned 13.3% of the science and engineering master's degrees in 1966, a percentage that increased steadily to nearly 36% in 1991 (see Table B-17). This varied by field.

The number of science and engineering master's degrees per 1,000 24-year-old women in the US population increased from 4 in 1966 to 15 in 1991 (NSF, 1994b:Table 57). Meanwhile, the number going to men went from more than 30 per 1000 in 1969-1970 to 26 in 1991 (after reaching a high of 32 in 1970 and a low of 21 in the early 1980s). Overall, in 1991, 21 master's degrees in science and engineering were awarded for every 1000 24-year-olds in the US population, up from 15 in 1966.

TABLE B-17   **Women as Percentage of Science and Engineering Master's-Degree Recipients, by Field, 1991**

Field	1966	1971	1976	1981	1986	1991
TOTAL	13.3	18.3	23.1	29.3	32.3	35.6
Physical/						
mathematical sciences	15.5	19.3	21.1	24.3	29.0	31.3
Physical sciences	11.4	14.4	15.6	20.1	25.0	28.4
Math/computer sciences	20.3	24.9	26.1	27.2	31.4	32.8
Environmental sciences	6.1	9.5	13.9	21.6	23.1	25.6
Life sciences	20.8	27.1	26.8	33.4	41.7	46.3
Agricultural sciences	4.4	6.2	14.1	22.8	31.2	36.2
Biological sciences	27.2	33.8	31.8	38.9	47.9	51.8
Social/behavioral sciences	22.8	28.7	34.0	43.2	48.9	53.7
Social sciences	20.2	26.2	29.0	36.8	41.2	45.6
Psychology	32.9	37.2	46.7	58.1	64.9	69.5
Engineering	0.6	1.1	3.5	8.1	11.4	14.0

SOURCE: Calculated from Table 18 in NSF, 1994b.

Underrepresented Minorities

NSF has collected information on the race, ethnicity, and citizenship of master's degree recipients biennially since 1977. Table B-18 shows that the proportion of science and engineering master's degrees awarded to members of underrepresented minorities (i.e., blacks, Hispanics, and American Indians) has increased slowly in the natural sciences and engineering, offset by declines in psychology and the social sciences, fields that traditionally have registered the largest shares of underrepresented minorities.

TABLE B-18 **Members of Underrepresented Minorities as Percentage of Science and Engineering Master's Degree Recipients, by Field, 1977-1991**

Field	1977	1981	1987	1991
TOTAL	7.8	7.5	7.0	7.3
Physical/ mathematical sciences	4.1	3.7	4.0	4.4
Physical/ environmental sciences	3.4	3.6	3.7	3.4
Mathematical/ computer sciences	5.1	4.5	4.1	5.3
Life sciences	4.2	4.4	5.4	5.3
Agricultural sciences	3.5	3.9	4.2	4.1
Biological sciences	4.6	4.8	6.1	6.0
Social/ behavioral sciences	11.3	11.1	10.2	11.1
Social sciences	11.6	11.7	10.8	11.7
Psychology	10.3	8.4	8.4	9.1
Engineering	3.2	3.4	4.5	3.9

SOURCE: Calculated from Table 4 in NSF, 1994c.

Non-US Citizens

Non-US citizens with temporary visas received almost 20% of the science and engineering master's degrees in 1991, almost double their share in 1977 (see Table B-19). Most were in physical or mathematical science and engineering programs, where they constituted about 30% of all master's-degree students. They were relatively unlikely to be in social-science or psychology programs.

TABLE B-19 Science and Engineering Master's Degrees Earned by Students Who Were Not US Citizens, by Field, 1977, 1985, and 1991

Field	1977 No.	%	1985 No.	%	1991 No.	%
TOTAL	8,282	9.9	13,256	16.3	18,013	19.5
Physical/ mathematical sciences	1,392	11.8	3,492	22.1	5,382	29.5
Physical/ environmental sciences	656	12.3	1,098	18.9	1,504	28.5
Mathematical/ computer sciences	736	11.3	2,394	24.0	3,878	29.9
Life sciences	1,141	10.5	1,080	13.1	1,352	18.2
Agricultural sciences	664	17.8	606	19.2	603	23.0
Biological sciences	477	6.7	474	9.3	749	15.6
Social/ behavioral sciences	2,204	5.0	2,866	8.0	3,583	8.7
Social sciences	2,033	5.6	2,570	9.5	3,270	10.3
Psychology	171	2.1	296	3.5	317	3.2
Engineering	3,545	21.8	5,818	26.7	7,692	30.5

SOURCE: Calculated from Table 4 in NSF, 1994g.

SCIENCE AND ENGINEERING DOCTORAL DEGREES

Doctorates in Science and Engineering

The number of science and engineering PhDs awarded annually tripled between 1958 and 1968 to about 18,000. Between 1968 and 1974, the number leveled off or fell in various fields, although the aggregate number peaked in 1971-1973 at nearly 19,400 per year, and fell to fewer than 18,000 per year by 1977, where it remained through 1981. Table B-20 shows the numbers of science and engineering PhDs awarded during 1983-1993 period.

TABLE B-20 **Science and Engineering Doctorates Awarded, by Field, 1983-1993**

Field	1983	1984	1985	1986	1987	1988	1989	1990	1991	1992	1993
TOTAL	18,393	18,514	18,713	19,253	19,710	20,748	21,534	22,688	23,787	24,454	25,184
Physical/ mathematical sciences	4,426	4,452	4,531	4,807	5,030	5,309	5,455	5,859	6,279	6,502	6,496
Physics/Astronomy	1,043	1,080	1,080	1,187	1,237	1,302	1,274	1,393	1,411	1,537	1,543
Chemistry	1,759	1,765	1,836	1,903	1,975	2,015	1,970	2,100	2,193	2,214	2,139
Mathematics	701	698	688	729	740	749	859	892	1,039	1,058	1,146
Computer/ information sciences	286	295	310	399	450	515	612	705	800	869	878
Environmental sciences	637	614	617	589	628	728	740	769	836	824	790
Life sciences	4,756	4,877	4,904	4,804	4,815	5,127	5,203	5,503	5,719	5,861	6,059
Agricultural sciences	1,015	997	1,111	997	976	1,015	1,088	1,176	1,074	1,063	969
Biological sciences	3,741	3,880	3,793	3,807	3,839	4,112	4,115	4,327	4,645	4,798	5,090
Social/ behavioral sciences	6,430	6,272	6,112	6,266	6,153	6,125	6,333	6,432	6,574	6,652	6,933
Social sciences	3,083	3,015	2,994	3,140	2,980	3,051	3,125	3,150	3,324	3,388	3,514
Psychology	3,347	3,257	3,118	3,126	3,173	3,074	3,208	3,282	3,250	3,264	3,419
Engineering	2,781	2,913	3,166	3,376	3,712	4,187	4,543	4,894	5,215	5,439	5,696

SOURCE: Calculated from Table 1 in NSF, 1994b.

In 1982, the number of science and engineering doctorates awarded annually rose above 18,000 for the first time since 1976. The growth rate was still low—about 2% per year—until 1988, when the increase was more than 5% over 1987. The number increased by around 3% per year from 1988 through 1993. Table B-21 shows the increases from 1988 to 1993 by field.

TABLE B-21 **Increases in Numbers of Science and Engineering Doctorates Awarded, by Field, 1988-1993**

			Increase	
Field	1988	1993	No.	Percentage
TOTAL	20,748	25,184	4,436	21.4%
Physical/ mathematical sciences	5,309	6,496	1,187	22.4
Physics/Astronomy	1,302	1,543	241	18.5
Chemistry	2,015	2,139	124	6.2
Mathematics	749	1,146	397	53.0
Computer sciences	515	878	363	70.5
Environmental sciences	728	790	62	8.5
Life sciences	5,127	6,059	932	18.2
Agricultural sciences	1,015	969	-46	-4.5
Biological sciences	4,112	5,090	978	23.8
Social/behavioral sciences	6,125	6,933	808	13.2
Social sciences	3,051	3,514	463	15.2
Psychology	3,074	3,419	345	11.2
Engineering	4,187	5,696	1,509	36.0

SOURCE: Calculated from Table 1 in NSF, 1994f.

Women

The number of women awarded science and engineering PhDs increased from 4,624 in 1983 to 7,537 in 1993, or 63.0%. As a result, the proportion of PhD awards to women increased from 25.1% in 1983 to 29.9% in 1993. They varied from field to field (see Table B-22).

TABLE B-22 Women as a Percentage of Science and Engineering Doctorate Recipients, by Field, 1983-1993

Field	1983	1984	1985	1986	1987	1988	1989	1990	1991	1992	1993
TOTAL	25.1	25.4	25.7	26.4	26.6	26.9	27.9	27.8	28.7	28.6	29.9
Physical/											
mathematical sciences	13.9	14.8	15.8	16.1	16.5	16.6	18.9	18.3	18.7	19.7	20.7
Physics/Astronomy	7.1	7.3	9.4	9.2	9.7	10.0	9.3	10.8	11.1	12.1	12.6
Chemistry	16.9	18.1	19.7	20.8	20.6	21.2	25.3	24.0	23.6	26.2	27.3
Mathematics	16.1	16.5	15.4	16.6	16.9	16.2	18.0	17.7	19.2	19.4	23.0
Computer sciences	12.6	12.5	10.6	12.0	14.4	10.9	17.6	15.6	14.6	13.8	15.6
Environmental sciences	15.2	17.3	18.0	17.0	18.2	19.9	20.3	19.4	22.1	23.4	20.8
Life sciences	28.7	27.6	28.7	30.2	31.8	33.0	34.0	33.8	34.6	35.2	37.6
Agricultural sciences	13.1	13.3	15.4	17.3	17.5	18.3	21.0	21.0	19.5	21.9	23.5
Biological sciences	33.0	31.3	32.6	33.6	35.4	36.6	37.5	37.3	38.1	38.2	40.3
Social/											
behavioral sciences	39.1	40.6	40.8	42.0	42.8	44.5	44.8	45.9	48.7	47.1	49.0
Social sciences	29.8	30.4	31.7	33.0	31.4	34.3	33.2	33.0	36.3	35.6	37.1
Psychology	47.7	50.1	49.4	51.2	53.5	54.7	56.1	58.3	61.4	59.1	61.1
Engineering	4.5	5.2	6.3	6.7	6.5	6.8	8.3	8.5	9.0	9.3	9.1

SOURCE: Calculated from Tables 1 and 2 in NSF, 1994b.

Women earning science and engineering PhDs were concentrated in particular fields. In 1993, nearly half (45%) were in the social and behavioral sciences, and 30% were in the life sciences (see Table B-23). The concentration in social and behavioral sciences was reduced over the previous 10 years, however, as more awards to women were made in the physical and mathematical sciences and engineering. Overall, the shift was 4.5 percentage points (to nearly 18%). The number of women receiving PhDs in the physical and mathematical sciences more than doubled from 1983 to 1993 (from 617 to 1,344). The number in engineering quadrupled (from 124 to 521), but fewer than 7% of women PhDs were in engineering.

TABLE B-23 **Science and Engineering Doctorates Awarded to Women, by Field, 1983 and 1993**

Field	1983 Number	Percentage	1993 Number	Percentage
TOTAL	4,624	100.0	7,537	100.0
Physical/ mathematical sciences	617	13.3	1,344	17.8
Physics/astronomy	74	1.6	194	2.6
Chemistry	297	6.4	585	7.8
Mathematics	113	2.4	264	3.5
Computer sciences	36	0.8	137	1.8
Environmental sciences	97	2.1	164	2.2
Life sciences	1,366	29.5	2,278	30.2
Agricultural sciences	133	2.9	228	3.0
Biological sciences	1,233	26.7	2,050	27.2
Social/behavioral sciences	2,517	54.4	3,394	45.0
Social sciences	920	19.9	1,305	17.3
Psychology	1,597	34.5	2,089	27.7
Engineering	124	2.7	521	6.9

SOURCE: Calculated from Table 2 in NSF, 1994f.

The percentage of science and engineering doctorates awarded to members of underrepresented minorities—American Indians, blacks, and Hispanics—has been very low and has increased slowly (see Table B-24). In fact, the percentage of doctorates received by black citizens declined during the last half of the 1980s.

TABLE B-24 Members of Underrepresented Minorities as a Percentage of Science and Engineering Doctorate Recipients, by Field, 1983, 1988, and 1993

Field	1983 No.	Percentage	1988 No.	Percentage	1993 No.	Percentage
All US Citizens	13,403	100.0	13,218	100.0	14,708	100.0
Underrepresented Minorities	547	4.1	628	4.8	843	5.7
American Indian	27	0.2	41	0.3	41	0.3
Black	283	2.1	260	2.0	363	2.5
Hispanic	237	1.8	327	2.5	439	3.0

SOURCE: Calculated from Table 3 in NSF, 1994f.

Non-US Citizens

In 1993, more than 8,000 science and engineering PhDs went to foreign citizens with temporary visas—nearly one-third of all the doctorates awarded by US universities (see Table B-25). Only 18.5% of PhDs awarded in 1983 went to foreign citizen with temporary visas. In 1993, they received just under half of the new doctorates in engineering, up from 42% 10 years earlier. They were awarded more than one-third (36%) of the PhDs in the physical and mathematical sciences and more than one-fourth (28%) of those in the life sciences.

TABLE B-25 Share of Science and Engineering Doctorates Earned by Students Who Were Not US Citizens, by Field, 1983 and 1993

Field	1983 Doctorates Awarded All	Temporary Visa No.	Percentage	1993 Doctorates Awarded All	Temporary Visa No.	Percentage
TOTAL	18,393	3,400	18.5	25,184	8,087	32.1
Physical/ mathematical sciences	4,426	926	20.9	6,496	2,363	36.4
Physics/astronomy	1,043	256	24.5	1,543	583	37.8
Chemistry	1,759	283	16.1	2,139	674	31.5
Mathematics	701	209	29.8	1,146	517	45.1
Computer sciences	286	72	25.2	878	349	39.7
Environmental sciences	637	106	16.6	790	240	30.4
Life sciences	4,756	629	13.2	6,059	1,694	28.0
Agricultural sciences	1,015	307	30.2	969	448	46.2
Biological sciences	3,741	322	8.6	5,090	1,246	24.5
Social/ behavioral sciences	6,430	675	10.5	6,933	1,247	18.0
Social sciences	3,083	596	19.3	3,514	1,099	31.3
Psychology	3,347	79	2.4	3,419	148	4.3
Engineering	2,781	1,170	42.1	5,696	2,783	48.9

SOURCE: Calculated from Table 4 in NSF, 1994f.

The number of non-US citizens with temporary visas increased 138% over a decade—from 3,400 in 1983 to 8,087 in 1993 (Table B-26). That increase was greater in the physical and mathematical sciences and in the life sciences. The rate of growth was lower than average in the social and behavioral sciences.

TABLE B-26 **Increase in Science and Engineering Doctorates Awarded to Non-US Citizens with Temporary Visas, by Field, 1983 and 1993**

Field	1983	1993	Difference No.	Percentage
TOTAL	3,400	8,087	4,687	137.9
Physical/ mathematical sciences	926	2,363	1,437	155.2
Physics/astronomy	256	583	327	127.7
Chemistry	283	674	391	138.2
Mathematics	209	517	308	147.4
Computer sciences	72	349	277	384.7
Environmental sciences	106	240	134	126.4
Life sciences	629	1,694	1,065	169.3
Agricultural sciences	307	448	141	45.9
Biological sciences	322	1,246	924	287.0
Social/ behavioral sciences	675	1,247	572	84.7
Social sciences	596	1,099	503	84.4
Psychology	79	148	69	87.3
Engineering	1,170	2,783	1,613	137.9

SOURCE: Calculated from Table 4 in NSF, 1994f.

Table B-27 shows the distribution of foreign citizens with temporary visas, by field. In 1993, roughly one-third were in engineering, and another one-third were in the physical/mathematical sciences. Around 15-20% were in each of the life sciences and the social sciences. Compared with 1983, temporary-visa holders moved away from the social sciences (by about 4.5 percentage points) and into the physical/mathematical sciences (by about 2 points) and the life sciences (by about 2.5 points).

TABLE B-27 **Science and Engineering Doctorates Awarded to Non-US Citizens with Temporary Visas, by Field, 1983 and 1993**

Field	1983	1993
TOTAL	3,400	8,087
Physical/mathematical sciences	27.2%	29.2%
Physics/astronomy	7.5%	7.2%
Chemistry	8.3%	8.3%
Mathematics	6.1%	6.4%
Computer sciences	2.1%	4.3%
Environmental sciences	3.1%	3.0%
Life sciences	18.5%	20.9%
Agricultural sciences	9.0%	5.5%
Biological sciences	9.5%	15.4%
Social/behavioral sciences	19.9%	15.4%
Social sciences	17.5%	13.6%
Psychology	2.3%	1.8%
Engineering	34.4%	34.1%

SOURCE: Calculated from Table 4 in NSF, 1994f.

STATISTICS ON GRADUATE EDUCATION OF SCIENTISTS AND ENGINEERS

The country of origin of temporary-visa holders shifted during the 1980s (see Table B-28). Citizens from eastern Asia increased their share of science and engineering PhDs awarded to temporary-visa holders from one-fourth to more than a half. Nearly all this increase was accounted for by students from the People's Republic of China, who increased their share from near zero in 1982 to 22% of all the science and engineering PhDs earned by temporary-visa holders in 1992.

TABLE B-28 **Region and Country of Origin of Foreign Citizens with Temporary Visas Earning Science and Engineering PhDs, 1983 and 1993**

Country	1983	1993
TOTAL	3,400 (100.0%)	8,087 (100.0%)
East Asia	958 (28.2%)	4,335 (53.6%)
Taiwan	438 (12.9%)	1,055 (13.0%)
PRC	3 (0.1%)	1,745 (21.6%)
Korea	136 (4.0%)	1,027 (12.7%)
West Asia	935 (27.5%)	1,538 (19.0%)
India	308 (9.1%)	789 (9.8%)
Africa	385 (11.3%)	374 (4.6%)
Europe	314 (9.2%)	838 (10.4%)
Other	808 (23.8%)	1,002 (12.4%)

SOURCE: Calculated from Table 5 in NSF, 1994f.

The annual reports of the Survey of Earned Doctorates conducted by the National Research Council for NSF have documented a substantial increase since 1970 in the time it has taken to obtain a PhD, whether measured in years since the bachelor's degree or in years registered in graduate school. According to these reports, which calculate the median time-to-degree (TTD) of all those obtaining PhDs each year, the figure has increased by about 30% over the last 20 years.

According to the latest report of the Survey of Earned Doctorates, total TTD (years from bachelor's degree to doctorate), or TTTD, went up by 29.6% from 1967 to 1993, from 8.1 to 10.5 years (Table B-29). The trend in registered time-to-degree (RTTD) was similar—31.5% (from 5.4 to 7.1 years). However, 1967 was near the postwar total-TTD low of 8 years reached in 1970. TTTD increased for decades (from 7 years in 1920 to 9 in 1962), fell during the 1960s to the low of 8 years in 1970, and then resumed its upward trend after 1970 (Bowen and Rudenstine, 1992:Figure 6.3).

Those figures are for all PhDs in all fields, including humanities, education, and the professional (which have had the highest TTDs historically). The patterns vary widely by field, even within the sciences and engineering. Engineering and physical sciences have always had shorter than average completion times; social sciences, longer.

The increase in TTD has slowed considerably since about 1987, even though the recession of the early 1990s might have increased the incentive to stay in school a year or two longer.

TABLE B-29 **Median Total Time-to-Degree for Doctorate Recipients, 1962-1993 (selected years)**

Field	1962	1967	1972	1977	1982	1987	1992	1993
All fields (including humanities)								
Registered	5.4	5.4	5.7	6.1	6.5	6.9	7.1	7.1
Total	8.8	8.1	8.2	8.7	9.6	10.4	10.5	10.5
All Science and Engineering								
Registered						6.4	6.7	6.7
Total						8.6	9.1	9.2
Physical sciences								
Registered	5.1	5.1	5.6	5.7	5.8	6.0	6.5	6.5
Total	6.5	6.0	6.5	6.9	6.9	7.4	8.1	8.3
Life sciences								
Registered	5.3	5.4	5.5	5.7	6.0	6.5	6.7	6.8
Total	7.8	7.2	7.0	7.3	7.6	8.8	9.4	9.4
Social sciences								
Registered	5.4	5.2	5.6	5.9	6.7	7.2	7.5	7.4
Total	9.0	7.7	7.5	8.0	9.2	10.4	10.6	10.4
Engineering								
Registered	5.0	5.2	5.5	5.6	5.7	5.8	6.2	6.3
Total	7.1	7.2	7.5	7.5	8.0	8.1	8.7	8.8

SOURCE: Calculated from Table 6 in NRC, 1995.

In conducting the research for their recent book *In Pursuit of the PhD,* Bowen and Rudenstine (1992:113-119), noticed that TTD figures were lower for their sample of 10 schools. They consulted demographers who suggested a different method for determining TTD that should be more accurate. The method used by the Office of Scientific and Engineering

Personnel (OSEP) and others determines the median number of TTD years for all those receiving their doctorates in a particular year. The demographers pointed out that this permits a bias if the cohorts entering graduate school are increasing or decreasing in size over time. Each entering class of PhD candidates has some fast finishers and some slow finishers. In a period such as the late 1950s and 1960s, when the number entering PhD programs was growing every year, the proportion of fast finishers showing up for their degrees a few years later increased and made the decreases in TTD larger than they would have been if cohorts had been steady. Similarly, when cohort sizes decrease, as they did in 1974-1984, the proportion of fast finishers getting their degrees a few years later goes down, increasing the apparent TTD. More recently, enrollments have gone up again, and that accounts for at least part of the decrease in TTD medians in the past several years.

Bowen and Rudenstine corrected for that bias by calculating average TTD of _entering_ cohort, rather than _graduating_ cohort. They asked, how long on the average, did it take those entering a PhD program (or getting their bachelor's degrees in year X to get their doctorates? They found that use of the entering-cohort method gave an increase in TTD of about 10% over the preceding 15-20 years, not 30%. They admitted that any lengthening in the already-long TTD is a serious problem but said that its magnitude and newness had been exaggerated.

A study of TTD by staff of OSEP reviewed the literature on the causes of increasing TTD (Tuckman, et al., 1990). They found that earlier studies had looked at sociological, demographic, economic, and institutional factors, although few had looked at them all and undertaken a causal analysis. They developed a model of TTD with five vectors of variables: family background characteristics, individual abilities and interests, tuition and financial aid, institutional environment and policies, and economic and social forces. They tested the model in 11 fields using data from the Survey of Earned Doctorates and found a variety of factors that affected registered time-to-degree (RTTD) or total time-to-degree (TTTD), including the availability and form of student support, labor-market conditions, sociodemographic characteristics of the doctorate recipients, and characteristics of the undergraduate and graduate institutions. Yet no factor or set of factors consistently explained the general upward trend in TTD. That might be because TTD is poorly measured (the study was based on the graduating, rather than the entering, cohort), or because the data are inadequate. They are aggregate data, and some measure the variables of interest only indirectly; other variables, such as increasing complexity of subject matter or the incentive for faculty to keep students longer as cheap labor on research projects, are not measured at all.

As for negative consequences, the following have been mentioned (Tuckman, et al., 1990):

● The increasing time spent in graduate school increases the time it takes for the supply of PhDs to respond to shifts in market demand, and that has both social and individual costs (if demand goes up, there are not enough qualified people; if it falls, highly capable people cannot be employed in their field of training).

●   Increasing TTD will discourage some highly qualified candidates from staying in science (perhaps some of the most qualified students, who can more easily find attractive alternatives).

●   Delayed start of career reduces the total years of productivity for society and the return on investment for the individual.

Bowen and Rudenstine (1992) also studied the effects of financial support in some detail in their 10-school sample. They found that it mattered. Students who received financial aid had much higher completion rates and shorter TTD than students who relied on their own resources. In the sciences, the form of the aid had an effect on completion and TTD; research assistantships had the best effect, fellowships a close second, and teaching assistantships the worst effect. They also found that the NSF fellowship program had been very successful in reducing median TTD (4.9 years versus 5.6 years for those who were not NSF fellows in an eight-university group). Interpreting such findings is problematic, however. Did the NSF fellows finish earlier because of the fellowship form of support itself or because they were selected through a rigorous process that selected more-motivated students?

In conclusion, both RTTD and TTTD have been increasing for a long time, with the exception of the 1960s. Presumably, the increases are caused in part by the increasing complexity of knowledge and techniques to be mastered in doctorate programs and in part by less-desirable or less-excusable reasons (e.g., an increase in tuition costs and a decrease in federal aid, which force students to work more during graduate school, or a desire of faculty to keep students working on research projects). They are also caused in part by the increasing participation of women and minority-group members, who generally have longer TTDs.

According to Bowen and Rudenstine, having outside aid does improve completion and TTD rates. The form of the aid—fellowships, research assistantships, or teaching assistantships—might have little independent effect.

Source of Support

The Survey of Earned Doctorates (SED) administered yearly by OSEP for NSF asks new PhDs to list their primary source of support during graduate school. The data for 1993 are displayed in Table B-30. It should be noted, however, that the nonresponse rate to this question was 34%, for unknown reasons (it was 23% in 1991, and 30% in 1992). It also should be noted that federally funded research assistantships are listed with other research assistantships under "university" because students often do not know the source of support for their research assistantships. Federal loans are listed under "personal." "Other" includes national fellowships, employer funds, and support from foreign governments, state governments, and other nonspecified sources. The "life sciences" include "health science" PhDs as well as the biological and agricultural scientists listed in the other tables in this appendix.

A brief analysis of the table shows that a relatively large percentage of the PhD recipients in social sciences are self-supporting—nearly half, compared with 10-15% of those in the physical sciences and engineering and a fifth of those in the life sciences.

PhDs in the life sciences receive the most direct federal support, probably resulting from the large fellowship and traineeship programs of the National Institutes of Health.

Most PhDs in the physical sciences and engineering, and to a lesser extent the life sciences, receive their primary support from their universities. That includes federally funded research assistantships, as well as other research and teaching assistantships.

TABLE B-30 **Primary Sources of Support for Science and Engineering Doctorate Recipients, by Broad Field, 1993 (percentages)**

Field	Personal	University	Federal	Other
TOTAL	23.8	61.4	7.5	7.3
Physical sciences	12.1	77.9	4.5	5.4
Life sciences	21.4	56.8	14.4	7.4
Social sciences	47.8	41.6	5.0	5.6
Engineering	14.7	69.3	4.9	11.1

SOURCE: Calculated from Table 11 in NRC, 1995.

POSTDOCTORATE EMPLOYMENT PLANS

According to the SED, among new science and engineering PhDs who had definite postgraduation plans, the percentage planning to work in academe (college or university) was 48% in the early 1960s (NRC, 1978:Table 30). That figure increased to 57.0% in 1970 before falling steadily to 44.1% in 1980 (NSF, 1993b:Table 15) and 40.4% in 1993 (NSF, 1994f:Table 7). Meanwhile, the proportion of new science and engineering PhDs going to business and industry grew from about 22% in the 1960s to 26.5% in 1970 and 36.2% in 1993.

Note that Table B-31 does not include those with definite plans for postdoctoral study in the United States, almost all at universities. These numbered 2,789 in 1970, 3,571 in 1980, 4,676 in 1990, and 5,739 in 1993 (NSF, 1993b:Table 15, 1994f:Table 7).

It also should be noted that the percentage of science and engineering PhDs who had definite plans at the time of the SED survey fell from 76.6% in 1970 to 72.0% in 1980, 64.0% in 1990, and 60.1% in 1993 (NSF, 1993b:Table 15, 1994f:Table 7).

TABLE B-31   **Science and Engineering PhD Recipients with Definite Postgraduation Commitments in the United States, by Field and Type of Employer, 1970-1991**

Field	1970 No.	Percentage	1975	1980	1985	1990	1991 No.	Percentage
TOTAL	9,216	100.0	8,187	7,285	6,614	7,175	7,403	100.0
College/university	5,263	57.1	4,287	3,228	2,851	2,952	3,099	41.9
Elementary/ secondary school	44	0.5	99	113	95	81	111	1.5
Government	1,015	11.0	1,365	1,142	885	871	890	12.0
Nonprofit organization	408	4.4	443	537	502	493	492	6.6
Industry/business	2,399	26.0	1,886	2,139	2,099	2,452	2,488	33.6
Self-employed	48	0.5	71	101	145	240	229	3.1
Other and unknown	39	0.4	36	25	37	86	94	1.3

SOURCE: Calculated from Table 5 in NSF, 1993b.

POSTDOCTORAL STUDY TRENDS

TABLE B-32 **Postdoctoral Study Plans of Recipients of Science and Engineering Doctorates from US Universities, 1985-1992**

PhD Recipients	1985	1987	1988	1989	1990	1991	1992
TOTAL	19,164	20,203	21,411	22,294	23,440	24,543	25,248
Postdoctoral plans	5,941	6,728	7,216	7,268	8,087	8,811	9,316
Fellowship	49.0%	48.0%	48.7%	49.7%	49.0%	49.9%	50.7%
Research associate	41.3%	42.9%	43.0%	40.5%	41.7%	41.5%	41.2%
Traineeship	4.5%	3.6%	3.9%	4.0%	4.1%	3.9%	3.3%
Other	5.2%	5.1%	4.4%	5.5%	4.9%	5.0%	5.1%

SOURCE: Calculated from Appendix Table A-3 in NRC, 1993.

TABLE B-33 **Postdoctoral Study Plans of Recipients of Science and Engineering Doctorates from US Universities, by Field, 1992**

PhD Recipients	Physical Sciences	Engineering	Life Sciences	Social Sciences	Total Science and Engineering
TOTAL	6,498	5,437	7,108	6,205	25,248
Postdoctoral plans	3,022	1,202	4,066	1,036	9,316
Fellowship	53.1%	34.4%	57.5%	64.7%	50.7%
Research associate	42.8%	58.8%	32.3%	19.2%	41.2%
Traineeship	2.2%	4.1%	2.6%	9.6%	3.3%
Other	1.9%	3.2%	7.7%	6.6%	5.1%

SOURCE: Calculated from Appendix Table A-3 in NRC, 1993.

TABLE B-34   **Science and Engineering Postdoctoral Appointees in Doctorate-Granting Institutions, by Field, 1982-1992**

Field	1982	1983	1984	1985	1986	1987	1988	1989	1990	1991	1992
All Science and Engineering	14,672	15,657	16,168	16,920	17,901	18,760	19,759	20,962	21,604	23,018	24,024
Science, Total	13,694	14,556	14,974	15,573	16,505	17,319	18,075	19,054	19,661	20,781	21,680
Physical sciences	4,281	4,444	4,386	4,517	4,843	4,953	5,187	5,355	5,507	5,623	5,772
Physics	1,326	1,350	1,320	1,342	1,527	1,548	1,578	1,678	1,715	1,763	1,954
Chemistry	2,805	2,973	2,906	2,995	3,151	3,246	3,429	3,462	3,580	3,627	3,573
Environmental sciences	335	415	488	375	417	420	499	459	605	645	709
Mathematical sciences	194	170	203	226	201	228	280	223	247	206	201
Computer sciences	46	82	63	74	74	100	91	78	71	157	149
Agricultural sciences	279	307	375	373	409	441	454	512	529	574	634
Biological sciences	7,756	8,355	8,707	9,164	9,722	10,346	10,752	11,518	11,799	12,648	13,287
Psychology	520	435	422	495	517	454	493	535	457	503	521
Social sciences	283	348	330	349	322	377	319	374	446	425	407
Engineering, Total	978	1,101	1,194	1,347	1,396	1,441	1,684	1,908	1,943	2,237	2,344
Chemical engineering	174	198	245	273	295	309	423	466	551	578	554
Materials	166	204	168	245	250	283	325	323	370	401	458
Mechanical	130	182	196	207	239	216	216	302	218	329	355
Electrical	176	174	171	176	172	175	186	193	241	300	307

SOURCE: Calculated from Table C-25 in NSF, 1992a; and, for 1991 and 1992, NSF, unpublished tables.

TABLE B-35 **Trends in Net Growth of Science and Engineering Postdoctoral Appointee Positions in Doctorate-Granting Institutions, by Field, 1982 and 1992**

	Growth, 1982-1992				Percentage Distribution of Postdoctoral Positions Among All Fields	
Field	1982	1992	Difference	Percentage	1982	1992
All Science and Engineering	14,672	24,024	9,352	63.7	100.0	100.0
Science, Total	13,694	21,680	7,986	58.3	93.3	90.2
Physical sciences	4,281	5,772	1,491	34.8	29.2	24.0
Physics	1,326	1,954	628	47.4	9.0	8.1
Chemistry	2,805	3,573	768	27.4	19.1	14.9
Environmental sciences	335	709	374	111.6	2.3	3.0
Mathematical sciences	194	201	7	3.6	1.3	0.8
Computer sciences	46	149	103	223.9	0.3	0.6
Agricultural sciences	279	634	355	127.2	1.9	2.6
Biological sciences	7,756	13,287	5,531	71.3	52.9	55.3
Psychology	520	521	1	0.2	3.5	2.2
Social sciences	283	407	124	43.8	1.9	1.7
Engineering, Total	978	2,344	1,366	139.7	6.7	9.8
Chemical engineering	174	554	380	218.4	1.2	2.3
Materials	166	458	292	175.9	1.1	1.9
Mechanical	130	355	225	173.1	0.9	1.5
Electrical	176	307	124	74.4	1.2	1.3

SOURCE: Calculated from Table C-25 in NSF, 1992a; and, for 1991 and 1992, NSF, unpublished tables.

TABLE B-36 Appointments of Postdoctoral Scientists and Engineers Who Were Not US Citizens in Doctorate-Granting Institutions, by Field, 1982 and 1992

Field	Growth, 1982-1992				Percentage of All Postdocs within Field		Percentage of All Non-US Science and Engineering Postdocs	
	1982	1992	Difference	Percentage	1982	1992	1982	1992
All Science and Engineering	5,961	12,627	6,666	111.8	40.6	52.6	100.0	100.0
Science, Total	5,304	11,053	5,749	108.4	38.7	51.0	89.0	87.5
Physical sciences	2,367	3,506	1,139	48.1	55.3	60.7	39.7	27.8
Physics	673	1,099	426	63.3	50.8	56.2	11.3	8.7
Chemistry	1,661	2,311	650	39.1	59.2	64.7	27.9	18.3
Environmental sciences	121	276	155	128.1	36.1	38.9	2.0	2.2
Mathematical sciences	126	109	-17	-13.5	64.9	54.2	2.1	0.9
Computer sciences	12	50	38	316.7	26.1	33.6	0.2	0.4
Agricultural sciences	116	275	159	137.1	41.6	43.4	1.9	2.2
Biological sciences	2,397	6,574	4,177	174.3	30.9	49.5	40.2	52.1
Psychology	65	127	62	95.4	12.5	24.4	1.1	1.0
Social sciences	100	136	36	36.0	35.3	33.4	1.7	1.1
Engineering, Total	657	1,574	917	139.6	67.2	67.2	11.0	12.5
Chemical engineering	133	415	282	212.0	76.4	74.9	2.2	3.3
Materials	138	331	193	139.9	83.1	72.3	2.3	2.6
Mechanical	100	211	111	111.0	76.9	59.4	1.7	1.7
Electrical	94	186	92	97.9	53.4	60.6	1.6	1.5

NOTE: Includes permanent residents and those with temporary visas.

SOURCE: Calculated from Table C-30 in NSF, 1992a; and, for 1991 and 1992, NSF, unpublished tables.

TABLE B-37 **Federally Supported Science and Engineering Postdoctoral Appointees in Doctorate-Granting Institutions, by Field, 1982 and 1992**

Field	Growth, 1982-1992				Percentage of All Postdocs within Field		Percentage of All Federally Supported Postdocs	
	1982	1992	Difference	Percent	1982	1992	1982	1992
All Science and Engineering	11,119	17,660	6,541	58.8	75.8	73.5	100.0	100.0
Science, Total	10,447	16,050	5,603	53.6	74.8	74.0	94.0	90.9
Physical sciences	3,600	4,589	989	27.5	64.1	79.5	32.4	26.0
Physics	1,156	1,641	485	42.0	87.2	84.0	10.4	9.3
Chemistry	2,307	2,730	423	18.3	82.2	76.4	20.7	15.5
Environmental sciences	255	556	301	118.0	76.1	78.4	2.3	3.1
Mathematical sciences	46	143	97	210.9	23.7	71.1	0.4	0.8
Computer sciences	25	113	88	352.0	54.3	75.8	0.2	0.6
Agricultural sciences	166	417	251	151.2	59.5	65.8	1.5	2.4
Biological sciences	5,825	9,695	3,870	66.4	75.1	73.0	52.4	54.9
Psychology	392	358	-34	-8.7	75.4	68.7	3.5	2.0
Social sciences	138	179	41	29.7	48.8	44.0	1.2	1.0
Engineering, Total	672	1,610	938	139.6	68.7	68.7	6.0	9.1
Chemical engineering	100	340	240	240.0	57.5	61.4	0.9	1.9
Materials	121	284	163	134.7	72.9	62.0	1.1	1.6
Mechanical	94	250	156	166.0	72.3	70.4	0.8	1.4
Electrical	118	229	111	94.1	67.0	74.6	1.1	1.3

NOTE: These are postdoctoral appointees for whom federal agencies and programs are "the source of the largest amount of their support" (those supported by federal loans are not included).

SOURCE: Calculated from Table C-27 in NSF, 1992a; and, for 1991 and 1992, NSF, unpublished tables.

TABLE B-38 Sources of Support for Science and Engineering Postdoctoral Appointees in Doctorate-Granting Institutions, by Field, 1992

Field	Total	Federal Sources Total	Fellow- ships (%)	Trainee- ships(%)	Research Grants(%)	Non- Federal Sources
All Science and Engineering	24,024	17,660	11.1	7.6	81.3	6,364
Science, Total	21,680	16,050	11.8	8.2	80.0	5,630
Physical sciences	5,772	4,589	7.5	0.8	91.7	1,183
Physics	1,954	1,641	4.4	0.2	95.4	313
Chemistry	3,573	2,730	8.5	1.2	90.3	843
Environmental sciences	709	556	7.9	1.1	91.0	153
Mathematical sciences	201	143	16.1	4.2	79.7	58
Computer sciences	149	113	1.8	0.9	97.3	36
Agricultural sciences	634	417	9.8	0.5	89.7	217
Biological sciences	13,287	9,695	13.9	11.9	74.2	3,592
Psychology	521	358	14.2	23.5	62.3	163
Social sciences	407	179	27.4	14.5	58.1	228
Engineering, Total	2,344	1,610	3.7	1.1	95.2	734
Chemical engineering	554	340	0.9	0.9	98.2	214
Materials	458	284	1.1	0.0	98.9	174
Mechanical	355	250	4.4	2.4	93.2	105
Electrical	307	229	3.5	0.0	96.5	78

SOURCE: Calculated from NSF unpublished data.

C

EMPLOYMENT TRENDS AMONG SCIENTISTS AND ENGINEERS WITH GRADUATE DEGREES

————————————

Michael McGeary
Study Director, Committee on Science,
Engineering, and Public Policy

————————————

Contents

EMPLOYMENT OF RECENT SCIENCE AND ENGINEERING MASTER'S DEGREE RECIPIENTS   166

OVERVIEW

This appendix has two parts: an original "cohort" analysis of data on the employment of recent science and engineering (S&E) PhDs since 1973 and a review of data on the employment of new science and engineering master's-degree recipients.

EMPLOYMENT TRENDS AMONG RECENT COHORTS OF SCIENCE AND ENGINEERING DOCTORATES

To understand better the career prospects of recipients of advanced degrees in science and engineering, a thorough knowledge of trends in the recent employment-related histories of new graduates is helpful. A rich database for such an analysis exists, and a preliminary study is reported in this appendix. The database is the Survey of Doctorate Recipients (see Box C-1 on page 148 for a description of the SDR database and its potential uses and limitations).

NSF publishes tables of data from the SDR on the entire population of U.S. scientists and engineers (the most recent was of the 1991 survey; see NSF, 1994d). The tables are examined below, but they do not provide information about <u>recent</u> science and engineering PhDs. For this study, OSEP was asked to produce two series of data tables: (1) tables on the employment activities of scientists and engineers who had received science and engineering PhDs in the 1-4 years before each survey, and (2) tables on the employment activities of those receiving science and engineering PhDs 5-8 years before each survey. This type of cohort analysis was apparently last done in response to the "new depression" in academic employment of the middle 1970s (see, e.g., NRC, 1983).

In this appendix, 4-year "classes" or cohorts are used to ensure minimal sample size when looking at specific fields, such as mathematics, chemistry, and biology. For example, the first set of tables gives information on those getting PhDs in 1969-1972 at the time of the 1973 survey, those getting PhDs in 1971-1974 at the time of the 1975 survey, and so on, through those who earned PhDs in 1987-1990 at the time of the 1991 survey.

The tables present data on workforce status (full-time, part-time, or unemployed), employment sector (academe, other education, business and industry, government, etc.), and tenure status of those employed in academe (4-year colleges, universities, and medical schools). There are tables and/or figures for the following:

All scientists and engineers (excluding psychologists)
> Physical scientists
>> Mathematicians
>> Computer scientists
>> Physicists/astronomers
>> Chemists
>> Earth/atmospheric/ocean scientists
> Life scientists
>> Agricultural scientists
>> Medical scientists
>> Biological scientists
> Engineers
> Social scientists
> Psychologists

Employment Status: Full-Time, Part-Time, and Not Employed

<u>1-4 Years Out</u> For those 1-4 years after receipt of PhD at the time of each survey since 1973, the SDR data (not reproduced here) show that unemployment rates and part-time employment rates have been low in all fields. Overall, the percentage of unemployed (defined as not working and looking for work) has varied between 1.2% and 1.6%. It was 1.5% in 1991 among those getting PhDs in 1987-1990. This trend, or lack of a trend, holds for each field. It does not rule out, however, substantial increases in unemployment since 1991.

The percentage not employed for all reasons (e.g., not looking, retired, or unemployed) has also been low and steady since 1973, about 3%.

The proportion of new PhDs employed part-time has increased by about 50%—from 2% in 1973 to 3.1% in 1991 (totaling about 1,100 of 58,000 in 1973 and 2,000 of 63,000 in 1991). This trend was shown in all science fields, except that part-time employment tripled among new social scientists, from 2% to 6%. Part-time employment did not increase among new engineering PhDs (it has been about 1% since 1973).

The category with the most significant change has been the proportion of recent doctorates employed in postdoctoral appointments. Just 8% of the 1969-1972 PhDs were postdoctorates in 1973, a percentage that increased steadily to 19% of the 1985-1988 PhDs in 1989 (the 1991 survey was delayed six months, so the postdoctorate percentage is lower—14%). Most postdoctorates were among new biology PhDs (2,000 in 1973 and 6,300 in 1989), and most of the rest were in physics/astronomy and chemistry (1,900 in 1973 and 2,800 in 1989).

<u>5-8 Years Out</u> For those 5-8 years out at the time of each survey, the pattern is similar except that few are in postdoctoral appointments. The percentage of unemployed is generally lower than for those 1-4 years out—between 0.7% and 1.3%—but it increased to 1.9% in 1991.

The percentage not employed for other reasons was up a little in 1991, but 97% were still employed. The proportion employed part-time doubled to 3.2% in 1991 but was still low.

Conclusion If there are major employment changes or problems, they have arisen mostly since 1991. The employment statistics are all relatively good, but some were slightly worse in 1991 than in 1987 or 1989. Even that is difficult to interpret, because the survey procedures were changed in 1991 and the response rate was much higher.[1]

Employment Sector: Academe, Industry, Government

Figure C-1 shows where all science and engineering PhDs were employed 1-4 years after receiving their doctorates, and Figure C-2 shows where they were 4 years later (5-8 years after receiving their doctorates.); Tables C-1 and C-2 give the numbers and percentages on which the figures are based. Figure C-1 confirms the steadily growing proportion going into postdoctoral positions during the 1970s and 1980s (8% in 1973 and 19% in 1989, as noted above)[2] as well as the growing proportion going into business and industry (22% in 1973 and 29% in 1991). A smaller proportion went directly into academic employment (49% in 1973 and 40% in 1991)(presumably, some were going into postdoctoral positions instead).

Figure C-2 shows where science and engineering are 5-8 years after receiving their doctorates. Not surprisingly, few are in postdoctoral appointments, although the percentage increased from 2% to 3% over the period (but it increased from 4.8% in 1973 to 9.2% in 1989 among biologists 5-8 years out). The proportion employed in academe fell. More than half the 1969-1972 PhDs were employed in academe 5-8 years later, compared with 45% of the 1983-1986 graduates in 1991. **This trend is the basis of a major conclusion of the report—that most new PhDs are employed outside academe.**

Another way of looking at the trend is to compare the same "class" 1-4 years and 5-8 years out (Figures C-3 to C-5). Over the period, there is an increasing falloff from the number of those on postdoctorates and employed in academe in the first 1-4 years to the number employed in academe plus postdoctorates after 5-8 years (this is true, although to different degrees, across fields).

The growth sector was business and industry. After 5-8 years, 26% of science and engineering PhDs were employed in business and industry as of 1973, a proportion that grew to about 45% in 1991 (Figures C-3 through C-5).

---

[1] As the report was going to press, after this was written, NSF released the preliminary results of the 1993 SDR. The unemployment rates were up slightly but still low (see text Figure 2-5).

[2] It is important to remember that some members of each 4-year cohort have already completed a postdoctoral assignment by the time of the survey. These figures are most useful for seeing trends.

The employment patterns differ from field to field (see Figures C-6 through C-18 for those 1-4 years out and Figures C-19 through C-31 for those 5-8 years out). Some fields such as chemistry and engineering, have long had a high percentage of PhDs working in industry; others have had high percentages working in academe. Within the sciences, however, the trends have been similar—a smaller proportion going into academe and the federal government, and a greater proportion going into business and industry (there was also noticeable growth in nonprofit employment among social scientists). Engineering is one field in which the percentage working in academe after 5-8 years, although relatively low, has increased (from 29% in 1979 to 32% most recently), as has the percentage working in business and industry (from 50% to 58%). The federal government was the big loser, going from 13% (1,600 of the class of 1969-1972 in 1977) to 5% (about 500 of the class of 1983-1986 in 1991).

Tenure Status

Table C-2 has some interesting data on trends in tenure and tenure status within academe among those 5-8 years after receiving the PhD. The number of academics with tenure fell both absolutely and relatively over the period. In 1979, for example, 20% of all those who had received their PhDs 5-8 years before (1971-1974) had tenure, and another 14% had tenure-track positions. The percentage with tenure after 5-8 years fell steadily to 12% in 1989, while the percentage in tenure-track positions grew to 17%. In absolute terms, the number with tenure after 5-8 years fell from 12,000 in 1979 to 6,500 in 1989, while the number in tenure-track positions went from 8,000 to 9,000. (The 1991 survey increased the percentage with tenure to at least 14%; the extent to which the change in survey methods contributed to this change needs to be explored.)

In another way of looking at the data, the total number in the tenure system of those 5-8 years after receiving the PhD fell from 20,000 in the 1979 survey to about 16,000-17,000 in the 1989-1991 survey, and the proportion with tenure decreased relative to those still in tenure-track jobs.

Meanwhile, a fairly steady number and percentage of PhDs 5-8 years out had non-tenure system positions over the period (about 7,000, or 12% of all PhDs 5-8 years out).

The figures differ from field to field, although the general trends hold. Biology is interesting because the percentage with tenure, low in 1979 at 18% fell to 7% in 1989, while those in tenure-track positions or not in the tenure system stayed about the same. Presumably, that reflects the high and growing proportion of postdoctorates and the lengthening time before biology PhDs enter faculty positions and begin their quest for tenure. In fact, as noted above, more than 9% of biologists were still in postdoctoral positions 5-8 years after receiving their PhDs. That in turn might be part of the explanation for the low and falling percentage of principal investigators under 35 years of age applying for National Institutes of Health research project grants, as reported in the recent National Research Council study of funding of young investigators (NRC, 1994a).

Impact of Employment Choices of Recent PhDs

The new data presented here on science and engineering 1-4 and 5-8 years after receiving their doctorates give a sense of the career-related flow of new PhDs. The flows also have an impact on the overall stock of PhDs. More than 14,000 new doctorates were added each year to the total stock of PhDs working in the United States, and small shifts in employment patterns have a cumulative impact over time on the whole. Table C-3 presents data on the employment of all US PhDs at the time of each survey.

- With 14,000 a year being added to a stock that was relatively young in 1973, the total number of employed science and engineering PhDs increased from 220,000 in 1973 to 437,000 in 1991.
- Although the percentage in academe (four-year colleges, universities and medical schools) fell from 57% to 49%, the absolute number increased from 125,000 in 1973 to 195,000 in 1991 (an increase of 56%).
- The overall percentage of those in academe with tenure grew from 58% in 1975 to 62% in 1983 and fell to 55% in 1991.
- The percentage employed in business and industry increased from 24% to 36%, or from 53,000 to 157,000 (an increase of 196 percent).

Conclusions

1. More than 14,000 new PhDs in science and engineering have found employment each year since the early 1970s. Unemployment rates of those out for 1-4 years or 5-8 years have been low compared with other occupations and fairly stable, at least through 1991. That does not reflect events since 1991, and it does not mean that all found work in their fields or found jobs that they expected or wanted.

As a result of the steady output of doctoral science and engineering, the overall number of people with science and engineering PhDs from U.S. universities working in the United States has nearly doubled since 1973. Academe has absorbed a large number, 70,000, or about 3,900 a year. Business and industry have absorbed another 104,000, or 5,800 a year. The latter has been the growth sector for PhD employment, and is likely to remain so for future PhDs.

2. Year by year, the proportion of new PhDs going into academe for employment has fallen steadily, with business and industry increasing their share of PhD employment. It is important to note that academe, while losing share, is still an important employer of new PhDs, and any changes in the academic employment market would have a substantial, if slowly declining, impact on the career prospects of new PhDs.

3.   The increasing proportion of new PhDs taking postdoctoral appointments has been an important feature of some fields, especially biology (accounting for more than half) and some of the physical sciences.   The percentage of those 5-8 years out, in postdoctoral positions, especially in biology, is increasing, indicating perhaps a lengthening of such positions or an increase in the practice of taking multiple postdoctorates.   Those trends might account in part for the decreasing percentage of PhDs with tenure 5-8 years out, because it postpones beginning of an independent faculty career.   Also, increasing numbers of postdoctorates are going into nonacademic employment.

4.   The data do not show a substantial increase in part-time employment or in nontenure positions in academe, at least through 1991.   However, a large percentage (12%) and number (7,000) of recent PhDs, all those 5-8 years out, have been in such positions through the period.   Who are they and what are they doing?

5.   This analysis should be extended by looking at data on such matters as salary (academe versus business versus government), primary activity (e.g., basic or applied research, development, R&D management, teaching, or consulting), and field-switching.

The Survey of Doctorate Recipients (SDR) is a biennial survey that has gathered employment-related information from a nationally representative panel of PhDs from U.S. institutions since 1973 (it does not include anyone who received a doctorate from a foreign institution). It is conducted by the Office of Scientific and Engineering Personnel (OSEP) of the National Research Council (NRC) for the National Science Foundation (NSF), National Institutes of Health (NIH), and other federal agencies. For each survey, a sample of new doctorate recipients since the preceding survey is added that is representative of all U.S. citizens and foreign citizens who stay in the United States. Although NSF publishes tables of information based on the entire sample, it is possible to use the SDR database to compare the employment situations of PhD "classes" over time. For this report, for example, we had tables produced of the employment characteristics of doctoral scientists and engineers who had received their PhDs 1-4 and 5-8 years before each survey to see how the employment situations of "new" or "recent" PhDs have changed over time by field (much more such work could be done, involving more detail and additional variables-e.g., citizenship and sex-to understand better the careers of doctoral scientists and engineers).

During the 1980s, the response rate to the SDR fell steadily. NRC studies in 1975 and 1989 indicated that nonresponse bias resulted in overestimates of the number of employed scientists and engineers, especially in academe but also overall (Spisak and Maxfield, 1979; Mitchell and Pasquini, 1991). In 1989, for example, the difference in academic employment was estimated to be about 5 percentage points. A recent NSF analysis concluded that the overestimates had been consistent over time and therefore did not affect the trend line of steady growth since 1973 (NSF, 1992b).

In 1991, several changes were made in the SDR that affect the comparability of the 1991 results with earlier data. The overall response rate was improved substantially, from 58% in 1989 to 80%. That improved the quality of the 1991 estimates, but, as NSF noted, "the improved response rates and the expected lessening of bias should be considered additional sources of changes in time series and longitudinal analysis" (NSF, 1994d:66). The 1991 survey was also fielded 7 months later than earlier surveys, and that explains at least part of the drop in proportion of those in postdoctoral-study positions in the group 1-4 years after the PhD (from 18.7% in 1989 to 14.0% in 1991).

Because of the changes in survey response rates and timing, time-series comparisons involving 1991 should be interpreted with caution. In this report, for example, we do not use 1991 data at all to look at postdoctoral-study trends. We do use 1991 estimates of employment status because they are the most-accurate data on the current situation, and if the reader understands the procedural changes described here, they still provide a useful comparison with (and correction of) earlier data.

In 1993, most of the questions were also changed, which substantially limited comparability for all but a few basic characteristics (e.g., unemployment). The only data used from the 1993 survey, which appeared as this report was going to press, are unemployment rates.

Box C-1: Methodological note

TABLE C-1 Scientists and Engineers 1-4 Years After Receiving PhD from US Institutions, by Field, Employment Status, and Sector of Employment, 1973-1991

TOTAL	1973	1975	1977	1979	1981	1983	1985	1987	1989	1991
Total Population	58,121	59,618	57,343	55,075	53,518	54,119	55,324	56,227	58,825	63,010
(percentage)	100.0	100.0	100.0	100.0	100.0	100.0	100.0	100.0	100.0	100.0
Postdoctoral Study	4,652	6,315	7,280	7,307	7,725	7,956	8,919	9,390	10,978	8,803
(percentage)	8.0	10.6	12.7	13.3	14.4	14.7	16.1	16.7	18.7	14.0
Total Employed	50,934	51,595	47,848	45,887	44,218	44,250	44,815	45,029	46,098	51,935
(percentage)	87.6	86.5	83.4	83.3	82.6	81.8	81.0	80.1	78.4	82.4
4 Year/University/ Medical School	28,170	27,017	24,062	23,410	21,150	20,646	22,175	21,976	22,139	25,174
(percentage)	48.5	45.3	42.0	42.5	39.5	38.1	40.1	39.1	37.6	40.0
-tenured	3,468	4,206	3,168	2,483	1,764	1,829	1,347	1,122	1,029	1,482
(percentage)	6.0	7.1	5.5	4.5	3.3	3.4	2.4	2.0	1.7	2.4
-tenure track				11,771	12,648	11,761	13,262	12,363	12,057	14,313
(percentage)	0.0	0.0	0.0	21.4	23.6	21.7	24.0	22.0	20.5	22.7
-other/no reports	24,702	22,721	20,894	9,156	6,738	7,056	7,566	8,491	9,053	9,379
(percentage)	42.5	38.1	36.4	16.6	12.6	13.0	13.7	15.1	15.4	14.9
Other Educational Institutions	1,326	1,472	1,618	802	923	969	892	764	827	911
(percentage)	2.3	2.5	2.8	1.5	1.7	1.8	1.6	1.4	1.4	1.4
Business/Industry	12,550	14,086	13,962	13,615	15,009	16,120	15,634	15,177	15,435	18,280
(percentage)	21.6	23.6	24.3	24.7	28.0	29.8	28.3	27.0	26.2	29.0
US Government	5,400	5,347	4,379	4,104	3,681	3,154	2,641	2,992	3,527	3,465
(percentage)	9.3	9.0	7.6	7.5	6.9	5.8	4.8	5.3	6.0	5.5
State/Local Government	806	999	1,141	1,124	886	959	1,117	1,259	1,453	1,144
(percentage)	1.4	1.7	2.0	2.0	1.7	1.8	2.0	2.2	2.5	1.8
Nonprofit Organization	2,468	2,398	2,386	2,555	2,409	2,193	2,176	2,515	2,545	2,626
(percentage)	4.2	4.0	4.2	4.6	4.5	4.1	3.9	4.5	4.3	4.2
Other/No Report	214	276	300	277	160	209	180	346	172	335
(percentage)	0.4	0.5	0.5	0.5	0.3	0.4	0.3	0.6	0.3	0.5
Total Not Employed	2,535	1,708	2,215	1,881	1,534	1,913	1,590	1,808	1,749	2,272
(percentage)	4.4	2.9	3.9	3.4	2.9	3.5	2.9	3.2	3.0	3.6
-seeking	811	783	927	716	622	682	670	775	686	940
(percentage)	1.4	1.3	1.6	1.3	1.2	1.3	1.2	1.4	1.2	1.5
-not seeking	287	348	353	480	345	285	297	465	498	668
(percentage)	0.5	0.6	0.6	0.9	0.6	0.5	0.5	0.8	0.8	1.1
-retired	23	16	24	11	9	2	0	90	71	19
(percentage)	0.0	0.0	0.0	0.0	0.0	0.0	0.0	0.2	0.1	0.0
-other/no report	1,414	561	911	674	558	944	623	478	494	645
(percentage)	2.4	0.9	1.6	1.2	1.0	1.7	1.1	0.9	0.8	1.0

NOTES: This table compares cohorts of scientists and engineers 1-4 years after receiving a doctorate from a US university (e.g., 1969-1972 PhDs in 1973, 1971-1974 PhDs in 1975, and so on). All fields are included except psychology (for field-level data, see Figures C-6 through C-18). All percentages are of the total population, including those not in the workforce.

Due to changes in survey procedures and timing in the 1991 survey, the 1991 estimates are not entirely comparable to those for the earlier survey years (see methodological note in Box C-1 for further information on comparability of 1991 estimates).

SOURCE: Special runs of data on employment status and employment sector of US doctoral scientists and engineers from the Survey of Doctorate Recipients.

TABLE C-2 Scientists and Engineers 5-8 Years after Receiving PhD from US Institutions, by Field, Employment Status, and Sector of Employment, 1977-1991

	Year of Survey:							
TOTAL	1977	1979	1981	1983	1985	1987	1989	1991
Total Population	58,334	59,514	57,456	55,734	53,985	54,013	54,812	55,598
(percentage)	100.0	100.0	100.0	100.0	100.0	100.0	100.0	100.0
Postdoctoral Study	1,179	1,208	1,153	1,185	1,355	1,228	1,651	1,325
(percentage)	2.0	2.0	2.0	2.1	2.5	2.3	3.0	2.4
Total Employed	55,446	56,879	54,914	52,507	51,504	51,233	51,782	52,082
(percentage)	95.0	95.6	95.6	94.2	95.4	94.9	94.5	93.7
4 Year/University/ Medical School	29,561	27,673	26,467	25,165	24,831	24,063	24,468	23,879
(percentage)	50.7	46.5	46.1	45.2	46.0	44.6	44.6	42.9
-tenured	14,407	12,149	11,257	9,822	8,113	7,163	6,502	7,844
(percentage)	24.7	20.4	19.6	17.6	15.0	13.3	11.9	14.1
-tenure track		8,171	9,026	8,483	10,138	9,165	9,658	9,081
(percentage)	0.0	13.7	15.7	15.2	18.8	17.0	17.6	16.3
-other/no reports	15,154	7,353	6,184	6,860	6,580	7,735	8,308	6,954
(percentage)	26.0	12.4	10.8	12.3	12.2	14.3	15.2	12.5
Other Educational Institutions	1,357	1,174	1,032	805	977	847	721	883
(percentage)	2.3	2.0	1.8	1.4	1.8	1.6	1.3	1.6
Business/Industry	14,945	16,981	17,974	18,285	17,830	18,568	19,418	19,156
(percentage)	25.6	28.5	31.3	32.8	33.0	34.4	35.4	34.5
US Government	5,556	6,525	4,682	4,573	3,998	3,536	3,074	3,255
(percentage)	9.5	11.0	8.1	8.2	7.4	6.5	5.6	5.9
State/Local Government	932	1,034	1,158	1,129	1,044	1,080	1,090	1,773
(percentage)	1.6	1.7	2.0	2.0	1.9	2.0	2.0	3.2
Nonprofit Organization	2,693	3,070	3,175	2,401	2,683	2,865	2,741	2,774
(percentage)	4.6	5.2	5.5	4.3	5.0	5.3	5.0	5.0
Other/No Report	402	422	426	149	141	274	270	362
(percentage)	0.7	0.7	0.7	0.3	0.3	0.5	0.5	0.7
Total Not Employed	1,709	1,427	1,389	2,042	1,126	1,552	1,379	2,191
(percentage)	2.9	2.4	2.4	3.7	2.1	2.9	2.5	3.9
-seeking	761	515	452	735	373	563	498	1,058
(percentage)	1.3	0.9	0.8	1.3	0.7	1.0	0.9	1.9
-not seeking	286	453	473	529	312	483	498	571
(percentage)	0.5	0.8	0.8	0.9	0.6	0.9	0.9	1.0
-retired	56	66	57	82	63	59	78	100
(percentage)	0.1	0.1	0.1	0.1	0.1	0.1	0.1	0.2
-other/no report	606	393	407	696	378	447	305	462
(percentage)	1.0	0.7	0.7	1.2	0.7	0.8	0.6	0.8

NOTES: This table compares cohorts of scientists and engineers 5-8 years after receiving a doctorate from a US university (e.g., 1969-1972 PhDs in 1977, 1971-1974 PhDs in 1979, and so on). All fields are included except psychology (for field-level data, see Figures C-19 through C-31). All percentages are of the total population, including those not in the workforce.

Due to changes in survey procedures and timing in the 1991 survey, the 1991 estimates are not entirely comparable to those for the earlier survey years (see methodological note in Box C-1 for further information on comparability of 1991 estimates).

SOURCE: Special runs of data from the Survey of Doctorate Recipients on employment status and employment sector of US doctoral scientists and engineers.

TABLE C-3A Employed Doctoral Scientists and Engineers, by Field, 1973-1991

Field	1973	1975	1977	1979	1981	1983	1985	1987	1989	1991
TOTAL	220,332	255,940	285,055	314,257	343,956	369,320	400,358	419,118	448,643	437,206
SCIENTISTS	184,551	213,507	240,005	263,915	286,917	307,775	334,505	351,350	373,860	367,440
Physical scientists	48,526	54,629	57,531	60,222	63,110	63,986	67,480	68,647	70,209	80,872
Chemists	30,769	35,825	37,412	39,659	41,910	41,298	43,735	44,136	45,649	48,967
Physicists/ Astronomers	17,757	18,804	20,119	20,563	21,200	22,688	23,745	24,511	24,560	31,905
Mathematical scientists	12,130	13,611	14,609	15,250	15,569	16,379	16,758	16,699	17,611	20,049
Mathematicians	10,661	11,864	12,846	12,843	13,024	13,589	13,957	13,878	14,867	16,546
Statisticians	1,469	1,747	1,763	2,407	2,545	2,790	2,801	2,821	2,744	3,503
Computer/ Information specialists	2,713	3,528	5,767	6,684	9,064	12,164	14,964	18,571	19,797	5,376
Environmental scientists	10,321	12,103	13,001	14,575	15,909	16,467	17,288	17,811	19,787	13,263
Earth scientists	8,552	9,500	9,715	11,083	11,990	12,523	13,202	13,577	15,138	9,745
Oceanographers	1,130	1,277	1,563	1,662	1,793	1,742	1,959	2,037	2,460	1,920
Atmospheric scientists	639	1,326	1,723	1,830	2,126	2,202	2,127	2,197	2,189	1,598
Life scientists	56,665	63,344	70,537	78,857	84,912	92,802	101,838	107,378	115,833	113,743
Biological scientists	36,798	39,036	42,069	45,617	49,621	55,205	59,871	61,985	67,250	88,188
Agricultural scientists	9,189	10,993	12,112	12,789	13,496	14,536	15,513	15,796	16,504	16,637
Medical scientists	10,678	13,315	16,356	20,451	21,795	23,061	26,454	29,597	32,079	19,047
Psychologists	24,782	30,001	33,652	37,848	42,829	46,645	52,182	56,378	60,596	65,672
Social scientists	29,414	36,291	44,908	50,479	55,524	59,332	63,995	65,866	70,027	68,465
Economists	9,674	11,814	12,970	13,978	15,990	16,958	17,925	17,837	18,588	19,241
Sociologists/ Anthropologists	65,311	7,910	9,471	10,198	11,007	12,056	12,692	12,933	13,529	18,094
Other social scientists	3,209	16,567	22,467	26,303	28,527	30,318	33,378	35,096	37,910	31,130
ENGINEERS	35,781	42,433	45,050	50,342	57,039	61,545	65,853	67,768	74,783	69,766
Aeronautical/ Astronomical	1,670	2,019	1,987	2,364	2,519	3,684	3,827	5,005	6,367	3,087
Chemical	4,458	5,368	5,603	6,166	7,146	6,992	7,122	6,923	7,959	10,633
Civil	3,100	3,772	4,066	5,157	6,089	5,317	6,396	6,479	6,951	7,512
Electrical/Electronic	7,057	8,538	8,284	8,597	10,630	12,696	14,248	12,601	15,088	16,994
Material science	4,462	4,784	5,244	5,732	6,085	7,422	7,259	8,088	8,280	6,230
Mechanical	3,257	4,033	4,648	5,245	5,370	5,657	6,594	6,711	7,390	8,680
Nuclear	1,264	1,680	1,773	2,286	2,061	2,329	2,377	2,151	2,437	1,903
Systems design	1,963	2,436	3,556	4,931	5,349	3,891	3,683	3,935	3,896	1,561
Other	8,550	9,803	9,889	9,864	11,790	13,557	14,347	15,875	16,415	13,166

NOTES: All numbers in the table are estimates derived from a sample.

All doctoral scientists and engineers employed in a science or engineering (S&E) field were categorized by their field of employment when that information was available. When it was not, or when the employment field was other than science or engineering, doctorate holders were categorized by their field of degree.

SOURCE: Calculated from NSF, 1991, and NSF, 1994d.

TABLE C-3B   **Employed Doctoral Scientists and Engineers, by Employment-Related Characteristics, 1973-1991 (percentage distribution)**

Characteristics	1973	1975	1977	1979	1981	1983	1985	1987	1989	1991
TOTAL	100.0	100.0	100.0	100.0	100.0	100.0	100.0	100.0	100.0	100.0
Type of employment										
Science/Engineering	93.6	93.9	91.9	91.7	91.4	88.6	91.3	90.3	90.4	89.7
Other/Unknown field	6.4	6.1	8.1	8.3	8.6	11.4	8.7	9.7	9.6	10.3
Sector of employment										
Business/Industry, Total	24.2	25.2	25.1	26.4	28.8	30.7	31.4	31.4	32.4	36.0
Not self-employed	22.2	22.9	22.5	23.1	24.6	25.8	25.6	24.8	25.1	27.1
Self-employed	2.0	2.3	2.6	3.3	4.3	4.9	5.8	6.6	7.2	8.8
Educational institution	58.7	58.2	57.5	55.5	54.4	53.1	52.9	52.2	51.5	47.2
University/4-year college	56.7	56.1	55.1	53.3	52.1	50.8	50.5	50.0	49.2	44.7
Other	2.0	2.1	2.3	2.2	2.3	2.3	2.4	2.2	2.2	2.5
Federal government (civilian)	8.3	7.4	7.5	7.6	7.3	7.0	6.6	6.6	6.5	6.3
State/Local government	1.9	1.9	1.9	1.9	1.9	2.1	2.1	2.2	2.3	2.4
Hospitals/Clinics	2.1	2.9	3.0	3.1	2.9	2.8	2.8	2.9	2.8	3.2
Other non-profits	3.6	3.3	3.6	4.0	3.7	3.2	3.4	3.7	3.6	3.6
Other/No response	1.2	1.0	1.5	1.5	1.1	1.1	.9	1.0	.9	1.4
Primary work activity										
Research and development	32.4	32.2	32.8	31.7	34.9	33.8	33.1	36.8	37.1	36.0
Basic research	15.5	14.9	15.3	15.2	16.0	15.5	15.3	15.1	15.1	14.0
Applied research	13.0	12.9	12.8	11.7	13.5	12.8	12.3	17.2	17.4	16.4
Development	3.9	4.4	4.7	4.8	5.3	5.5	5.5	4.5	4.7	5.6
Management/Administration	20.9	20.2	21.3	23.0	17.6	16.7	17.4	16.2	16.4	15.6
of Research and Development	11.9	11.2	10.8	13.7	9.5	8.5	8.7	8.1	7.9	7.6
of Other	9.0	9.0	10.5	9.3	8.1	8.2	8.7	8.1	8.5	8.0
Teaching	36.3	35.6	31.9	29.4	30.6	29.3	27.9	26.2	25.1	22.7
Professional services	3.3	4.0	4.7	5.8	6.7	7.1	7.9	7.8	8.2	9.1
Reports/Statistics/										
Computer activity	1/	1/	1/	1/	1/	1/	1/	2.8	2.9	3.6
Consulting	1.8	2.2	2.2	2.9	3.5	3.5	3.5	3.3	3.7	4.4
Other/No response	5.2	5.8	7.2	7.2	6.7	10.2	10.2	6.9	6.6	8.5
Federal support										
Receiving support	45.2	43.0	42.0	40.3	36.9	32.3	32.3	43.7	44.2	40.7
Not receiving support	50.3	53.5	53.7	54.4	46.8	52.3	52.3	52.7	53.0	55.7
Status unknown/No response	4.5	3.5	4.2	5.3	16.3	15.4	15.4	3.6	2.7	3.5

1/ This category was first introduced in 1987 to conform to other data series produced by NSF.

NOTE: All numbers in the table are estimates derived from a sample.

SOURCE: Calculated from NSF, 1991, and NSF, 1994d.

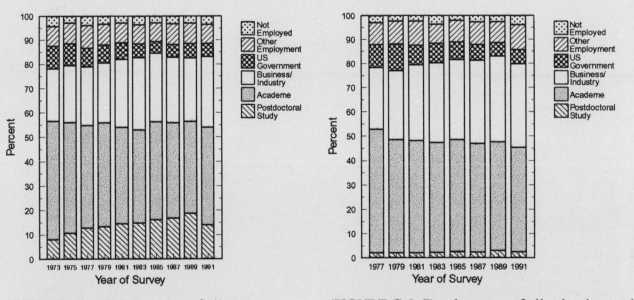

FIGURE C-1 Employment of all scientists and engineers 1-4 years after US PhD.

FIGURE C-2 Employment of all scientists and engineers 5-8 years after US PhD.

SOURCE: Tables C-1 and C-2

NOTES: See notes to Table C-1 and methodological note in Box C-1 for important information on the comparability of 1991 estimates with earlier estimates.

Not employed includes those seeking work (i.e., unemployed), not seeking work, retired, otherwise not working, or not reporting employment status.

Other employment includes other education (junior colleges, 2-year colleges, technical institutes, and elementary, middle, and secondary schools); state and local governments; hospitals and clinics; private foundations and other nonprofit organizations; other employers; and those who did not respond to the employment-sector question.

Business/industry includes self-employed.

Academe includes those employed at 4-year colleges, universities, and medical schools (including university-affiliated hospitals and medical centers).

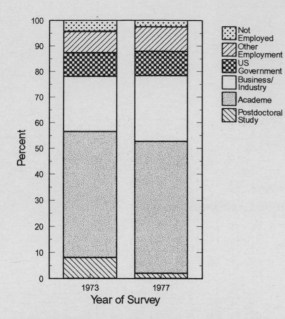

FIGURE C-3 1969-1972 science and engineering PhD recipients 1-4 and 5-8 years later.

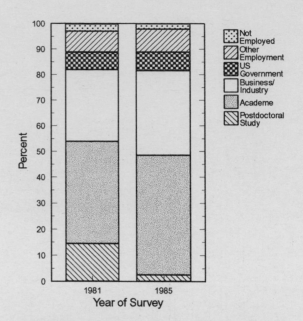

FIGURE C-4 1977-1980 science and engineering PhD recipients 1-4 and 5-8 years later.

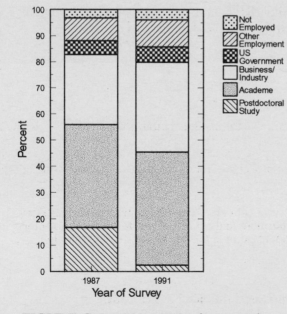

FIGURE C-5 1983-1986 science and engineering PhD recipients 1-4 and 5-8 years later.

SOURCE: Tables C-1 and C-2.

NOTES: See notes to Table C-1.

NOTES: Figures C-6 through C-18 compare cohorts of scientists and engineers 1-4 years after receiving a doctorate from a US university (e.g., 1969-1972 PhDs in 1973, 1971-1974 PhDs in 1975, and so on). Figures C-19 through C-31 compare cohorts of scientists and engineers 5-8 years after receiving a doctorate from a US university (e.g., 1969-1972 PhDs in 1977, 1971-1974 PhDs in 1979, and so on). All percentages are of the total population, including those not in the workforce.

Due to changes in survey procedures and timing in the 1991 survey, the 1991 estimates are not entirely comparable to those for the earlier survey years (see methodological note in Box C-1 for further information on comparability of 1991 estimates).

SOURCE: Special runs of data from the Survey of Doctorate Recipients on employment status and employment sector of U.S. doctoral scientists and engineers.

FIGURES C-6 THROUGH C-31

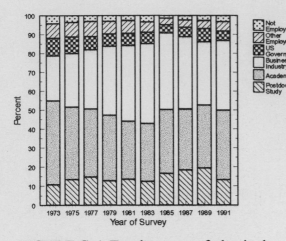

FIGURE C-6 Employment of physical scientists 1-4 years after US PhD.

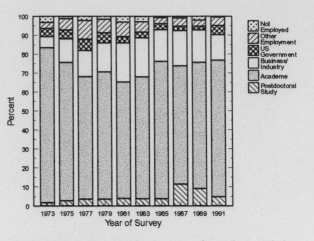

FIGURE C-7 Employment of mathematicians 1-4 years after US PhD.

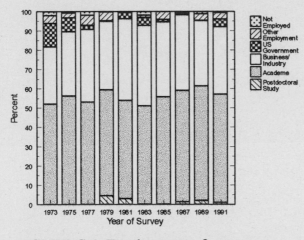
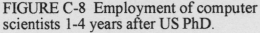

FIGURE C-8 Employment of computer scientists 1-4 years after US PhD.

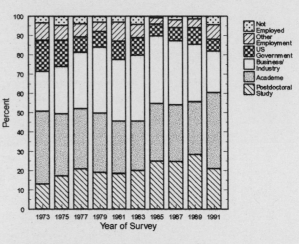

FIGURE C-9 Employment of physicists/astronomers 1-4 years after US PhD.

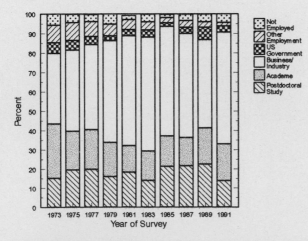

FIGURE C-10 Employment of chemists 1-4 years after US PhD.

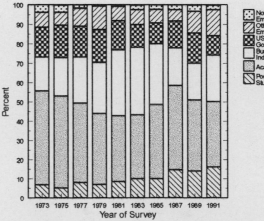

FIGURE C-11 Employment of environmental scientists 1-4 years after US PhD.

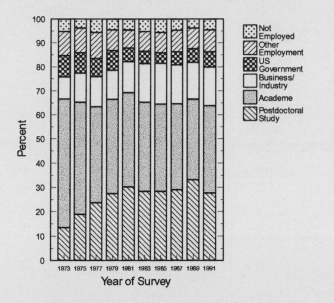

FIGURE C-12 Employment of life scientists 1-4 years after US PhD.

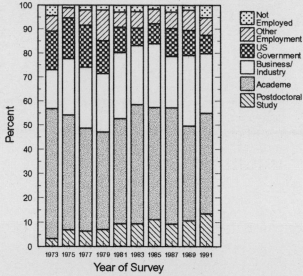

FIGURE C-13 Employment of agricultural scientists 1-4 years after US PhD.

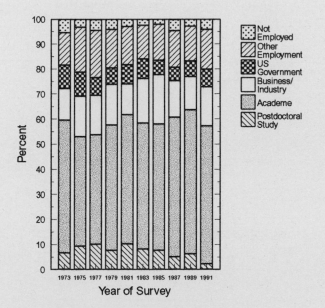

FIGURE C-14 Employment of medical scientists 1-4 years after US PhD.

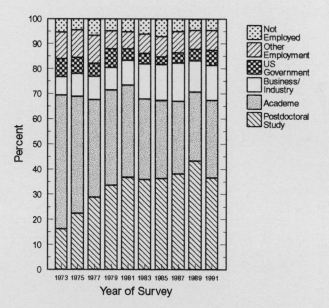

FIGURE C-15 Employment of biological scientists 1-4 years after US PhD.

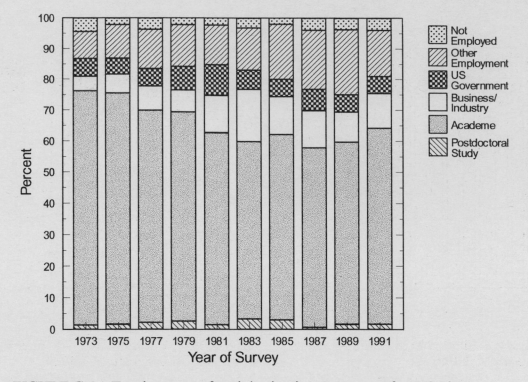

FIGURE C-16 Employment of social scientists 1-4 years after US PhD.

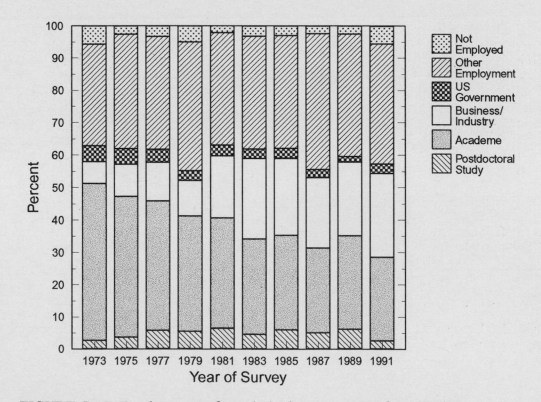

FIGURE C-17 Employment of psychologists 1-4 years after US PhD.

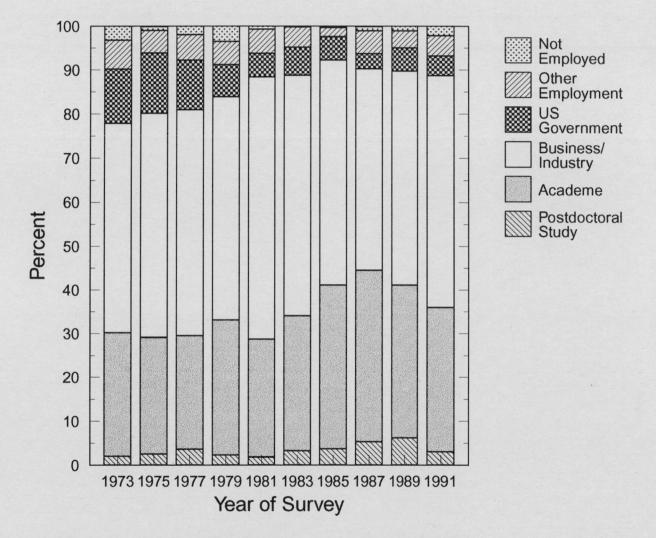

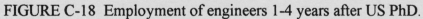

FIGURE C-18 Employment of engineers 1-4 years after US PhD.

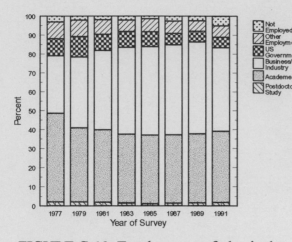

FIGURE C-19 Employment of physical scientists 5-8 years after US PhD.

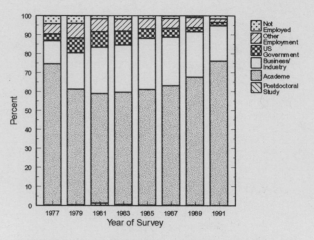

FIGURE C-20 Employment of mathematicians 5-8 years after US PhD.

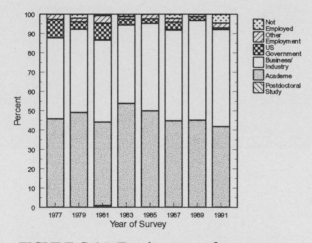
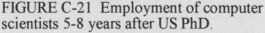

FIGURE C-21 Employment of computer scientists 5-8 years after US PhD.

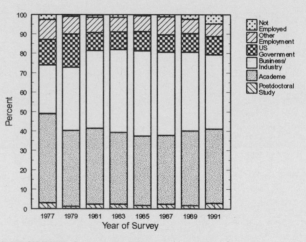

FIGURE C-22 Employment of physicists/astronomers 5-8 years after US PhD.

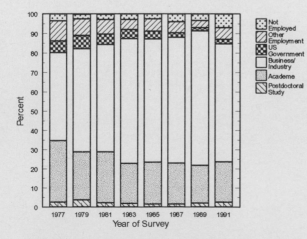

FIGURE C-23 Employment of chemists 5-8 years after US PhD.

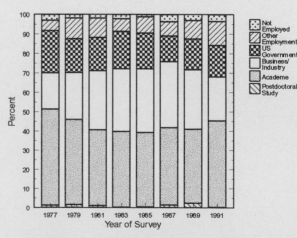

FIGURE C-24 Employment of environmental scientists 5-8 years after US PhD.

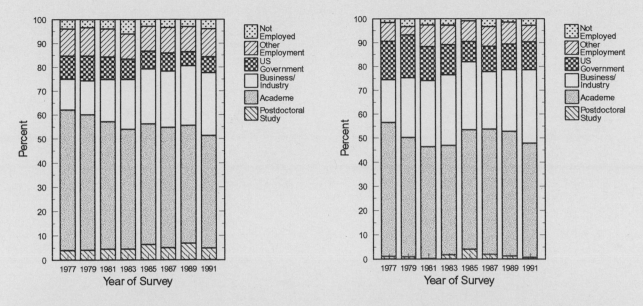

FIGURE C-25 Employment of life scientists 5-8 years after US PhD.

FIGURE C-26 Employment of agricultural scientists 5-8 years after US PhD.

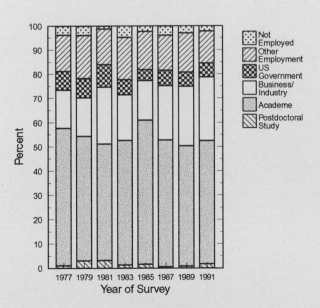

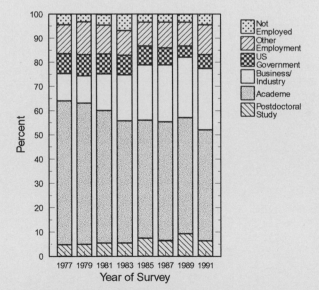

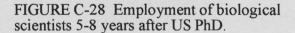

FIGURE C-27 Employment of medical scientists 5-8 years after US PhD.

FIGURE C-28 Employment of biological scientists 5-8 years after US PhD.

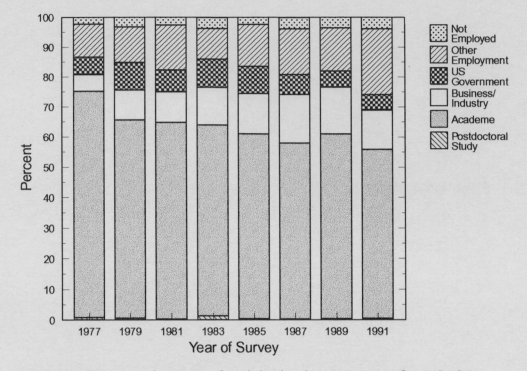

FIGURE C-29 Employment of social scientists 5-8 years after US PhD.

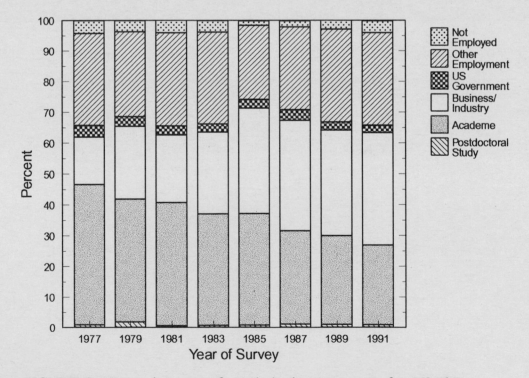

FIGURE C-30 Employment of psychologists 5-8 years after US PhD.

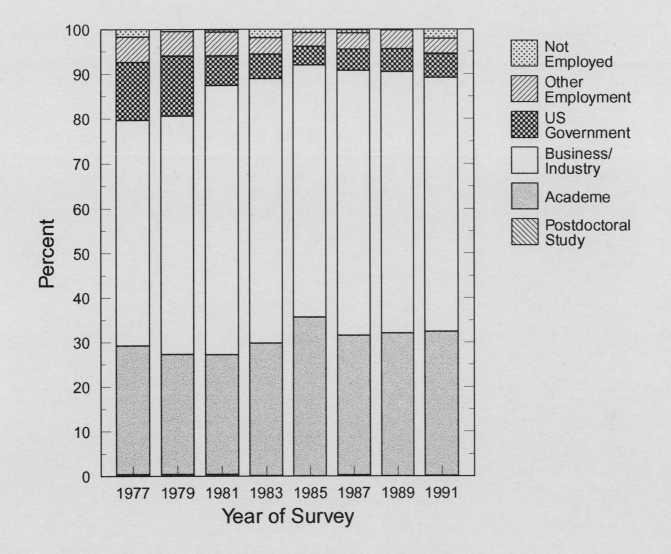

FIGURE C-31 Employment of engineers 5-8 years after US PhD.

EMPLOYMENT OF RECENT SCIENCE AND ENGINEERING MASTER'S DEGREE RECIPIENTS

The National Science Foundation conducts biennial surveys of recent recipients of master's and bachelor's degrees in various science or engineering fields. The latest published data are from the survey administered in the spring of 1990 to a sample who received science and engineering degrees during the 1987-1988 (1988) and 1988-1989 (1989) academic years (NSF, 1992a). Surveys conducted in 1982 (NSF, 1984), 1984 (NSF, 1986), 1986 (NSF, 1987), and 1988 (NSF, 1990a) are also reported here. A more recent survey was fielded in 1993 and is scheduled to be published shortly.

The NSF survey of recent college graduates and master's-degree recipients collects information on demographic and education characteristics and on early career-development experiences, such as employment status, reasons for unemployment, and attributes of employment including occupational classification, major activity, and salary. The survey is based on a nationally representative sample and is used to derive national estimates of the numbers and demographic, education, and employment characteristics of recent graduates in science and engineering.

How Many Science and Engineering Master's Degree Recipients Continue Graduate Study?

The number of new science and engineering master's-degree recipients in 1989 continuing as full-time students in 1990 was 16,200, or about 23% of the estimated 70,400 who received master's degrees in 1989 (another 4,900, or 7%, were part-time students)(Table C-4). The comparable percentage and number of continuing students among new master's-degree recipients in the 1980s surveys were about 21% and 10,000 - 13,000.

TABLE C-4 **Graduate-School Status One Year Later of Recipients of New Master's Degrees in Science and Engineering, 1982-1990**

Status	Master's Received in				
	1981	1983	1985	1987	1989
New science and engineering master's	46,700	47,500	61,100	58,100	70,400
Full-time students					
Number	9,800	10,300	13,000	12,200	16,200
Percentage	21.0%	21.7%	21.3%	21.0%	23.0%
Part-time students					
Number	4,300	4,200	4,700	3,300	4,900
Percentage	9.2%	8.8%	7.7%	5.7%	7.0%

SOURCE: Calculated from Table B-28 in NSF, 1984; Table B-28 in NSF, 1986; Table B-31 in NSF, 1987; Table B-31 in NSF, 1990a; and Table B-31 in NSF, 1992b.

Continued Education of New Science and Engineering Master's-Degree Recipients

The tendency to continue graduate studies full-time varies across fields but has increased in most fields since 1982. Barely 7% of those receiving master's degrees in computer science in 1989 were full-time students the next year, compared with 60% of those with new physics/astronomy master's degrees (Table C-5). The proportion of new master's-degree recipients going to graduate school part-time also varies from field to field but has gone down since 1982. The ratio of full-time to part-time graduate students a year after receipt of master's degrees also varies by field. In fields where the master's degree is usually considered the working degree, the ratio is more nearly equal (e.g., 2.2:1 in engineering and 1:1 in computer science and technology) than in fields where the PhD is considered the minimal professional credential (e.g., 3.6:1 in physics/astronomy, 22.6:1 in biology, and apparently higher in chemistry).

TABLE C-5 Science and Engineering Master's-Degree Recipients Continuing in Graduate School the Next Year, 1982 and 1990 (percentages)

| | Master's Received in 1981 | | Master's Received in 1989 | |
	Full-Time Student	Part-Time Student	Full-Time Student	Part-Time Student
All science and engineering master's	21.0	9.2	23.0	7.0
Physical sciences	33.3	11.1	43.5	6.5
Physics/Astronomy	50.0	*a*	60.0	16.7
Chemistry	33.3	13.3	43.8	*a*
Other Physical sciences	25.0	25.0	11.1	*a*
Mathematics/Statistics	17.1	9.8	21.6	7.8
Computer sciences	8.0	10.0	7.1	7.1
Environmental sciences	17.6	5.9	20.0	8.0
Life sciences	27.9	9.3	32.0	4.1
Agricultural sciences	25.0	9.4	27.8	8.3
Biological sciences	29.1	9.1	36.1	1.6
Social sciences	23.9	8.5	27.5	7.3
Psychology	33.3	16.7	41.9	7.0
Engineering	15.2	7.2	17.3	7.7

a Too few cases to report.

SOURCES: Calculated from Table B-28 in NSF, 1984, for 1981 data; and Table B-31 in NSF, 1992b, for 1989 data.

How Many Recent Science and Engineering Master's-Degree Recipients Are Unemployed?

Unemployment rates among recent science and engineering master's-degree recipients in the labor force are low. In 1990, among those awarded master's degrees in 1988 and 1998, unemployment was 1.8% overall, ranging from a low of 1.1% of mathematicians and statisticians to a high of 3.6% of psychologists (Table C-6). In most fields, the unemployment rate among recent master's-degree recipients was lower in 1990 than in 1982 and 1984 (in the aftermath of the 1980-1982 recession), but slightly higher than in 1988.

TABLE C-6 Unemployment One Year Later Among Recipients of Master's Degrees in Science and Engineering, 1982-1990 (percentages)[a]

| Field of Degree | Master's Received in | | | | |
	1980-1981	1982-1983	1984-1985	1986-1987	1988-1989
All science and engineering master's	3.7	3.5	2.1	1.7	1.8
Physical sciences	3.0	3.6	1.4	2.9	2.1
Physics/Astronomy	[b]	[b]	[b]	[b]	2.2
Chemistry	2.0	6.3	1.3	3.1	1.9
Other Physical sciences	[b]	[b]	[b]	[b]	[b]
Mathematics/Statistics	4.1	2.7	1.5	1.1	1.1
Computer sciences	0.6	1.1	0.4	1.1	1.5
Environmental sciences	6.9	4.3	6.1	1.9	2.7
Life sciences	2.5	4.3	4.2	1.3	2.1
Agricultural sciences	1.6	4.3	4.6	0.3	2.5
Biological sciences	3.0	4.3	4.0	1.9	1.9
Social sciences	6.8	5.6	3.4	3.2	2.1
Psychology	9.3	2.7	4.4	2.5	3.6
Engineering	2.1	3.0	1.2	1.7	1.7

[a] Full-time graduate students are excluded.

[b] No rate computed for groups in which labor force is smaller than 1,500.

SOURCES: Calculated from Table B-45 in NSF, 1984; Table B-45 in NSF 1986; Table B-49 in NSF, 1987; Table B-47 in NSF, 1990a; and Table B-47 in NSF, 1992b.

How Many New Science and Engineering Master's-Degree Recipients Are Employed in Their Fields or Other Science and Engineering Occupations?

Although unemployment rates are comparatively low for those with master's degrees, not all are working in the fields of their degrees or in other science and engineering occupations. Overall, in 1990, fewer than two-thirds of science and engineering master's-degree recipients were working in the same fields as their degrees, and fewer than one-fifth were working in other science and engineering occupations (Table C-7). Exactly 17% were not employed in science and engineering occupations. This split varied by field, however, with 7.5% of engineers and 8% of computer scientists working outside science and engineering, compared with 37% of social scientists and 46% of psychologists. Only one-fourth of physicists and astronomers were working in their fields (25% were working in computer science and "other physical sciences," and 25% in engineering occupations) (NSF, 1992b:Table B-39).

TABLE C-7 Employed New Science and Engineering Master's-Degree Recipients Working in Fields of Degrees or in Science and Engineering Occupations, 1990 (percentage)[a]

Field of Degree	Same Field as Master's	Another Science and Engineering Occupation	Non-Science and Engineering Occupation
All 1989 science and engineering master's	64.7	18.1	17.0
Physical sciences	41.7	41.7	16.7
Physics/Astronomy	25.0	50.0	25.0
Chemistry	55.6	33.3	11.1
Other Physical sciences	25.0	50.0	25.0
Mathematics/Statistics	57.9	26.3	15.8
Computer sciences	78.2	13.9	7.9
Environmental sciences	65.0	25.0	10.0
Life Sciences	52.5	19.7	27.9
Agricultural sciences	52.2	26.1	21.7
Biological sciences	52.6	15.8	31.6
Social sciences	44.0	20.0	36.0
Psychology	41.7	12.5	45.8
Engineering	78.2	14.4	7.5

[a] Exclusive of full-time graduate students.
NOTE: Percentages may not add to 100 because of rounding.
SOURCE: Calculated from Table B-39 in NSF, 1992b.

Who Employs New Science and Engineering Master's-Degree Recipients?

In the last decade, nearly 60% of employed new science and engineering master's-degree recipients were working in the private sector (Table C-8). Less than 20% were employed by educational institutions, split about evenly between four-year colleges and universities and other institutions (two-year colleges and elementary and secondary schools).

TABLE C-8 **Type of Employer One Year Later of Recipients of Master's Degrees in Science and Engineering, 1982-1990[a]**

| | Master's Received in | | | | |
Employer	1981	1983	1985	1987	1989
All employed science and engineering master's	34,100 100.0%	34,400 100.0%	45,600 100.0%	43,700 100.0%	51,700 100.0%
Educational institutions	6,000 17.6%	4,900 14.2%	6,800 14.9%	7,400 16.9%	9,300 18.0%
4-year college/ university				4,000 9.2%	4,600 8.9%
Other educational institution				3,400 7.8%	4,600 8.9%
Business and industry	20,000 58.7%	20,000 58.1%	25,400 55.7%	25,200 57.7%	30,700 59.4%
Nonprofit organization	900 2.6%	1,700 4.9%	1,600 3.5%	1,400 3.2%	1,000 1.9%
Federal government	2,200 6.5%	2,500 7.3%	3,900 8.6%	2,300 5.3%	3,600 7.0%
State/local government	2,500 7.3%	2,800 8.1%	4,100 9.0%	2,900 6.6%	2,900 5.6%
Other	2,300 6.7%	2,400 7.0%	3,600 7.9%	4,400 10.1%	4,200 8.1%
No report	100 0.3%	100 0.3%	200 0.4%	100 0.2%	[b]

[a] Full-time graduate students are excluded.

[b] Too few cases to report.

SOURCES: Calculated from Table B-32 in NSF, 1984; Table B-32 in NSF, 1986; Table B-36 in NSF, 1987; Table B-36 in NSF, 1990a; and Table B-36 in NSF 1992b.

Field-to-Field Differences in Employment Sector

The tendency to work in industry or for other types of employers varies by field. In 1990, for example, more than three-quarters of computer scientists worked in the private sector, compared with less than a third of life scientists (Table C-9).

TABLE C-9 Type of Employer of New Recipients of Master's Degrees, by Field of Science and Engineering, 1990[a]

Employer	Physical Sciences	Mathematics/ Statistics	Computer Sciences	Environmental Sciences	Life Sciences	Social Sciences	Psychology	Engineering
ALL	2,400	3,800	10,100	2,000	6,100	7,500	2,400	17,300
Educational institutions	800 33.3%	1,600 42.1%	800 7.9%	200 10.0%	2,300 37.7%	2,400 32.0%	700 29.2%	600 3.5%
Four-Year college/ university	300 12.5%	400 10.5%	500 5.0%	200 10.0%	1,200 19.7%	1,200 16.0%	300 12.5%	500 2.9%
Other educational institution	400 16.7%	1,100 28.9%	300 3.0%	100 5.0%	1,100 18.0%	1,200 16.0%	400 16.7%	100 0.6%
Business and industry	1,200 50.0%	1,700 44.7%	7,800 77.2%	1,200 60.0%	1,900 31.1%	2,700 36.0%	900 37.5%	13,200 76.3%
Nonprofit organization	100 4.2%	100 2.6	100 1.0%	[b]	100 1.6%	300 4.0%	100 4.2%	100 0.6%
Federal government	100 4.2%	200 5.3%	400 4.0%	200 10.0%	600 9.8%	700 9.3%	100 4.2%	1,400 8.1%
State/local government	100 4.2%	[b]	200 2.0%	200 10.0%	700 11.5%	1,000 13.3%	100 4.2%	600 3.5%
Other	100 4.2%	300 7.9%	800 8.0%	200 10.0%	600 9.8%	400 5.3%	400 16.7%	1,400 8.1%
No report	[b]	[b]	[b]	[b]	[b]	[b]	[b]	[b]

[a] Full-time graduate students are excluded.

[b] Too few cases to report.

SOURCE: Calculated from Table B-36 in NSF, 1992b.

D

RESPONDENTS TO CALL FOR COMMENTS

The committee solicited comments on the current graduate education system from academia, industry, and students. These comments helped the committee formulate its views. The respondents to the call for comments are listed below.

Mary E. Adamson
Miles Inc.
Mobay Road
Pittsburgh, PA

John Ahearne
Executive Director
Sigma Xi
Research Triangle Park, NC

Jame S. Allen
Glaxo Research Institute
Research Triangle Park, NC

Lawrence F. Ayers
Executive Vice President
Utilities and Mapping Sciences
Intergraph Corp.
Huntsville, AL

John C. Bailar
Department of Epidemiology and
  Biostatistics
Montreal, Quebec, Canada

J.F. Bagley
University Programs Focus Group
Battelle
Pacific Northwest Laboratories
Richland, WA

Mary B. Bennett
Director of Operations
Glaxo Research Institute
Research Triangle Park, NC

William O. Berndt
Office of the Vice Chancellor for
  Academic Affairs
University of Nebraska
Omaha, NE

U. Narayan Bhat
Office of the Dean
Research and Graduate Studies
Southern Methodist University
Dallas, TX

Rockey K. Bandlish
Raleigh, NC

Peter Bingham
President
Philips Laboratories
Briarcliff Manor, NY

Marc H. Brodsky
Executive Director and
  Chief Executive Officer
American Institute of Physics
College, Park, MD

Mary-Dell Chilton
Agricultural Biotechnology
CIBA-Geigy Corp.
Research Triangle Park, NC

Walter Cohen
Office of the Dean
Sage Graduate Center
Cornell University
Ithaca, NY

Henry H. Dearman
Dean, Graduate School
University of North Carolina
Chapel Hill, NC

Philip H. Francis
Vice President, Technology
Schneider North America
Palatine, IL

Chad Gaffield
Acting Dean
University of Ottawa
School of Graduate Studies & Research
Ottawa, Ontario, Canada

David L. Goodstein
Vice Provost
Professor of Physics and Applied Physics
California Institute of Technology
Pasadena, CA

Eileen G. Gorman
Glasgow Business Community 707
Newark, DE

William Green
Graduate Coordinator, Mathematics
School of Mathematics
Georgia Institute of Technology
Atlanta, GA

N.A. Gjostein
Director, Materials Research Laboratory
Ford Motor Company
Dearborn, MI

Lowell M. Greenbaum
Vice President for Research
Dean, School of Graduate Studies
Medical College of Georgia
Augusta, GA

R.Z. Gussin
Corporate Vice President
Science and Technology
Johnson & Johnson
News Brunswick, NJ

Dennis Guthrie
Manager, University Relations
DOW
Midland, MI

Robert P. Guertin
Dean
Graduate School of Arts and Sciences
Tufts University
Medford, MA

Lawrence H. Hare
Director, Operations
Martin Marietta Specialty Components,
 Inc.
Largo, FL

Thomas P. Hogan
Dean
Graduate School
University of Scranton
Scranton, PA

Rae Ann Hallstrom
Babcock & Wilcox
Barberton, OH

Thomas M. Hellman
Vice President
Environmental Affairs
Bristol-Myers Squibb Co.
New York, NY

Roy C. Herrenkohl
Vice Provost for Research and
 Dean of Graduate Studies
Whitaker Laboratory
Bethlehem, PA

Joseph W. Helmick
Dean of Graduate Studies and Research
Texas Christian University
Fort Worth, TX

C. Dernis Ignasis
Office of the Vice President
University of Maryland Eastern Shore

Robert Carl Johnson
The Graduate School
Office of the Associate Provost and Dean
Miami University
Oxford, OH

Marie-Louise Kagan
Syracuse, NY

Fritz R. Kalhammer
Vice President
Strategic Research and Development
EPRI
Palo Alto, CA

Ronald S. Kane
Assistant Vice President
 for Academic Affairs
Graduate Studies
New Jersey Institute of Technology
Newark, NJ

Cliff Kottman
Intergraph Corp.
Reston, VA

Frederick J. Krambeck
Senior Consultant
Mobil Research and Development
 Corporation
Paulsboro Research Laboratory
Paulsboro, NJ

Michael A. Kriss
Director
Community Outreach Program
Center for Electronic Imaging Systems
University of Rochester
Rochester, NY

Henry S. Leonard
Professor and Director of
  Graduate Studies
Northern Illinois University
DeKalb, IL

Diandra L. Leslie-Pelecky
Center for Materials Research & Analysis
University of Nebraska
Lincoln, NE

Charles N. Li
Dean
Graduate Division
University of California, Santa Barbara
Santa Barbara, CA

Bill Linder-Scholer
Cray Research, Inc.
Eagan, MN

Pat M. Loman
Shell Development Company
Westhollow Technology Center
Houston, TX

Carl D. McAulay
General Manager
Fred L. Hartley Research Center
Brea, CA

C. Gordon McCarty
Miles, Inc.
Mobay Road
Pittsburgh, PA

Kenneth O. McFadden
Vice Presdent, Research Division
W.R. Grace & Company
Columbia, MD

Otto Von Merring
Professor and Director
Center for Gerontological Studies
University of Florida
Gainesville, FL

Richard A. Milburn
Senior Vice President
Grumman International
Arlington, VA

J.C. Mihm
Senior Vice President
Phillips Petroleum Company
Bartlesville, OK

Steve Mitchell
Bioacoustics Research Program
Cornell Lab of Ornithology
Ithaca, NY

Nancy K. Morgan
Corporate Product Integrity
Mattel, Inc.
El Segundo, CA

Roger Morton
Business Unit Manager
Depth Imaging
Eastman Kodak Company
Rochester, NY

John H. Nelson
Vice President
Science and Technology
McCormick & Company, Inc.
Sparks, MD

Jack Nelson
Acting Dean
Office of the Dean
Temple University
Philadelphia, PA

James M. Pearson
Manager, Doctoral Recruitment
University Relations
Eastman Kodak Company
Rochester, NY

Timothy J. Pettibone
Dean, The Graduate School
New Mexico State University
Las Cruces, NM

Robert D. Phemister
Office of the Dean
College of Veterinary Medicine
Cornell University
Ithaca, NY

Henry C. Pitot
Professor of Onocology and Pathology
McArdle Laboratory for Cancer Research
Madison, WI

Gary W. Poehlein
Vice President for Interdisciplinary
  Programs
Georgia Institute of Technology
Atlanta, GA

Joseph A. Potenza
Provost
Office of the Provost and the
  Graduate School
Rutgers
New Brunswick, NJ

Frank L. Powell
Associate Professor of Medicine
University of San Diego
La Jolla, CA

J.W. Powers
Manager, Chemistry Laboratory
Packaging Products Group
Muncie, IN

Frederic Quan
Manager of Research Contracts
Corning, Inc.
Technology Sales and Licensing
Corning, NY

Mary Lee Seibert
Assoicate Provost and
  Dean of Graduate Studies
Ithaca College
Ithaca, NY

Raymond Seltzer
Ciba Additives
Ciba-Geigy Corporation
Ardsley, NY

Peter R. Schneider
Office of IBM Vice President,
  Development and Environmental Affairs
International Business Machines
Somers, NY

Leslie B. Sims
Dean
University of Iowa
Iowa City, IA

James A. Schafer
University of Alabama, Birmingham
Birmingham, AL

Mary Ellen Scott
Cleveland, OH

John T. Snow
Dean, College of Geosciences
American Meteorological Society
Boston, MA

David Sorensen
Executive Director
3M Coporate Technical Planning
  and Coordination Department
St. Paul, MN

Gene Strull
Technology Consultant
Baltimore, MD

Susan Schwartz-Giblin
Professor Physiology
Vice Dean, Graduate School
Hahnemann University
Philadelphia, PA

Robert E. Thach
Dean, Graduate School of Arts and
  Sciences
Washington University
St. Louis, MO

Roger Thies
College of Medicine
University of Oklahoma
Oklahoma City, OK

Steadman Upham
President, Western Association
  of Graduate Schools
Graduate School
University of Oregon
Eugene, OR

Ed Wasserman
Central Research and Development
E.I. du Pont de Nemours
Wilmington, DE

Robert Wheeler
Department of Mathematical Sciences
Northern Illinois University
DeKalb, IL

Linda S. Wilson
President
Radcliffe College
Cambridge, MA

Chauncey Wood
Dean of Graduate Studies
McMaster University
Hamilton, Ontario, Canada

E

PANELISTS

A number of panels provided input to the committee deliberations on graduate education. These panelists, which represent faculty, graduate school deans, students, post-doctorates, women, minorities, and industry are listed below.

John A. Armstrong
South Salem, NY

Robert H. Atwell
President
American Council on Education
Washington, DC

Albert T. Bellino
Managing Director, College and University
Relations, Recruiting and
  Retention, Internal Communications,
  and Advertising
Banker's Trust
New York, NY

Erich Bloch
Distinguished Fellow
Council on Competitiveness
Washington, DC

Joseph Bordogna
Assistant Director
Engineering Directorate
National Science Foundation
Arlington, VA

Dennis Brown
Provost and Senior Vice President,
  Academic Affairs
Drexel University
Philadelphia, PA

Sarita E. Brown
Principal Partner, Education Trust
American Association for
  Higher Education
Washington, DC

Leonard N. Carter, Jr.
Postdoctoral Fellow
Center for Space Physics
Boston University
Boston, MA

Paul Christiano
Provost
Carnegie Mellon University
Pittsburgh, PA

Edward E. David, Jr.
EED, Inc.
Bedminster, NJ

Frank A. DeCosta, III
Member, Technical Staff
Mitre Corporation
McLean, VA

Denice D. Denton
National Research Council Board on
  Engineering Education
Assistant Professor
University of Wisconsin
Washington, DC

Mildred S. Dresselhaus
Professor
Masssachusetts Institute of Technology
Cambridge, MA

Richard Fink
Amherst College
Amherst, MA

Gideon Fredier
Dean of Engineering
George Washington University
Washington, DC

Bob Frosch
Kennedy School of Business
Harvard University
Cambridge, MA

Mark Furth
Glaxo Research Institute
Research Triangle Park, NC

Charles A. Gray
Vice President, Technology
Cabot Corporation
Bilterica, MA

Paula Therese Hammond
Postdoctoral Associate
Harvard University
Cambridge, MA

Barry J. Hardy
Computer-Aided Molecular Design Group
Physical Chemistry Lab
Oxford University
Oxford, UK

Bradley T. Hargroves
Mitre Corporation
McLean, VA

Richard Herman
Dean of Science
University of Maryland
College Park, MD

Ruth Kirschstein
Deputy Director
National Institutes of Health
Bethesda, MD

Leonard Kline
Associate Director for Career Entry
Office of Personnel Management
Washington, DC

Joyce Ladner
Vice-President, Academic Affairs
Howard University
Washington, DC

Neal Lane
Director
National Science Foundation
Bethesda, MD

Jules B. Lapidus
President
Council of Graduate Schools
Washington, DC

Peter McGrath
President
National Association of State
  Universities and Land Grant Colleges
Washington, DC

Feniosky Pena-Mora
Massachusetts Institute of Technology
Cambridge, MA

Thomas D. Pollard
Johns Hopkins University
School of Medicine
Baltimore, MD

Cornelius J. Pings
President
Association of American Universities
Washington, DC

Theodore Poehler
Vice-Provost of Research
Johns Hopkins University
Baltimore, MD

James L. Powell
Franklin Institute
Philadelphia, PA

Simon Ostrach
Wilbert J. Austin Distinguished Professor
  of Engineering
Case Western Reserve University
National Academy of Engineering
  Home Secretary

Roland Schmitt
Clifton Park, NY

Gerald M. Stancil
New Jersey Alternate
  Teacher Certification Program
East Orange, NJ

Frank Wazan
Dean of Engineering
University of California, Los Angeles
Los Angeles, CA

Luther S. Williams
Assistant Director
Directorate for Education and
  Human Resources
National Science Foundation
Washington, DC

Linda S. Wilson
President
Radcliffe College
Cambridge, MA

F

CALL FOR COMMENTS: SUMMARY OF RESPONSES

The committee solicited comments from more than 1,000 persons: graduate students, postdoctoral students, professors, university administrators, industry scientists and executives, and representatives of scientific societies. More than 100 responses were received, of which about half came from industry.

The committee noted several trends in the responses. There were general support for the current concept of PhD education (with a variety of suggestions for improvement, as outlined below), support for closer ties between the universities and industry, support for improved student counseling, and opposition to artificial limits on enrollments.

Although the call for comments was not a formal survey, we thought it would be useful to summarize the information gathered to indicate the diversity of views held by those with a stake in the success of our system of graduate education.

EMPLOYER EVALUATION OF PHD TRAINING

Overview

Industry and academic administrators generally responded favorably to the current concept of PhD training. Most comments affirmed US superiority in graduate education, but with the observation that there is always room for improvement. No substantial dissatisfaction was described. The following statement typifies the general sentiment: "We may see some specific difficulties in the relationship between academe and the profession it is intended to serve, but the structure itself is generally sound."

Preparation for Industry

However, some concerns were expressed about the level of additional education that is needed before recent graduates become fully participatory employees. Here is an example of a response from one major industrial employer that hires 150-400 advanced-degree people into its laboratories each year from many universities and in many disciplines:

Even "the best of the crop" take anywhere from 6 months to 2 years to become good, productive industrial researchers. Most recent graduates, particularly those who have not summer-interned, do not have the foggiest idea of what industrial research is all about. Some even think that using or developing technology to do something useful is not research and if it is a product that makes a profit, is even slightly dishonorable.

Preparation for Teaching

Almost everyone expressed support for better preparation of graduate students for teaching. Respondents generally cited numerous reasons for this improvement, including the following:

- Students pay high tuition for instruction, and they deserve better. Courses taught via recitation do not help students learn or graduate students teach.
- It is wrong to assume that anyone working on a PhD is automatically able to teach.
- Students aiming at careers in academe should take formal teacher-training courses to learn pedagogy as well as they learn research.

For example, the following comment is from a graduate dean and provost:

I have long been concerned about the teaching expectations of graduate students—all graduate students, not just in the sciences and engineering. How we can expect that an individual will intuit teaching skills is an amazement. While teaching is somewhat an art, there are many skills and techniques that need to be learned before an individual should be turned loose to teach a course. We do our graduate students no service, and certainly provide no service to the teachers, if we expect them to function in that capacity. ...They also need to be prepared to be academic advisors. It is not enough to walk into a class and conduct that experience. If graduate students are to be teachers, they need to know how to interact outside the classroom with undergraduate students, providing them the support that they should have during their undergraduate experience.

This is another:

The universities are not doing any better in training PhDs for academe either. Except for the recent initiatives taken by some universities in giving them pointers on effective teaching, generally their training is in a narrow area of research and they are faced with on-the-job training.

Master's versus PhD Degrees

Expectations for those with master's degrees and PhDs are slightly different. Here is an overview from a major company:

In the case of PhDs we are looking for high intelligence and creativity, the ability to originate and conduct independent research, a research background involving at least a solid thesis research experience, and the potential breadth of talent to move from one research field to another. The flexibility required by the latter point is important to us because we cannot hire new talent every time we wish to enter new research fields.

We are also looking for excellent communication and interpersonal skills, so that with proper training they can develop into potential management candidates both in the research organization and in management positions in our operations. We have had a good track record in our research organization in supplying high-caliber talent to our operations.

In the case of MS candidates, we are looking for the same kind of talents, except we do not expect experience in conducting research.

Changing Environment

Another consistent comment was on the changing environment—in both the industrial world and the academic world. The following comment is from the dean at a major graduate school:

> Graduates are not necessarily being well trained to participate in much of our high educational system as faculty: facilities for front-line research in sciences are not likely to get less costly. Not many colleges and universities will be able to afford the kinds of equipment required for faculty to make significant contributions to science in many areas. If this is true, most academic PhD positions will be in institutions which do not have essential facilities for what is viewed by these fields as cutting-edge research. Either the faculty in such institutions will have to carve out areas of research which don't rely on expensive equipment, or they will have to change their expectations of being significant players on the national and international science scene. It may be that there should be some effort devoted to training PhDs for research appropriate to those other institutions, either for enhancing their instructional roles or for providing them with realistic lines of research.

This is an industry perspective:

> In my judgment, educating and training students to do research as well as conducting basic research are still the primary objectives of graduate programs. However, it must be responsive to changing national policies and industrial needs.... I would agree that the American graduate system has been/is a great success. However, to ignore the indicators that show change is needed would be a mistake. Clearly, the challenge ahead is to retain the best of the system while making the changes that will strengthen the nation's outstanding research universities and make them more responsive to the nation's needs.

Yet another comment is the following:

> The days when a person could do a PhD thesis in surface thermodynamics (as I did) and reasonably expect to work in the field for a career are over—and I think will never return. One must be ready with the skills to change one's area of

focus several times over a career. Most PhD education is training people in the exact opposite direction, and I think this needs to be changed promptly.

Broad versus Specialized Education

Respondents indicated some general concerns about the level of specialized training some graduates receive:

Unfortunately, the training the graduates receive in universities is not directed to any specific career path. Most of the time, after some necessary training in their background, graduate students are pushed into narrow specialization. The consequence of such training is that many of them lack the breadth for work in industry. From what I have seen from the job offers received by our engineering students, they are successful with relatively less effort if their research topic and/or their assistantship experience is closely related to the prospective job description.

And they recommended a broader education for graduate students. One stated,

we may place a new employee in a position which exploits any special expertise he/she may have gained in order to provide "a soft landing," but [he or she] will eventually be called upon to handle a wide range of problems that go far beyond the training received during the completion of the PhD.

A vice president of an applied-research organization wrote, "Everything else being equal, individuals with graduate training cutting across areas of engineering, management and business will turn into better candidates for employment than more narrowly educated specialists."

But one industry respondent warned, "It's a terrible idea to turn [PhDs] into some kind of generalists who don't know anything deeply."

Nevertheless, here is a comment from an international corporation:

Why are industries such as ours not more accepting of PhDs with little or no experience? Because many fresh PhDs see their research area as their sole focus, at least for the immediate future. They generally tend to be very narrow. And, more important, they generally have no meaningful understanding of the *business* of business. Some might say that such understanding is the responsibility of business to provide. I say no. A highly trained scientist and engineer cannot be very effective if she/he has no knowledge at all of how a company is organized and why, lacks understanding about the principal staff and operating functions, is ignorant of the rudiments of accounting and finance, is unaware of product liability issues that directly affect product development, etc., etc. Industry cannot be expected to deliver such training and education in a short period of time. True, with years of experience working in industry such knowledge is slowly acquired—but it is an extremely inefficient transfer mechanism. Meanwhile, in the early years when the new technologist is working without awareness of these forces and boundary conditions, that person cannot be as effective as she/he otherwise might be. Careers are throttled.

And this is another:

Most of the new PhDs that we hire seem to be relatively well prepared for careers in our organization. I would urge, however, that rather than move towards increasing specialization, which occurs very early in their training, the students should be given a broad array of courses in related areas early in their training. I have the impression that, also from day one in their program, students are now put into laboratories and given a research project so that they can develop the knowledge and skills in their specific area of activity to allow them to complete for grants in the future. However, it has been my observation that this type of training limits their ability to participate in multidisciplinary teams that are often necessary in the industrial setting.

CHANGING THE CURRENT GRADUATE EDUCATIONAL SYSTEM

How should this change the current graduate educational system? Respondents agreed that the apprenticeship system of learning research should be preserved. At the same time, many in industry expressed a desire for mentors to be more open to the changing needs of industry. Some professors and administrators favoring apprenticeship thought that their programs already produced the kind of flexibility that industry desires. For example, a dean noted, "We must not change [apprenticeship]... however, ...[it] can also produce a very narrow specialist who is confined and limited by departmental or disciplinary perspectives, even though the obvious trend within the sciences is a breaking down of these barriers and a movement towards greater interdisciplinary perspective."

Expanded Experiences

There was also a general concern that students need to expand the experiences they have during graduate school:

It is our general finding that US graduate schools successfully continue their tradition of producing well-educated scientists and engineers that are capable of making important contributions in their chosen fields. We also believe that the effectiveness of these graduates could be enhanced through practical ("hands-on") experiences/traineeships, functioning as a member of a (multidisciplinary) team, strengthened interpersonal skills, ability to communicate clearly the purpose (including the "strategic" value and relevance of the activity in question), and substantial knowledge of the business environment/culture (including project management fundamentals, time/effort/budget deliverables, sensitivity to human resource concerns, safety, intellectual property, etc.).

Skill Expansion

In general, employers do not feel that the current level of education is sufficient in providing the following skills and abilities for the people that they are interested in employing:

- Communication skills (including teaching and mentoring abilities for academic positions).
- Appreciation for applied problems (particularly in an industrial setting).
- Teamwork (especially in interdisciplinary settings).

For example:

We look for top-notch technical skills and some evidence of ability to "reduce to practice" the technologies the candidate has been involved in. If we look at new graduates, we look for curiosity about and an appreciation for practical applications of science. As we move away from independent, stand-alone research, and toward more team projects, we screen and hire candidates based on their ability to work in teams, to lead collaborations and teams in an effective way. Skills like project management, leadership, planning and organizing, interpersonal skills, adaptability, negotiation, written and oral communication and solid computer knowledge/utilization and critical for an industrial R&D scientist/engineer. If you walk on water technically but can't or won't explain or promote your ideas and your science, you won't get hired. If you do get hired, your career will stall.

GRADUATE-EDUCATION ISSUES

Respondents were also asked about a number of key graduate-education issues.

Limiting Enrollments

Industry and administrators seemed to agreed that limiting enrollments was the job of market forces; professors disagreed. As a justification of limitations, they often cited an internal necessity, such as resource or space limitations, rather than a desire to affect the overall market. An industry respondent wrote, "Limiting enrollments is a drastic action to take since the law of supply and demand will usually bring about a correction, albeit several years out of phase. In a few particular disciplines, e.g., chemical engineering, limiting enrollment at the PhD level may need to be seriously considered." A dean wrote:

I would be hard pressed to argue that the world can ever have too many persons trained in the methods of inquiry.... The experience of students graduating with PhDs in the humanities in the 1970s showed us that good minds well trained will find a way to make a difference in places that didn't even know they needed or wanted PhD holders. Such may be the case with science and engineering....

This is from a graduate adviser:

> I am skeptical about the utility of attempts to manage enrollment; it is simply too hard to predict what is appropriate, let alone optimal. We at [our university] have been asked to control graduate enrollment, but I suspect that the real controls are still market mechanisms.

Time to Degree

There was nearly uniform agreement that the time to degree completion or initial employment is becoming longer. Many respondents favored shortening the time to degree, but others noted that adding teacher training, minor degrees, and other projects for graduate students could add to the time to degree and make it less easy to identify. A dean remarked, "It is not clear that 7 to 12 years of graduate work is either required or appropriate for most positions in business or industry."

National Goals

A question about national goals for graduate education drew a common response: there are none. A common impression was that graduate education, though considered the "best in the world," is generally rudderless without the external stimuli of the type provided, for example, by Sputnik and the Cold War. A professor at the New Jersey Institute of Technology wrote, "The problem is one of national focus and goals and not the education to support them. There does not seem to be a unifying technological endeavor or an idealized goal with technological underpinnings, to inspire our students and engender popular support."

Conclusion

In conclusion, the themes of the anecdotal information collected via the committee's call for comments indicates that although employers are generally pleased with the result of US graduate education, they have some specific concerns as to the breadth, versatility, and skill development in that education. Furthermore, they are concerned that the graduate education system as it exists today—although acceptable for the past employment world—is less and less acceptable in today's more global world.

INTERESTING IDEAS

Many interesting ideas were suggested by the respondents, and they are summarized below. The committee did not have the resources to evaluate all suggestions fully, so it presents them here for further thought and discussion. They are divided into three categories: career preparation, information needs, and funding. Each is summarized as action items and advice for universities, industry, students, and the federal government.

After the responses were received, the committee decided to conduct a separate survey on information needs; a summary of the survey results is provided in Appendix G.

Career Preparation

Universities should

- Initiate more collaborative arrangements with employers.
- Initiate more opportunities for research programs in association with industry.
- Eliminate tenure so that diverse teams of full-time and adjunct faculty can work together.
- Elevate manufacturing to the same level as the arts.
- Enrich the science and engineering curriculum to include training in interpersonal communication, technical writing, team skills, business-process management, accounting, and competitive assessment.
- Seek industrial appointments and sabbaticals for their faculty.
- Require that graduate students who teach be supervised on their first assignment by persons who can give them advice feedback on style and method.
- Help students to complete their education expeditiously.

- Continue to train research scientists of the highest caliber.
- Replace half the PhD candidates' course load for the first year with some form of apprenticeship.

Industry should

- Provide more internships in which academic fundamentals can be applied in real-world problems.
- Seek persons who have the ability to conceptualize, apply, develop, and continuously improve processes or products that can be sold at a profit.
- Support more "centers of excellence" to eliminate duplication of effort.

Industry is looking for

- Persons trained and specialized in the traditional scientific disciplines who can integrate skills with science.
- Persons with good writing skills.
- University-trained graduate students who are knowledgeable about safety, quality, statistics, and communication and who have good interpersonal skills.
- Highly technical employees and general managers.
- Persons who can negotiate with, work with, and lead others on a team (broadly trained scientists).
- Persons who can originate and conduct independent research.

Students should

- Take courses dealing with "applied interdisciplinarianism."
- Take a minor and more courses outside their specialties.
- Submit a proposal detailing the plans for their primary research efforts.

Information Needs

Universities should

- Collect benchmarking data to monitor the quality of approved programs and to try to satisfy hiring patterns of employers who regularly draw from particular program.
- Improve student counseling so that those planning PhD in the basic sciences understand, in advance, what the government gauges as appropriate for a PGY1 PhD salary.

●   Assess the needs for professors and doctoral-level industrial personnel, translate the results of this assessment into a set of goals, and design strategies to achieve the goals.

●   Offer students some comment about job prospects and frank cautions where job prospects are poor, as in physics. Disclosure of programs' completion rates and completion times would help prospective students to make informed choices.

Funding

Universities should

●   Reduce their size by establishing quality criteria for doctoral programs.

●   Refocus their funds through wider use of fellowships than of institutional grants.

●   Provide adequate preparation of scientist by using methods that do not depend on external funding sources. Dependence of doctorates in the sciences on external (federal) funding makes programs vulnerable.

●   Stop defending lower quality programs--some institutions are better prepared to deliver first-class PhD education.

●   Bring the cost of graduate research assistants in line with the cost of laboratory technicians.

●   Improve teaching by establishing a policy that senior graduate students can apply for federal grants to supplement their support and in exchange teach graduate courses.

The federal government should

●   Grant more fellowships directly to students, which would separate financial support from the research process.

●   Set guidelines so that no professor can be funded for more than five research assistantships; this would curtail empire building and encourage collaboration.

●   Create a category of funding open to all faculty members, regardless of seniority.

●   Restrict the number of foreign students on federal grants; this would force institutions to look inward for their supply of graduate students and make more of an effort to coach them.

●   Levy a surtax on employment of foreign graduate students, i.e., require more money for scholarship funds for each foreign student used.

•   Eliminate NSF graduate fellowships and redirect the money to research funding. Their fellowships are outdated and send the erroneous message to students that the nation needs more scientists.

•   Provide, with state governments, financial support for advanced graduate students to visit public universities and liberal-arts colleges for one semester as professorial interns.

Industry should

•   Help to change the science and engineering culture by setting aside a small amount of R&D money for internships for graduate students.

•   Cooperate with funding agencies in preparing and reviewing requests for proposals without requiring rights to intellectual property as long as there is no direct monetary support.

G

SUMMARY OF RESPONSES TO SURVEY ON INFORMATION NEEDS

In gathering data for this study, the committee asked scientists and engineers who have recently completed graduate degrees to describe the information they feel is necessary for students to make sound decisions about graduate education. We asked three questions about each of several topics:

- "What do you know today that you wish you knew when you were a student?"
- "What are the top 8-10 key areas that students need to know about in order to make academic and career decisions?"
- "When do you think students need this information?"

We found the responses to the questions interesting enough to warrant the detailed summary offered below. One surprising result was that students did not desire career *placement* information as much as career *guidance* information. They also have a strong interest in information on the graduate education process itself. As a result, the committee may consider developing a document to provide such guidance.

On the topic of the *graduate education process*, students need to know more about:

- The focus of graduate education. In particular, students should use research to "train the mind" rather than simply to acquire techniques used in the "real world."
- The chronology of a PhD program, and what is required at each step.

- The differences between careers in specific subfields (e.g., astrophysics, plasma physics, particle physics). Which are the 'successful' fields of research? Which offer the best job opportunities?
- The extent to which one should narrowly specialize within a particular subfield. For some positions (e.g., post-doctoral positions) and fields, specialization is considered an asset. For others (e.g., industry positions) it is considered a liability.
- Alternative areas of study beyond pure science (students need to be assured that alternative areas are worthy).
- Maturity as an asset in graduate school. Although the "traditional" path is to enter graduate school directly from a bachelor's degree program, a year or two of experience allows the student to mature.
- The political nature of science. Graduate school is more than classes. It is: choosing an adviser, defining a thesis project, giving seminars on your subject, networking, and many more activities which require "people skills." Students need to understand in detail how advisers have influence over a student's future.
- The importance of research: Students should know that they will be evaluated in terms of their research productivity as a graduate student and as a postdoctorate.
- Developing a successful grant may take as much effort as completing a master's thesis.
- The importance of student funding as a criterion for judging the quality level of a program.
- The importance of the difference between state universities and private universities in regard to their treatment of foreign students.
- Alternatives to an American PhD that can be pursued abroad. For example, in the British system, a graduate degree requires only a thesis (no classwork) and has a typical time-to-degree of 3 years.

CAREER GUIDANCE INFORMATION

- The importance of working in a field before making the decision to enter that field. For example, bright young college students who become technicians in an area learn a great deal about professional jobs in that area as well as inside information on how the field operates.
- The importance of the university one attends and the standing of one's faculty adviser (the "prestige factor") if one plans to go into academia or research.
- The difficulty of obtaining and retaining tenured faculty positions.
- The typical career structure in science and the range of differences, versus stereotypes portrayed in the media. Some jobs are "high-paying and wonderful"; others are "slave labor."

- The potential to successfully advance in a career as an academic or industrial scientist. What are the attrition rates between graduate school and tenure?
- The sectors that employ scientists in given fields and subfields, and the average age of scientists in those areas.
- A realistic comparison between careers in science and careers requiring other advanced degrees, such as an M.D., J.D., or MBA.
- The variance in salaries and competition levels among fields and subfields.
- The importance of seeking career information from academics, industrial scientists, and others with nonacademic careers instead of relying only on universities to provide such information.
- Acknowledgement that the employment market for scientists and engineers upon graduation is unpredictable. Many students assume that positions will be available when needed. There are no such guarantees.
- Students would benefit from knowing how a career evolves beyond the 'first job'. Departments could maintain a list of the career paths of their graduates. (Descriptions of career paths could remain anonymous.)
- An overview of the working world in a given field. What are the opportunities, expectations, pressures, and rewards; how do employers view and treat their employees.
- Quality information and discussion forums for young scientists made available on the Internet to balance the advice they receive from senior scientists.
- The counterintuitive concept that earning a PhD is considered by some to "overqualify" a person for many types of positions (e.g., performing technical work that does not require research skills). Sometimes one is more employable with a bachelor's or master's degree than with a PhD.
- Some potential employers, such as the National Institute of Standards and Technology, do not generally hire permanent employees through normal procedures. One must first win a very prestigious award - the National Research Council post-doctoral fellowship - before being considered for permanent employment.
- Most industry employers do not advertise openings for scientists and engineers at the PhD level.

KEY VARIABLES

To the question "What are the top 8-10 key variables that students need access to in order to make graduate education decisions?" there was no unanimity of responses. The most common answers were:

- A realistic view and recent history of the job market;

● An understanding of the funding situation in science and engineering as a function of scientific discipline, age, race, sex, geography, and time since degree.

The remaining responses, as with the first question, fell under the two broad categories of program information and employment information.

PROGRAM INFORMATION

(Note: All of the following items will vary by field and subfield.)

- Funding profiles and researcher population growth.
- Length of time-to-degree and time to first permanent position.
- Rate of retention from entry into the graduate program to degree completion.
- Frank assessments, 1: Opinions about available schools (including information on quality, cost, location, and research facilities) from students' points of view.
- Frank assessments, 1A: Experiences of recently graduated young scientists.
- Frank assessments, 2: Independent opinions about faculty advisers.
- Frank assessments, 2A: A list of seasoned, knowledgeable, accessible senior investigators with mentoring skills. No printed materials can substitute for the experience they can share or the vision they can impart.
- Required proficiency level in the necessary academic skills demanded by the profession (e.g., how proficient in math must a physics major be?).
- Minimum acceptable GRE scores and GPA.
- How much time is need to acquire the PhD skills.
- The ability to minor in a discipline remote from the major discipline.
- The amount of salary and financial aid that can be expected.
- Living costs for graduate education as a function of geography.
- The availability of a career placement system for science and engineering graduate students.
- History-of-science publications that would help students understand the development of various fields.

EMPLOYMENT INFORMATION

Respondents consider this area very important - especially because advisers may not have a full understanding of potential employment settings, especially nonacademic settings. Students need to know more about the following, by field:

-        Placement record of various programs.
-        Alternative career paths at various levels of education, including B.S. and M.S. levels.
-        Realistic notions of career demands (time, financial, personal) in various areas of study, versus the intellectual rewards.
-        Frank assessments of what it is like to work in a given field. Preconceptions are often misconceptions. For example, do undergraduates realize how much writing scientists do? Do they know how much time, energy and skill must be devoted to obtaining research grants? Do they have any idea of the day-to-day frustrations and rewards of working in industry versus academia?
-        Starting salaries.
-        Main source of employment. If it is an industry, what is the long-term prognosis for the health of that industry?
-        Employment prospects after 1, 2, 5, 10, 20 years.
-        Average hours worked per week.
-        How well does one's desired standard of living match the typical income level of the profession?
-        How many of an institution's graduates succeed in their field of study?
-        Rate of employment turnover for recent graduates.
-        How many jobs are there per job-seeker? (In today's tight job market, several correspondents on the Young Scientists' Network have used the estimate of one job for every six science and engineering graduates.)
-        Qualities and skills valued by industrial employers.
-        Grant-related opportunities available to young scientists as both graduate students and postdoctorates. How many years will they have to wait to gain independence?

The third question asked was, "When do you think students need this information? Do they need it at one stage or at many stages? Which information is needed at what stages?" The responses could be summarized as follows:

"The information needs to be available at many stages. People come gradually to new understandings and new questions, and reassess their progress continually. So the information needs to be available and findable when they're ready for it."

REFERENCES

AAU (Association of American Universities)
1990   *Institutional Policies to Improve Doctoral Education*. Washington, D.C.: Association of American Universities/Association of Graduate Schools.

ACS (American Chemical Society)
1993   *Starting Salaries of Chemists and Chemical Engineers: 1993*. Washington, D.C.: American Chemical Society.

AMS (American Mathematical Society)
1994a   1993 Annual AMS-IMS-MAA Survey (Second Report). *Notices of the American Mathematical Society* 41(July/August):598-601.
1994b   1994 Annual AMS-IMS-MAA Survey (First Report). *Notices of the American Mathematical Society* 41(November/December):1121-1128.

APS (American Physical Society)
1995   *Graduate Student Packet*. College Park, Md.: American Physical Society and American Institute of Physics.

ASEE (American Society for Engineering Education)
1987   *A National Action Agenda for Engineering Education*. Washington, D.C.: American Society for Engineering Education.

Atkinson, Richard C.
1990   "Supply and demand for scientists and engineers: A crisis in the making." *Science* 248(April 27):425-432.

Bowen, William G., and Neil L. Rudenstine.
    1992   *In Pursuit of the PhD*. Princeton, N.J.: Princeton University Press.

Bowen, William G., and Julie Ann Sosa
    1989   *Prospects for Faculty in the Arts and Sciences*. Princeton, N.J.: Princeton University Press.
    1991   "Measuring time to the doctorate: A reinterpretation of the evidence." *Proceedings of the National Academy of Sciences* 88: 713-717.

CGS (Council of Graduate Schools)
    1990   *The Doctor of Philosophy Degree: A Policy Statement*. Washington, D.C.: Council of Graduate Schools.

COSEPUP (Committee on Science, Engineering, and Public Policy)
    1993   *Science, Technology, and the Federal Government: National Goals for a New Era*. Washington, D.C.: National Academy Press.

CRS (Congressional Research Service)
    1992   *Foreign-Born Science and Engineering Doctorate Students in U.S. Institutions*. CRS Report for Congress 92-469. Washington, D.C.: Library of Congress.

Fechter, Alan
    1990   "Engineering shortages and shortfalls: Myths and realities." *The Bridge* (Fall):16-20.

Good, Mary, and Neal Lane
    1994   "Producing the finest scientists and engineers for the 21st century." *Science* 266:742.

Goodstein, David
    1993   "Scientific Ph.D. problems." *American Scholar* 62(Spring):215-220.

Kirby, Kate, and Roman Czujko
    1993   "The physics job market: Bleak for young physicists." *Physics Today* (December):22-27.

Leslie, Larry L., and Ronald L. Oaxaca
    1990   "Scientist and Engineer Supply and Demand." Final Report to the Division of Science Resources, National Science Foundation, Washington, D.C.

Mitchell, Susan, and Daniel Pasquini
    1991   *Nonresponse Bias in the 1989 Survey of Doctorate Recipients: An Exploratory Study*. Office of Scientific and Engineering Personnel, National Research Council, Washington, D.C.: National Academy Press.

NCES (National Center for Education Statistics)

1991 *Projections of Education Statistics to 2002.* NCES 91-490. Office of Educational Research and Improvement, U.S. Department of Education. Washington, D.C.

1993 *Condition of Education 1993.* NCES 93-290. Office of Educational Research and Improvement, U.S. Department of Education. Washington, D.C.

1994 *Faculty and Instructional Staff: Who Are They and What Do They Do?* NCES 94-346. 1993 National Study of Postsecondary Faculty. Washington, D.C.: U.S. Department of Education.

NRC (National Research Council)

1964 *Federal Support of Basic Research in Institutions of Higher Learning.* Washington, D.C.: National Academy of Sciences.

1969 *The Invisible University: Postdoctoral Education in the United States.* Washington, D.C.: National Academy of Sciences.

1975 *Personnel Needs and Training for Biomedical and Behavioral Research: The 1975 Report.* Washington, D.C.: National Academy of Sciences.

1978 *A Century of Doctorates: Data Analyses of Growth and Change.* Washington, D.C.: National Academy Press.

1981 *Postdoctoral Appointments and Disappointments.* Washington, D.C.: National Academy Press.

1983 *Departing the Ivy Halls: Changing Employment Situations for Recent PhDs.* Washington, D.C.: National Academy Press.

1993 *Summary Report 1992: Doctorate Recipients from United States Universities.* Washington, D.C.: National Academy Press.

1994a *The Funding of Young Investigators in the Biological and Biomedical Sciences.* Washington, D.C.: National Academy Press.

1994b *Meeting the Nation's Needs for Biomedical and Behavioral Scientists.* Washington, D.C.: National Academy Press.

1995 *Summary Report 1993: Doctorate Recipients from United States Universities.* Washington, D.C.: National Academy Press.

Forthcoming
  Science Education Standards. Washington, D.C.: National Academy Press.

NSB (National Science Board)

1985 *Science Indicators: The 1985 Report.* NSB 85-1. Washington, D.C.: National Science Board.

1993 *Science and Engineering Indicators: 1993.* NSB 93-1. Washington, D.C.: U.S. Government Printing Office.

NSF (National Science Foundation)
1984   *Characteristics of Recent Science/Engineering Graduates: 1982.* NSF 84-318. Washington, D.C.: National Science Foundation.
1986   *Characteristics of Recent Science/Engineering Graduates: 1984.* Washington, D.C.: National Science Foundation.
1987   *Characteristics of Recent Science/Engineering Graduates: 1986.* NSF 87-321. Washington, D.C.: National Science Foundation.
1989   *Future Scarcities of Scientists and Engineers: Problems and Solutions.* Division of Policy Research and Analysis, Washington, D.C., November 13, Working Draft.
1990a   *Characteristics of Recent Science/Engineering Graduates: 1986.* NSF 90-305. Washington, D.C.: National Science Foundation.
1990b   *The State of Academic Science and Engineering.* NSF 90-35. Washington, D.C.: National Science Foundation.
1991   *Characteristics of Doctoral Scientists and Engineers in the United States: 1989.* NSF 91-317. Division of Science Resources Studies. Washington, D.C.: National Science Foundation.
1992a   *Academic Science and Engineering: Graduate Enrollment and Support, Fall 1990.* NSF 92-323. Washington, D.C.: National Science Foundation.
1992b   *Characteristics of Recent Science and Engineering Graduates: 1990.* NSF 92-316. Washington, D.C.: National Science Foundation.
1992c   *Using the Survey of Doctorate Recipients to Measure the Number of Academic Research Personnel.* NSF 92-315. Washington, D.C.: National Science Foundation.
1993a   *Academic Science and Engineering: Graduate Enrollment and Support, Fall 1991.* NSF 93-309. Washington, D.C.: National Science Foundation.
1993b   *Science and Engineering Doctorates: 1960-91.* NSF 93-301. Washington, D.C.: National Science Foundation.
1993c   *Human Resources for Science & Technology: The Asian Region.* NSF 93-303. Washington, D.C.: National Science Foundation.
1993d   *Foreign Participation in U.S. Academic Science and Engineering: 1991.* NSF 93-302. Washington, D.C.: National Science Foundation.
1993e   *Indicators of Science and Mathematics Education 1992.* NSF 93-95. Washington, D.C.: National Science Foundation.
1994a   *Selected Data on Graduate Students and Postdoctorates in Science and Engineering: Fall 1992.* NSF 94-301. Arlington, Va.: National Science Foundation.
1994b   *Science and Engineering Degrees: 1966-1991.* NSF 94-305. Arlington, Va.: National Science Foundation.
1994c   *Selected Data on Federal Support of Universities and Colleges, Fiscal Year 1992: Selected Data Tables.* NSF 94-312. Arlington, Va.: National Science Foundation.
1994d   *Characteristics of Doctoral Scientists and Engineers in the United States: 1991.* NSF 94-307. Arlington, Va.: National Science Foundation.
1994e   *Guidelines for the NSF Graduate Research Traineeship Program.* NSF 94-140. Arlington, Va.: National Science Foundation.

1994f   *Selected Data on Science and Engineering Doctorate Awards: 1993.* NSF 94-318. Arlington, Va.: National Science Foundation.

1994g   *Science and Engineering Degrees, by Race/Ethnicity of Recipients: 1966-1991.* NSF-94-306. Arlington, Va.: National Science Foundation.

Unpublished
    Detailed tables in the Fall 1992 NSF/NIH Survey of Graduate Science and Engineering Students and Postdoctorates.

PCAST (President's Council of Advisors on Science and Technology)
1992   *Renewing the Promise: Research Intensive Universities and the Nation.* Washington, D.C.: U.S. Government Printing Office.

Rawls, Rebecca L.
1994   "Demand." *Chemical & Engineering News* (October 24):43-48.

Sapolsky, Harvey M.
1994   "Financing science after the Cold War." Pp.159-176 in David H. Guston and Kenneth Keniston, eds., *The Fragile Contract: University Science and the Federal Government.* Cambridge, Mass.: MIT Press.

Spisak, Andrew, and Betty D. Maxfield
1979   *The Effects of Nonresponse Bias on the Results of the 1975 Survey of Doctoral Scientists and Engineers.* National Research Council. Washington, D.C.: National Academy Press.

Stricker, Lawrence J.
1994   "Institutional factors in time to the doctorate." *Research in Higher Education* 35:569-587.

Tuckman, Howard, Susan Coyle, and Yupin Bae
1990   *On Time to the Doctorate: A Study of the Increased Time to Complete Doctorates in Science and Engineering.* Office of Scientific and Engineering Personnel. Washington, D.C.: National Academy Press.

U.S. Bureau of the Census
1994   *Statistical Abstract of the United States: 1994.* 114th Edition. Washington, D.C.: U.S. Government Printing Office.

Vetter, Betty M.
1993   "Setting the Record Straight: Shortages in Perspective." Occasional Paper 92-4, Commission on Professionals in Science and Technology, Washington, D.C.